VILLEPIN

TOWARD A NEW WORLD

DOMINIQUE de
VILLEPIN

TOWARD A NEW WORLD

SPEECHES, ESSAYS, AND INTERVIEWS
ON THE WAR IN IRAQ, THE U.N.,
AND THE CHANGING FACE OF EUROPE

WITH ADDITIONAL DEBATE AND COMMENTARY

MELVILLE HOUSE PUBLISHING
HOBOKEN, NEW JERSEY

ISBN: 0-9749609-8-5

Designed by David Konopka
Cover photo: Frédéric de La Mure

Melville House Publishing
P.O. Box 3278
Hoboken NJ 07030

mhpbooks.com

First Melville House edition

Library of Congress Cataloging-in-Publication Data

Villepin, Dominique de.
  [Autre monde. English]
  Toward a new world : speeches, essays, and interviews on the war in Iraq, the UN, and the changing face of Europe / Dominique de Villepin.
    p. cm.
  ISBN 0-9749609-8-5
  1. France--Foreign relations--20th century. I. Title.
  JZ1587.V55 2004
  327.44--dc22

                                        2004015246

TOWARD A NEW WORLD

PREFACE

BY STANLEY HOFFMANN

Stanley HOFFMANN (France and the United States)

Hoffman is a Professor at Harvard University where he has been teaching Intellectual and Political French History, the Sociology of War, and International Politics, since 1995. From 1969 to 1995, he was president of the Center for European Studies at Harvard. He is the author of many books, including In Search of France, Essays on France, De Gaulle, Artist of Politics, *and* A Moral Code for Cold Monsters. *His most recent book is* Is America Really Imperialist?

The speeches delivered by Dominique de Villepin since becoming France's chief diplomat merit attention for several reasons. First, they provide keys to France's foreign policy as de Villepin sees and dreams it. Second, they belong to a tradition too often eclipsed by the accidents of the moment and the many different personalities and styles that have run the Quai d'Orsay.[1] Finally, they are of interest because they permit us to dispel some grave misunderstandings and to respond to a great deal of slander and imprecation. They also offer us something we need so greatly, an elevated and noble vision of the international order we need to build.

The diplomacy of Dominique de Villepin is founded on an assessment of the present state of international relations that is hard to argue with. We live in a world characterized by interdependence, a world in which violence, as well as the economy, has become globalized. It is also a world characterized by "crisis, fear, and anxiety." This is not only the fault of terrorism—which has inserted well-armed and mobile nonstate actors into the international system alongside states and multilateral institutions—it is also a consequence of more traditional interstate conflicts. Unresolved tensions, such as those between Israel and the Palestinians, or India and Pakistan, are capable of setting off regional catastrophes and

---

[1] The Quai d'Orsay is the familiar name for the building housing the French Ministry of Foreign Affairs in Paris. Its name serves as shorthand for the Ministry, just as Foggy Bottom does for the U.S. Department of State.

boiling over into other areas. Countries situated in explosive political contexts also become major sources of instability when they seek to acquire weapons of mass destruction. To these anxieties, we must add the anguish we feel when we consider the scale of the problems faced by underdeveloped countries, the famines, AIDS, the drug use and the arms traffic, and the paucity of the resources that rich countries devote to fighting them.

The world being what it is, there is no shortage of urgent diplomatic projects to tackle. For de Villepin, the first imperative is our duty to "lay the foundations for the international system of the 21st century," now that the bipolar system of the Cold War is dead and since the "New World Order" briefly imagined by the first President Bush—something like a return to the original conception of the United Nations—was never more than a sketch. It was insufficient, in any case, to address today's host of international and transnational problems, as well as the conflicts which for the last fifteen years have been tearing apart disintegrating states from the Balkans to Africa.

The second imperative concerns peace. "Only a world at peace will be a more secure world," and for de Villepin, this implies an international community that makes "the new requirements of democracy, liberty and the rule of law" integral parts of its credo. This is necessary because the traditional rules of power have been turned on their head; we have experienced a *révolution de la puissance*. Military force remains essential, but in the era of asymmetrical conflicts, where "the weak can shake the strong by infiltrating the interstices of power," it can no longer pretend, nor should it pretend to be completely effective. "Total control" is no longer possible, and this is why "Much more than force is necessary to manage today's world." What strikes Dominique de Villepin is the new impotence of power, "*le vide de la puissance.*" Because power "now flows via channels of influence rather than authority," it must renounce the dream of *realpolitik* and the law of the strongest. It should instead find its legitimacy in the international community, and accept its norms (including those concerning international criminal justice). Moreover, "the obsession with security risks leading to greater insecurity." "The real power, from now on, is the kind of power that creates order and meaning."

This gives rise to a third imperative: justice. Justice must be sought for ethical reasons, but it is also in the interest of the rich and powerful to seek justice. The word that appears the most frequently in these texts is an appealing one: *partage*, sharing. This concern for justice also implies the respect of human rights, the abolition of the death penalty and torture, and informs the fight against political "disappearances." It includes the recognition and protection of economic and social rights.

Finally, one theme appears again and again in these speeches: the necessity of avoiding a "clash of civilizations," which some feel is the grim destination towards which international relations are inexorably heading. The most winning texts are those in which de Villepin speaks—as a diplomat and as a poet—of the diversity of cultures, the dialogue between them, and the ways in which they mutually enrich one another. De Villepin denounces both the isolationist impulse and the temptation to pursue empire as rejections of diversity. And "A world without diversity has joined itself to death." In Addressing the French Senate, he underlines the diversity of the Islamic world and the interpenetration of the worlds of Islam and the West. Here, de Villepin argues that the clash of ignorance is more dangerous than the clash of cultures, observing that the most fervent believers in a clash of cultures—literalists, fundamentalists—are often themselves among the most ignorant, and that fundamentalism itself is often a product of humiliation. In one very beautiful speech given in Israel in May 2003, he celebrates France's debt to the Jewish people and to its Jewish community, and while denouncing anti-Semitism, calls on Israel to end the current deadlock and make peace with the Palestinians.

The future international order sketched by de Villepin remains founded on states, but also on the realization that sovereignty is being eroded by the various aspects of interdependence. In de Villepin's vision, national identities continue to assert themselves, but must today be balanced with collegiality and collective identities, vital to the construction of regional ensembles. Such relationships are mutually reinforcing: in France's case, de Villepin argues, "giving the European Union the identity it needs to be influential in the world, far from weakening our national identity, will on the contrary magnify its strength." Regional cooperation is a factor of peace and the advancement of democracy.

In this new world, no single culture, no single state is capable of imposing its dominance. However, before "an identity inflected towards the desire of the other" can triumph, "a genuine worldwide democracy" must be established, one in which collective responsibility can be exercised and where the "sharing of sovereignties" will provide "new margins of maneuver."

Certain texts make recommendations on what might be done to defuse thorny situations like the Palestinian conflict. In one of these, a speech given in Israel, de Villepin exhorts leaders to make "courageous choices, compromises, [and] openings," and, after the first disappointments of the "Road Map," calls for accelerating the peace process, arguing that the extension of the timetable is a mistake.

It has often been said that Dominique de Villepin's writing is heavy on pretty phrases and high sentiments and light on practical ideas that can guide diplomatic action. After my reading, I think such criticism is unjustified. Concrete propositions are certainly not lacking: to aid in the fight against terrorism, he proposes that the UN create a cooperation and assistance fund equipped with its own resources to help poor countries strengthen their national anti-terrorism programs. To reinvigorate the international system, he proposes major reforms at the United Nations. These include the creation of a disarmament corps and a human rights corps, which would strengthen the UN in two areas where its resources for action are woefully insufficient. Next, de Villepin argues for an expansion of the Security Council and the addition of a monthly meeting where it would meet as a "Council of Peace." In the Palestinian conflict, he suggests considering the deployment of an international presence to the occupied territories. And certainly, in the speeches de Villepin has devoted to Iraq, specific suggestions were not lacking. In the case of the European Union, he argues for a Europe-wide education plan and major reforms in economic governance, including the establishment of a Euro Zone Council to coordinate budgetary policies. He has also fought for a much closer relationship with Russia, and the development of a new Transatlantic Charter more focused on joint activities and the establishment of procedures "to better manage our divergences."

There are many ways one can judge the originality of this vision, first by comparing it to some of his predecessors. There doesn't seem to be any fundamental disagreements between de Villepin and his immediate predecessor, Hubert Védrine, but the tone is quite distinct. Védrine has a more Kissingerian style, a more *realpolitik* feel, and is more suspicious of lyrical flights, whether they concern democracy, European integration, or international organizations. His criticism of the U.S. "hyperpower" and of the dangers it could create is more direct. This is yet another paradox from the world of French politics; one would expect the darker world view to belong to the Gaullist, yet the universe of Védrine the Socialist turns out to be bleaker than de Villepin's. Both men are skeptical of projects to spread democracy by force. But while Védrine once famously raised his voice against the exportation of democracy, in Warsaw, where Madeline Albright had gone to support the cause at a colloquium of more or less democratic states, de Villepin has ceaselessly promoted democracy as a requirement for world order, and he has even evoked the project of world democracy as well, something that would give Kissinger a start, as it would many other conservatives (but not neoconservatives).

De Villepin's relationship to de Gaulle is more complex. On one hand, the voluntarism and activism that de Villepin stands for, his perspective on the international system, the conviction that lives in everything he says and writes, his message that it is France's mission to address the world, and the interest he has in other cultures, all of that is profoundly Gaullist. His devotion to the nation and the state that fashioned it—the French nation—is equally so. But the differences and innovations on de Villepin's part are no less striking. Dominique de Villepin dreams of a world very different from the one de Gaulle saw (de Gaulle, the man who defied a destiny he knew to be implacable, the man in whom hope constantly battled an acute awareness of "the insignificance of things," the man who , based on his military training and his reading of history drew the conclusion that the sword was the world's axis). The visions of the two men are as different as the warrior's *Marseillaise* of Rouget de l'Isle and the *Marseillaise de la paix*. In contrast to the cyclical universe of the *Général*, de Villepin's world is oriented body and soul towards a better future, and this conception and its inspiration remind me of the vision of Jean Jaurès—not the Jaurès of *"rien ne fait de mal,"* but rather the Jaurès who felt that even from evil, good could be distilled, and who believed that the greatest curse for the workers in capitalist societies was not so much the exploitation of their labor as their privation of culture.

Elsewhere in my work, I have described French foreign policy in the 20th century as being dominated by two obsessions: Germany, a threat to France's security since the 1860s, and the fear of decline.[2] During the second half of the 20th century, France's European policy, in spite of the battles between the federalists and the proponents of intergovernmental cooperation, and through successive compromises, succeeded in transforming Franco-German antagonism into friendship. It also sought to make Western Europe an amplifier for French influence, an ambition that proved more difficult, both because of the preponderant weight of its ally, the United States (indispensable for French security during the Cold War, but indifferent to France's concern for its stature and its autonomy), and due to the limits of French resources and the ambitions of other European countries. De Villepin's foreign policy continues to want to breathe into Europe— which "only thrives by sharing"—the will to become a real power and the "melting-pot for a tamed globalization" . Like his German counterpart Joschka Fischer, de Villepin was a member of the Convention on the Future of Europe, presided by the former French president Valéry Giscard d'Estaing. In this forum, he exhorted his colleagues to "reject hesitation and the absorption in purely national interests"

---

[2] "France: Two Obsessions For One Century," in *A Century's Journey*, Robert A. Pastor, ed., Basic Books, New York, 1999.

and found a "new era in which Europe will be more effective, more democratic and will take its deserved place on the international scene." Dominique de Villepin is not a reluctant or conditional European.

These developments, however, are not sufficient to chase away the specter of France's decline as a world power. Those nostalgic for the past see the progression of European integration as a threat to France's independence, and, when there is not unanimous support for its policies, a barrier to France's action in the world. Others feel that the current situation in France—an ageing population, a stagnant economy, domestic obstacles attributed as much to the government as to a costly and rigid welfare state—adds to the distance between a disturbing reality and a diplomacy with international pretensions. For the voluntarists in the Élysée and the Quai d'Orsay, such calls for modesty are themselves contributing to the decline. The debate is certainly nothing new. The last big wave of *déclinite*—literally "declinitis"—towards the end of the IVth Republic, coincided with the beginning of a period of astonishing economic modernization, and occurred just before de Gaulle's return to power. What characterizes the current trend is that it puts France's relationship to the United States at the center of the discussion. But speaking first of the internal reforms, which all agree are of capital importance, some, like de Villepin, want to preserve a "national compromise," the force of which resides in "the balance that it has been able to keep between the sacredness of individual liberties and public solidarity, initiative and protection." This camp defends a very old model, ""an ambitious and unified France, served by a modern state." [3] Others want an *État modeste*, to use the expression of the French sociologist Michel Crozier, a state that no longer smothers private initiative, in a society that would resolutely apply the methods of economic liberalism

---

[3] *Le Monde*, October 8 2003, p. 19.

and renounce the succor of the welfare state: in other words, something very much like the American model celebrated in the United States and elsewhere for the last two decades. (Having some experience with this system myself, and having written no small amount on the "*mal français*," it is my opinion that confrontations between idealized models lead to little, and that compromises are necessary.)

The role of the United States in the world, Washington's hegemony in a unipolar system, is also a topic at the heart of the French debate. On the one hand, some want to avoid irritating the "Imperial Republic," becoming a target of its wrath and risking isolation, while others think that it is simultaneously in France's interest and in the interest of the world to channel the "hyperpower" the U.S. has become, and lead it to place its great power at the service of justice and law, even if that course involves some rough sailing. This is where the Gaullist inspiration is particularly clear: de Gaulle, who understood the limits of French "hard power" better than anyone, always thought that one of the most valuable elements of "soft power"—France's ability to persuade and its force of attraction—at his disposal was his ability and his will to tell the truth, even to the most powerful. And so he did, during the Vietnam War, during the crisis in the Middle East in 1967, and in service of a policy of "*détente, entente* and cooperation" with the Soviet Union after 1962. Dominique de Villepin seems to me elegantly to assume this legacy. This is not only because among the allies of the United States, the place of favorite has long since been occupied by Great Britain (which has often learned that this privilege doesn't always mean it will be listened to). It is also because the role of the independent and plain-speaking ally, the friend who is willing to say out loud what many think but do not dare express, is just as important.

Should we, in this context, say that French diplomacy has an American—or rather anti-American—fixation? I don't think so, even if the "will to be worthy of our rank and our mission in the world... making our convictions clear and refusing bad compromises" is sometimes viewed by Washington as systematically hostile, generally because Washington judges everything in relation to its policies of the moment.

Let us talk, then, about the Iraq crisis. First of all, as de Villepin notes, "while in the U.S. we hear too many giving voice to anti-French sentiments," you will not find "a single phrase, not a single even remotely aggressive word about the United States on the lips of any of the French officials dealing with this crisis." De Villepin is absolutely right about this. What was a fundamental policy disagreement did not erupt into a shouting match, even though provocation was not lacking on the American side. De Villepin both spoke frankly and avoided burning bridges.

Second, relative to what we might call the official background, that is, the crisis created by Iraq's repeated violation of the Security Council resolutions ordering him to abandon his WMD programs after the first Gulf War and to cooperate with the UN inspectors, France had always signaled that if it was not possible to disarm Iraq peacefully, it would join a military operation, and it supported the Anglo-American mobilization as an effective form of pressure. The disagreement with Washington was first of all about the inspections. The United States had decided to halt the inspections (and refused to restart them, as the British had requested). Given the dangers of a military operation, France, among many other countries, wanted to give inspections another chance. "The use of force," de Villepin had warned, "could stir up rancor and hatred, and feed a confrontation of identities, a clash of cultures, and it is precisely one of the major responsibilities of our generation to avoid such a thing." De Villepin made many suggestions for strengthening the inspection regime, including increasing the number of inspectors, creating a specialized corps to continue watching certain sites after inspection, creating a center to coordinate findings, and so on. All of this was founded on assumptions opposite from those the Americans had made: that "going ahead without taking precautions in a highly divided region of extreme cultural and religious sensitivities" was very dangerous, and that the risk of "misunderstandings, tension and humiliation" was so grave that every route to a peaceful disarmament had to be tried. The French view was that war would only serve to nourish terrorism, and what we have learned in the interval about Iraq's weapons of mass destruction, which have not materialized, also tends to support the French position.

But in the third place, beyond the issue of Saddam's WMDs and the threats they may or may not have posed, there was actually a deeper reasoning behind the French efforts to avoid war. The main American objectives, in fact, were regime change, and then with Saddam Hussein taken care of, the transformation of the political landscape of the entire Middle East. Now, it is highly unlikely that this will just happen by itself after victory in Iraq. It was a simplistic idea, an illusion. More probably, such a project would require more crises and more wars. As for regime change, de Villepin argues that this was not the objective sought by the international community, to whom he addresses a fundamental question: "Who, and in the name of what, will decide whether a regime is good or bad?" Similarly, the use of force, de Villepin, points out, is probably not the best means to help the progress of democracy in the Middle East. While it is understandable that Iraq's poorly informed and poorly prepared occupiers would be hesitant to let the Iraqis, divided and full of internecine rancor, choose their own destiny, on the other hand, imposing a western-style pluralist democracy on a people both proud and inexperienced is just as likely to end up producing an unsatisfactory government.

None of this is likely to resolve the issues raised by murderous regimes[4]. But we come here to a fourth point, which is essential. Can one country claim the sole right to topple a regime and "abusively" extend the principle of self-defense (which was done by associating Saddam Hussein and al-Qaeda) to include the preventative use of force, not only against terrorists, but also against states? This, in a nutshell, is the problem of the limits of the "right of the strongest." De Villepin urges us not to open this "Pandora's Box," arguing instead that force should be placed at the service of law. For de Villepin, the primacy of law is a "requirement of morality and politics and a condition of justice, but also of effectiveness." Citing Thucydides, he affirms that "only moderation can make power acceptable," and that the collective norms that seek to temper power place it "at the disposition of laws founded on humanism." During this crisis, the American hawks saw only weakness and an attempt to hide impotence in these appeals to the rule of law and legitimacy. But if what has occurred since the American victory in Iraq has not confirmed the apocalyptic fears of de Villepin and others who opposed the war, the optimistic triumphalist vision of the American leaders has proven even more erroneous. It is only through ongoing efforts with immense human and financial costs that the United States is avoiding the worst. And the American public seems little inclined to go on making these sacrifices over the long term so that the simplistic vision of its leaders can finally become reality.

---

4 For more suggestions, see S. Hoffmann in *L'Amérique vraiment impériale?* Stanley Hoffman and Fréderique Bozo, Paris, Éditions Louis Audibert, 2003.

And this brings us to our final point, for it is in anticipation of this reality that de Villepin has sought to inflect the American position on the political and material reconstruction of Iraq. The occupation is a magnet for the attacks that prevent order from being reestablished in Iraq. It also often slows reconstruction efforts made by the Iraqis themselves. For these reasons, it must be made as brief as possible; it is the Iraqis who must rebuild their country, and it is the United Nations, not merely the occupying authority, that must direct this work. The resolution unanimously voted by the Security Council on October 15, 2003 takes a small step in this direction, a direction U.S. leaders had initially rejected as unrealistic.

In the end, what I like about Dominique de Villepin is his high purpose, both political and ethical, ambitions based on an accurate reading of the problems that face us in this world, and on the idea the international community holds the key to their solution. "The emergence of public opinion as a force on the global scene marks the beginning of a new era. The world is now a totality: no longer can it be divided up through the shadowy calculations of the great powers." For the moment, there is a great deal of wishful thinking in these remarks, but they call us to act, precisely because we are engaged in a race against time, "a race between the forces of unity and the forces of disorder," that demands that we move faster. They call us to "share power, which in reality expands the scope of responsibility, of legitimacy, and thus the scope of action as well." It's a call not for the creation of a world that would have a single model—American values, and American-style democracy and capitalism—but for that of a world where multiple cultures and identities are respected, so long as they accept certain internal and external rules of conduct and responsibility. It's a call for a world where national interest will no longer be determined in terms of "arrangements of men, cannons or factories," but in terms of service to a disoriented and overwhelmed humanity. And it is a call, where global politics are concerned, not to traditional multipolarity—which would be unrealistic and even dangerous in a world where America's preeminence is a fact, insofar as multipolarity has historically meant "rivalry or competition"— but to a cooperation of world actors, not to manage a balance of armed peace, but to manage in common the problems that confound even the most powerful;,

What I like above all about this man, whom I have never met personally, is the generosity of his mind and his heart, capable of offering his country an internationalist and globalist ideal rather than a narrow defense of its national interests. In an earlier work, he called for a Europe of the heart, a "living mosaic of languages and cultures" to which "each citizen adheres with conviction," because "the time of a Europe limited to *de facto* bonds is today behind us."[5] Similarly, here, he asks that political consciousness assume a universal dimension, and affirms that "to dream the dream of two shores is to want to reconcile the best of ourselves with the best of the other." The old Gaullist that I am can tell that though they lived in different inner and outer universes, Dominique de Villepin and Charles de Gaulle have the same passion for France—the passion of Michelet—and for what the *Général* called the cause of man. They seek greatness through greatness of mission, not through greatness of force. And that is why those who only believe in force and in the sempiternal forms of power politics fail to understand him, or even consider him, as do certain Americans, their enemy, or else as certain French do, an incautious man. But for the same reasons, across the world, so many people have been touched by his remarks, even among the American public.

---

5 *Le cri de la gargouille* (Paris: Albin Michel, 2002).

In the same book, de Villepin celebrated the *passeurs* who in literature, music, philosophy, or in public life build "bridges across the ages" and serve as mediators between the past and new times, awaken consciences and seize occasions. I don't know if Dominique de Villepin sees himself as a *passeur* between the international relations of the past and present, and the better world he can see. But I hope he is one, with all of the force of the means at his disposal and the power of his faith. This lucid idealist is a true revolutionary.

PART ONE

IRAQ AND WAR

WE MUST NOT CUT CORNERS

COMMENTARY PUBLISHED IN *LE MONDE*, OCTOBER 1, 2002

"The International Community is at a critical moment in its history . . . "

In a speech before the United Nations General Assembly on September 12, 2002, United States President George W. Bush gave his support to a return to Iraq by The United Nations Monitoring, Verification and Inspection Commission (UNMOVIC) and the International Atomic Energy Agency (IAEA), to resume the search that had broken off in December, 1998 for "weapons of mass destruction"; such finding would in turn, according to Bush, justify a "regime change." However, other voices in the Bush administration openly questioned the inspections process and whether to abide by it; some seemed to advocate more immediate, unilateral and coercive measures. This was at odds with France's position in support of the inspections. France held that the prevention of the proliferation of weapons of mass destruction, not regime change, was the sole legal and legitimate basis for suggesting coercive measures; and that U.N. member states should abide by the collective authority of the Security Council in deciding how to react to the inspectors' reports.

Confronted with the Iraqi crisis, the international community is at a critical moment in its history. Every State must face up to its responsibilities. More than ever, France is determined to hold a clear course.

Yes, Iraq is a potential threat to the region's and international security. Yes, the fight against the proliferation of weapons of mass destruction presents an essential challenge for the future of every one of us. Yes, Iraq has defied the international community by concealing programmes concerning these weapons: if she does not yet have nuclear capabilities, all the indications make us think that she has reconstituted biological and chemical capacities.

Faced with this challenge, our duty is to combine firmness with clear-sightedness. In the wake of the 11 September attacks, thanks to our mobilization in the fight against terrorism we obtained results. With regard to Iraq, we must renew this unity through a shared determination: to combat the proliferation of weapons of mass destruction. This is clearly the priority. France in no way condones Baghdad's activities, but any action aimed at regime change would be at variance with the rules of international law and open the door to all kinds of excesses.

Since President Bush's recent speech, recognizing the primordial role of the United Nations, the debate has been able to resume in this forum, in which a broad consensus has emerged. In the face of such unity, on 16 September, Baghdad made known its acceptance of the unconditional return of the international inspectors. Their work has to lead to the elimination of every weapon of mass destruction and prevent any future rearmament. Let us not forget that a larger number of these weapons were destroyed as a result of the inspections between 1991 and 1998 than during the Gulf War.

The danger presented by Iraq concerns all the world's peoples and, in the first place, those of the Middle East. It is with them that we shall be able to find a lasting solution. These countries have made it known that they would support action decided on by the United Nations. It is for us to heed that message.

Today, all attention is focused on the discussions which are going to begin at the Security Council. The two-step approach proposed by President Chirac makes it possible to maintain the international community's unity, strengthen the legitimacy of the action and satisfy our demand for efficacy: Iraq must comply with international law; if she refuses to obey it, then all the appropriate conclusions will need to be drawn. This path is the only one capable of ensuring control at every stage of the crisis.

So initially it's important to agree, within the Security Council, on an inspection regime guaranteeing that the inspectors will be able to carry out their mission in full with no hindrance. In the event of the Iraqi regime violating these obligations, it would be for the Council to decide on measures to be taken. We must not cut corners. We do not want to give a blank check to military action, since we want to shoulder our responsibility to the end. This is why we cannot accept a resolution authorizing right now the recourse to force, without going back to the United Nations Security Council.

France shares the United States' determination to resolve a crisis which threatens us all. But she refuses the risk of an intervention which would not take all the demands of collective security fully into account.

Going beyond the Iraqi crisis, it is the international community's fundamental principles which are at stake: stability, fairness, responsibility.

Stability remains a strategic demand. While Iraqi disarmament constitutes an imperative, it must be carried out under conditions which strengthen international order, without adding new factors leading to further disorder in a region which already has too many, without bringing new risks of clashes in that area at the heart of the world's fault lines. For France, order does not signify either weakness or impotence, but the exercise of determination and clear-sightedness to bring about the lasting settlement of the crises.

Fairness is the second pillar of peace. Against a background of emergency situations and interdependence, the hallmark of our era, injustice creates rebellion, rebellion disorder and disorder violence, in a vicious circle, repeated in country after country, region after region, continent after continent. At a moment when it is determined to resolve the Iraqi disarmament problem, the international community must adopt the same approach to the Middle East crisis with a view to rejoining the path to finding a settlement.

Finally, collective responsibility is a moral and political necessity. Moral, because democracies become totally meaningless if they fail to honour abroad the principles underpinning them at home. Political, because only collective decisions secure the legitimacy necessary for far-reaching, coherent and effective action. Force can be only a last resort.

The decisions to be taken tomorrow are going to shape the new face of the world. The treatment of the Iraqi crisis will influence its spirit and structures. Collective security will depend on the international community's determination to enforce the law.

But if it is to last, the new order has to be built on the basis of sharing and exchange. Against a background of growing fear and intolerance, worsening tension and incomprehension, the task of bringing our peoples closer together demands the patient assertion of a community of values and rules, and recognition of a single destiny. Success in this rests too on respect for the Other achieved through genuine dialogue.

LET US BE UNITED AND RESPONSIBLE

INTERVIEW WITH *LE FIGARO*, OCTOBER 28, 2002

"What is at stake is the attitude of the international community when faced with a crisis—in this case the Iraq crisis—and its capacity to respond."

In the aftermath of George W. Bush's September 12 speech, negotiations on U.N. Security Council Resolution 1441, detailing the process of weapons inspections and the repercussions for defiance, grew lengthy and tense. France, joined by Germany, and Russia, advocated the position that only the Security council could determine the need for force, in response to the findings of the weapons inspectors. while the American position was that Iraq had already violated its agreement to inspections.

The United States presented a resolution about Iraq that did not satisfy France. What changes would you like to make?

DV—The discussions involve the team of weapons inspectors and the use of force. We reached an agreement on the idea of a two-step process. First, the Security Council must establish the basic conditions under which the inspectors could enter Iraq. Next, if Baghdad does not fulfill its obligations, the Security Council would examine the issue again on the basis of reports from the UN inspectors.

Insomuch as we have agreed on this approach with the Americans and all of our partners, the resolution presented by the United States must not contain any mechanisms that could bypass this prearranged plan.

The American resolution, without waiting for the inspectors' report, already claims Iraq is guilty of "material breach." By referring to "grave consequences" in the same paragraph—which in diplomatic jargon spells the use of force—doesn't the American resolution allow for the automatic recourse to force you wish to avoid?

We must eliminate all ambiguity. We obviously do not have any objections to the resolution's mentioning of Iraq's past failures. But above all it should take into account the new reality once the inspectors return as well as the resulting obligations for Iraq. Indeed, the main goal of the new resolution is to ensure that these obligations are met, now and in the future. If Iraq decides to shirk them, the Security Council will have to convene again and draw the necessary conclusions. Once this plan is adopted, we must stick to it: there cannot be a two-step process along with a blank check that could justify unilateral action at any moment.

Then the American resolution does not address your demands?

In its present state, for the reasons I just explained, it contains contradictory elements. Therefore, there is work to do. We want to take the lead and concentrate on the essential: install a rigorous inspections regime and define a clear mechanism governing the eventual use of force.

Will France present a different resolution than the American one?

We are currently working with the American resolution and naturally presenting some amendments. Otherwise, we have circulated a document that summarizes our propositions. We now have a double objective: finalize a resolution quickly and with the greatest possible consensus within the Security Council. That is why I proposed a meeting of the Security Council's foreign ministers in order to remove the final barriers. I discussed this idea with several of my colleagues, including Colin Powell, and they were very receptive.

If the United States calls for a vote on their resolution, would France go so far as to use its veto?

From the beginning, France has adopted a clear position that we will not agree to a resolution that does not respect the principles we are defending. But I believe we will be able to come to a resolution acceptable for everyone.

Do you think that a consensus is possible?

For us the important thing is that the Security Council be engaged at each step of the process. A collective responsibility is not something that can be delegated. The action taken by the international community must be based on both a firm sense of morality and international legality.

Doesn't France, especially in the United States, risk being seen as the country blocking any action in Iraq?

The relationship between France and the United States is not at stake. That is excellent. We are working in the spirit of solidarity and cooperation. As seen in the recent Security Council debate, the ideas we are defending enjoy broad support. What is at stake is the attitude of the international community when faced with a crisis—in this case the Iraq crisis—and its capacity to respond. These stakes are very important, and extend even beyond Iraq.

WAR IS NOT INEVITABLE

INTERVIEW WITH *LE PARISIEN*, DECEMBER 9, 2002

"We want peace and stability. There is no hidden agenda."

Resolution 1441 was adopted unanimously on November 8, 2002, and Iraq met its demands by submitting a declaration detailing the status of its nuclear, biological and chemical weapons programs on December 7. According to 1441's timetable, UNMOVIC, the inspections commission, was scheduled to give its final report on January 27, 2003.

Saturday, Iraq handed over a 12,000 page document that is supposed to settle once and for all the question of the status of its WMD programs. In your opinion, does this make war more or less likely?

DV—War is not inevitable. As far back as September, many observers had already decided that war was unavoidable. But with United Nations Resolution 1441, which sent a very clear message to Saddam Hussein and was passed unanimously with the support of Russia, China and Syria, we have been able to create a chance for peace. So let's keep working in this direction. Now, we have never stopped calling on Iraq to disarm, and we will not stop calling very strongly for this. The present situation is unacceptable, and Iraq's weapons of mass destruction must be eliminated.

What do you think of the work of the inspectors so far?

DV—So far, their work has taken place under favorable conditions. That having been said, Iraq has a heavy responsibility to bear, and one it should not try to avoid. We live in an increasingly dangerous world, and the proliferation of weapons of mass destruction is not limited to Iraq, so it is crucial to demonstrate that by working together, in a collective framework, we can produce political solutions. Should it prove to be the case that Iraq is not complying with Resolution 1441, it will then be necessary to return to the Security Council and examine all the options, including a recourse to force.

When will France make known its reaction to the document produced by Baghdad?

DV—Let's wait until the experts have had a chance to evaluate it. Then we will work together with our partners in the Security Council to come up with an appropriate response. At the same time, we need to step up our efforts to find a political solution in the Middle East if we are going to avoid creating an enduring rift and aggravating feelings of injustice and suspicion. Our objectives are simple: we want peace and stability. There is no hidden agenda.

Isn't the warlike rhetoric of the Americans making this difficult?

DV—In September, President Bush made the decision to go through the United Nations, and we showed that we can work with the Americans in a relationship of trust. That's the spirit in which we want to continue. A rush to war is not in anyone's interest. Resolution 1441 rejects any automatic recourse to force, and we are holding to that principle.

THREE TEMPTATIONS

INTERVIEW WITH *PARIS MATCH*, PUBLISHED JANUARY 16, 2003

"From time to time, your idealism can begin to sound a bit naïve..."

In the weeks following Iraq's declaration, and before UNMOVIC issued a report on its findings, the United States continued a massive military buildup in the Persian Gulf. Meanwhile, other incidents provoked concern: On November 29, a terrorist attack on a hotel frequented by Israeli tourists in Kenya killed thirteen people. On December 12, North Korea announced plans to restart its nuclear program, raising the specter of a new proliferation crisis. On December 30, Pyongyang expelled the last IAEA inspectors from its territory, and on January 10, declared that it was withdrawing from the Non-Proliferation Treaty.

Until the end of January, France holds the rotating presidency of the United Nations Security Council. Faced with the U.S. buildup to war in Iraq, what is France's role? What results are you determined to achieve?

DV—France should energize the Security Council and call on each of its members to guarantee security by acting together. Given the strong interdependence between these regional crises, several urgent issues are on the agenda. Each of these conflicts needs to be addressed in its wider context, and we must neither be satisfied with temporary measures, nor fail to address latent problems that can degenerate later. It's the same with fires: If you don't go for heart of the blaze, it is going to spread around the edges.

Do you mean to say that these crises could have been better managed in the past?

DV—Serious questions must be dealt with in a global way. Today, political conflicts have profound and far-reaching consequences: smuggling, organized crime, the proliferation of criminal networks and so forth. We must do everything in our power to keep disorder from overflowing into neighboring countries and at the same time address the roots of the problems. We have to be permanently on guard and, in particular, we must identify the fault lines. This is how we can reduce the uncertainty the world faces.

Is it likely that within the Security Council we will see an "antiwar front" made up of France, Russia and China rise up in opposition to the United States and Great Britain in an attempt to prevent them from going to war against Iraq?

DV—We have no interest in setting ourselves against one another. To deal with the Iraq crisis, and now that of North Korea, we need to work together. We need to pool our abilities and make our diversity work for us. The diplomatic work should be collective, not competitive. With the Americans, we should work to complement their approach with alternatives, enrich the discussion and, through taking an active role, deepen our cooperation.

Do Bush and his team understand the French position and France's efforts to avoid confrontation with Iraq?

DV—They are aware of what France and its particular approach to the situation have to offer them. Regardless of its great power, the United States is a country that can feel quite alone in the world. It can feel drawn towards a standoff with the other members of the international community. Such a thing would be dangerous for it, as it would be for us. We all know it.

Isn't it true that France has become their bête noire, constantly forcing them to change strategies and go through the UN?

DV—No. I work very closely with Colin Powell, and it's a relationship of trust. If one wants to be effective, it is better to confront crises together, with respect for morality and the rule of law. We need to develop an approach that encourages leadership by example. Our work, our collective ambition is to create more stability and build a better world. In Iraq, we must disarm Saddam to bring peace to the region. In Korea, our policy is to promote reconciliation between North and South Korea. I'd like to point out, moreover, that the Korean situation is the last living vestige of the Cold War. Four decades have passed without a peace treaty being signed: 37,000 U.S. soldiers are stationed in South Korea. North Korean missiles can be launched at Seoul or Tokyo at any time. We are going to try to move the situation forward by using the channels that exist under the bilateral framework agreement and also by working at the regional and multilateral levels, whether that involves the IAEA or the Security Council.

As president of the UN Security Council, what, concretely, does France plan to do on Iraq?

DV—Affirm the special role of the UN in the Iraq crisis by taking a hard line with Iraq and supporting the work of the weapons inspectors there. We have complete confidence in Mr. Blix and his teams. And where there are gray areas, it will be our responsibility to clarify them. Iraq must accept the principle of active cooperation. If it makes its moves to disarm credible, then we will have no reason to go to war. If it fails, then we will have to put another resolution before the UN. France has its own perspective, intends to preserve its freedom to act, and will assume all of its responsibilities here. Force can only be a last resort. The Middle East does not need a new conflict. At every stage, we must evaluate the effectiveness of our decisions and be sure that we can anticipate their consequences.

Speaking frankly, does it look today as though the war in Iraq can be avoided? The U.S. mobilization in the region—120,000 troops— makes it look as though it has already been decided.

For France, war is not a foregone conclusion. The American military deployment is first of all proof of America's determination to make Iraq disarm, a determination that France shares. We must be extremely demanding here and apply as much pressure as possible to see the disarmament process through to the end. It was in this spirit that last week I wrote to each of the members of the Security Council, and asked them to provide the inspectors with any special information they might have on Iraq's weapons. We need to make sure the inspectors have every advantage we can give them.

For the moment, the inspections don't seem to have uncovered much.

DV—Let's note first of all that the inspections are proceeding under favorable conditions. The quality and the capacity of the inspections are increasing with each passing week. They have already brought all new weapons development to a standstill. We want to go farther and completely eliminate Iraq's capacity for weapons of mass destruction. That's why we must persevere under the framework set up by the UN. Collective security requires collective responsibility. We are all accountable, and we must find ways to make our efforts more effective every day.

So what if they find nothing? Even if the inspectors are given more time after January 27 as Tony Blair has asked?

DV—We have chosen the path of cooperation and it is this path that optimizes the security interests of the international community. Given time, the inspections will provide us with an accurate picture of Iraq's weapons programs, as long as Iraq cooperates actively and the inspectors have the means necessary for carrying out their mission. We should constantly be asking ourselves how we can better meet our objectives, whether these be in the field of non-proliferation, the fight against terrorism, the reduction of uncertainty, or the promotion of security and stability.

From time to time, your idealism can begin to sound a bit naïve....

DV—In a world rife with disorder, it is very important to defend moral principles with conviction and to set the bar very high where the respect for the rule of law is concerned. Giving these principles concrete form requires a great deal of thought. After reflection, it is our responsibility to set standards publicly. The world urgently needs standards and it needs justice, particularly in the Middle East.

On Monday, December 21, you will be at the United Nations in New York to address a meeting on terrorism that you and your colleagues in the Security Council have organized. Why? Do you have the impression that countries are not doing enough in the fight against terrorism?

DV—Opportunism is one of terrorism's defining characteristics: it is ready at all times to exploit the world's vulnerabilities, fears and divisions. Our countries have done a great deal to mobilize against this threat, but they should do more. The meeting has a triple objective: First of all, to ensure better cooperation between countries. Second, to increase the level of readiness across the board by providing technical assistance to countries that for various reasons are more fragile or are facing bankruptcy. Finally, to launch more initiatives, and use every means available to frustrate the plans of our adversaries.

No one sounds more Gaullist than yourself at the moment!

DV—The line developed by the President of the Republic is both purposeful and clear. The example set by de Gaulle is at the heart of my own efforts, which are guided by the desire to preserve France's independence and the will to be worthy of our rank and mission in the world. This means making our convictions clear and refusing bad compromises. We must have the courage to defend a certain idea of France and to share this spirit of peace and solidarity with less fortunate countries. To make this possible in today's turbulent world, we must be constantly in motion, seizing the initiative.

CLEAR CHOICES

REMARKS MADE AT A U.N. PRESS CONFERENCE, JANUARY 20, 2003

"Given that we can disarm Iraq by peaceful means, it is our responsibility not to jeopardize the lives of innocent civilians or soldiers, not to jeopardize the stability of the region and even widen the gap between our peoples and cultures and thus nurture terrorism."

By mid-January the massive presence of American troops at the Iraqi frontiers suggested that an American military intervention was inevitable. On January 18th, the United States announced it would increase further still the numbers of troops already mobilized. On January 20th the British government announced its decision to send troops, also. In the revolving position of president of the Security Council, France called for the Council to meet on January 20. Afterwards, a press conference was held.

Today in the context of the French presidency of the Security Council I presided over a meeting on terrorism. The fight against terrorism is a priority for us. It is a priority for France and for the international community North and South.

We hope to give added impetus to this struggle in terms of four objectives: first of all the necessity of concluding negotiations on the General Convention Against Terrorism and the new Convention Against Nuclear Terrorism. We have also proposed that a fund be created to cooperate with and help states that wish to strengthen their national resources. Moreover, we need to improve our control over radioactive sources in the world. Secondly, it is imperative to define a new calendar. There could be a new ministerial meeting of the Security Council in September, in addition to the general assembly. Thirdly, we need to reassert our joint desire to act together. All relevant United Nations organizations, including the General Assembly, will be mobilized for an extraordinary session should this prove necessary. We have also intensified our efforts on other fronts, as in the G8 and the Financial Action Task Force on Money Laundering. In addition to this we must put an end to dysfunctions in the international community that help support terrorism. I am referring to criminal networks and financial centers that encourage shady movements of funds. Unity is the key to success. It is essential to maintain it. Terrorism is a fact that is a permanent threat to the whole world, alongside transactions involving weapons of massive destruction, regional crises, networks and illegal financing.

I would now like to say a few words about Iraq. The crisis in Iraq is a trial for all of us. We are faced by enormous challenges. Why are they enormous? Because we cannot isolate Iraq from the other questions relating to proliferation. What we do for Iraq in relation to proliferation, we should also do for every other crisis. If war is the only way to solve the problem, we immediately find ourselves in an impasse. The international community must demonstrate initiative and imagination in clear and unambiguous fashion. We must also preserve international unity. Unilateral military intervention should be seen as a victory for strong-armed tactics and an assault on the primacy of law and international morality.

We all made a joint choice in favor of inspections in Iraq. A choice in favor of legitimacy that was approved by the international community at large. It is also a choice in favor of efficacy. Inspections are taking place under satisfactory conditions. We already know, and this is an established fact, that Iraqi programs of massive destruction have been interrupted, even frozen. This is confirmed every single day by the information we receive on the ground. We ask that everything be done to strengthen this process. This is also a choice in favor of responsibility. If we give ourselves the appropriate means, the inspections can be brought to their conclusion. Once Mr. Blix and Mr. El Baradei have presented their report to the Security Council on January 27th, we must examine all the possible consequences in order to make any necessary adjustments in terms of resources and personnel. And lastly, it is a choice in favor of firmness. Iraq must understand that it is high time for it to cooperate actively, that it must provide the international community with a complete and global outline of its weapons programs. We shall not accept any shady zones.

Given that we can disarm Iraq by peaceful means, it is our responsibility not to jeopardize the lives of innocent civilians or soldiers, not to jeopardize the stability of the region and even widen the gap between our peoples and cultures and thus nurture terrorism. The consultations that have taken place since the beginning of the Iraqi crisis are exemplary in terms of their unity. This must be the basis of the way we handle other crises, particularly in North Korea and the Middle East.

With regard to North Korea it is important to know what we are talking about when it comes to the preservation of multilateral instruments, nonproliferation, particularly the NPT, as well as stability in the region and elsewhere. Here again, we believe that gradual but firm steps are better suited to the situation. All channels can be used simultaneously: bilateral contacts, regional and multilateral consultations, particularly in relation to the IAEA and the Security Council. It is indispensable that the states in the region, particularly Japan and South Korea, be involved in every stage in the process.

Now we come to the most long lasting of the crises: the Middle East. On the one hand, terrorism hits out at innocent people and on the other the sentiment of injustice is nourishing extremist sentiments. What are our priorities at this point?

We believe that after the elections the roadmap adopted by the Quartet on December 20th should be published and that its implementation should be immediate. In line with the roadmap it is imperative to have elections in the Palestinian Territories on a peace platform and an international conference on the Middle East. France wishes to make a firm commitment along with its partners and to set an example by officially recognizing at the end of a clearly defined deadline the state of Palestine within its provisional frontiers. However, we must already begin to consider the question of guarantees: a guarantee of security for Israel, a guarantee of justice for the Palestinian people and of course guarantees of economic development for the whole of the region.

I have to admit that this preliminary intervention has been quite long but we are convinced, and this is the French approach, that all of the world's problems are interconnected. And problems on a world scale require solutions on a world scale and within the framework of the United Nations global security.

Here we get the impression that France is inconsistent, that it is making every effort to restrain the superpower whereas it is ready to send its own troops into battle. A France that always gives in to pressure. Firstly, is this impression justified? Secondly, President Chirac has requested that the inspectors be given a little more time to complete their work in Iraq. You have just stated quite clearly that you believe that the process needs to be reinforced and improved but that the process should continue. Last week Colin Powell said that he believed that by the end of the month there would be enough elements to justify a second resolution authorizing a war in Iraq. Is there any chance in the next two or three weeks that Iraq will abandon its demands in favor of longer inspections?

DV—France's position on Iraq, as on all subjects, is guided by strong principles: law, morality, solidarity and justice. These principles have guided France all through the preparation of resolution 1441. This resolution stresses the necessity of advancing toward the disarmament of Iraq in the search for collective security. I wish to remind you that the objective of the international community, and there is only one objective, is Iraqi disarmament. And we have given ourselves the means to achieve this goal: the inspectors who are working on the ground have information from the ground. And we have established a simple principle: these inspectors make a report to the Security Council, which enables it to have a satisfactory evaluation of what is happening on the ground and, based on that, to face up to its responsibilities. With regard to the whole planet, France is true to the principles it upholds. And I believe I can say that the international community generally recognizes this fact.

Today it is patently obvious that a choice must be made: either to continue in the path of cooperation or to advance, because we are getting impatient with the situation in Iraq, to advance along the path of military intervention. Today we believe there is nothing to justify envisaging military action. The inspectors have been working on the ground for fewer than sixty days. For two months we have held the opinion that the setting up of inspections and the work they have conducted—more than three hundred inspections per month—constitutes satisfactory work. But of course we can improve this work, and France is actively committed to enabling the inspectors to conduct their work in an ever more effective manner. And we have set ourselves as a principle, quite naturally, that we shall seek the active cooperation of Iraq. That is the goal we are working toward. And we can clearly see, day after day, that the inspectors are in a position to have more information. Moreover, it is obvious today that Iraq can no longer pursue new programs, even if it wants to, because of the number of inspectors on the ground. That is the choice the international community has made, and the choice that France supports. However, we may decide to change at any given time. We are not the ones who would be changing. It is the people who might wish to decide in favor of a military intervention who would be changing. The international community has chosen cooperation. And we say that as long as cooperation can continue to advance, then we must continue along the path we have chosen. If we decide to change step and if the United States decided at some stage to envisage unilateral military action, our first question would concern the legitimacy of such an action.

Our second question would concern the efficacy of the intervention. Because it is one thing to intervene militarily in Iraq, even to attack Saddam Hussein's regime, to get rid of Saddam Hussein and to bring down the regime. It is another thing to have a united Iraq, to have the Middle East secure and stable. Moreover, what would be the consequences for the international community in terms of security? What new divisions would we see appearing on the international scene? What frustrations and feelings of injustice would be nourished? Our feeling is that in terms of efficacy this intervention is leading us into an adventure in which we would have no control at any time over the situation and the issues. The choice is therefore quite simple. Either we continue patiently but with the conviction that at the end of the road we shall disarm Iraq through cooperation, and this is the conviction that France is expressing. And it is also the conviction that the inspectors are expressing. We shall see their report on January 27th. Either we consider that there is a military shortcut and that by means of this shortcut we can hope to achieve our goal more quickly. We say, let us be careful, the world is ill, the world is in a state of great disorder. Can the world afford to take such initiatives when we know that they may set a precedent?

Because the problem of proliferation concerns not just Iraq but also North Korea and other states. Must we then envisage a military intervention or will one military intervention suffice by some magical effect to solve all the other problems on the planet? Let's be responsible. Let us acknowledge that the world situation is serious and that we must tackle all of its problems at the same time and with the trump card that we hold today. And we believe that must stress the value of this trump card: the unity and unanimity of the international community. You know that France played its part in adopting resolution 1441 alongside our American friends in order to preserve that unanimity. This unanimity is of precious importance to the international community. Before taking the risk of breaking this unanimity, let's take time to think. That is the whole point of our consultations. I met Colin Powell yesterday, we shall be having lunch with the Secretary General of the United Nations and the fourteen other Ministers for Foreign Affairs. This is a real opportunity for us to take counsel from each other and I am convinced that today it is possible for us agree on a given route that is effective and firm within the framework of resolution 1441.

Are you firmly convinced that military action is not justified? Is France ready to oppose its veto if it receives insufficient assurance or if it is convinced that Iraq is not manifestly violating its obligations? And I get the impression that you are suggesting that even if there were some proof, you might decide that military force is still not justified, that it could have too many repercussions.

DV—The French attitude in the case of a second resolution or if the United States were to decide to continue along their path, and we have said this since the beginning, the French

President has said it clearly: we will not be involved in any military intervention that does not have the support of the international community, the support of the United Nations. Moreover, we believe that military intervention would be the worst solution and that recourse to force must be a final resort, always supposing that all other pathways have been exhausted. At that point we can talk about the right to veto. As a permanent member of the Security Council, France accepts all its responsibilities in accordance with the principles it holds dear. And I say again in response to the question I was asked concerning the inconsistency of France: you may take it from me that when it comes to respecting principles, we shall stand by them to the end. On the question of military intervention and the legality of any such action, our feeling is very simple: for as long as we can continue to explore cooperation, as long as we can advance through cooperation with the inspectors, there is no reason to choose the worst of all solutions, military intervention.

Going from what you say, and having heard Mr. Powell, we get the impression that you are not at all on the same wavelength. He has confronted you, you and the other members of the Security Council, with an ultimatum: rally to our position, otherwise you'll see what happens. Is that the result of your recent exchanges? You mentioned that you had an exchange of views with him yesterday. How far do you intend to go? And what do you think about his efforts and the efforts that have been made with a view to exiling Saddam Hussein?

DV—We have an excellent relationship with our American friends. And it is all the better for the fact that we speak frankly to each other. That is the whole meaning of the French diplomatic action and we have observed, week after week, that there is great trust in this relationship. It so happens that on this particular question we may have different positions. And it is precisely on a question of principles that we differ: the feeling that today the international community can hope to look for the means that will enable us to find the solutions to the crises in the world and, as I have said, terrorism, proliferation and regional crises, and that it is important to take the pulse of the world, to assess the feelings in the world, the feelings of frustration and feelings of injustice.

Let's pay attention to the people in the world. Deciding on an intervention is one thing, solving the problems is another. Unfortunately, there is no magic wand for solving problems, much as we might wish there were. It is only through effort, determination, energy and imagination that we can make things possible. And it is this very energy, these very efforts and this very patience that we are devoting to international cooperation. Because it is the only way to solve the question of Iraq, to solve the question of North Korea tomorrow, the only way to recover the initiative in the Near East. Look at the situation we are in: one of the oldest crises on the planet, which the international community seems to be ignoring today and allowing the existing situation of injustice to continue. How do you expect the Arab world to react to these situations? France is accountable on an international level for seeing that the principles of law, morality, justice and solidarity are respected. Moreover, we say that it is time to ask the questions, all the questions, if a military intervention is to be envisaged. What will the result be tomorrow? Yet again, the problem is more difficult than changing regime. And that is the very reason why we have fixed a simple objective: Iraqi disarmament. And you ask me about exiling Saddam Hussein. Let's not be diverted from our goal. Our goal is Iraqi disarmament, not other solutions, some of which may today seem to be totally fantastical.

Today you convoked the Ministers for Foreign Affairs of the major powers to speak on terrorism and here we are speaking essentially about Iraq. Do you think the discussions have been diverted and that if we speak too much about Iraq, we run the risk of feeding terrorism?

DV—We believe that all questions are linked. It is one planet. And when you have a situation of weakness in the international community, when the world is running a fever, it is quite obvious that the fever exists at the head and at the extremities. It exists everywhere. We cannot isolate different parts of the planet. We are witnessing a multiplicity of crises. Just consider the multiplication of attacks the planet has experienced since September 11. There is obviously a link between all of these situations. And that is why the choice of remedy is so important. That is why we believe that the true wealth of the international community is its unity, its unanimity. We will be effective only if we act together. And all the temptations, fear, force and skepticism lead nowhere. The international community needs to be mobilized. And there are not, contrary to what some people would like to believe, on one side those who want to act and on the other, those considered to be inconsistent or skeptical and who are content to merely pretend to act. No, there are those who believe that certain actions are effective and others who think that other actions are more effective. And it is our conviction that cooperation and inspections represent the true face of the international community. Today we must be able to run the risk of peace, of constructing peace, which is sometimes far more demanding than making war.

A CHANCE FOR PEACE

ADDRESS TO THE U.N. SECURITY COUNCIL, AFTER A PRESENTATION BY
U.S. SECRETARY OF STATE COLIN POWELL, FEBRUARY 5, 2003

*"The Iraqi authorities must provide the
inspectors with answers to the new elements presented by Colin Powell."*

On January 27th, UN inspectors Dr. Hans Blix and Mohamed El Baradeï presented a report citing satisfactory cooperation by Iraq with the inspections to date, and adding that while there was no proof of Baghdad's destruction of weapons of mass destruction, nor was there any proof of the existence of such weapons.

However, on January February 5th American Secretary of State Colin Powell made a dramatic presentation to the Security Council of what he called "proof"—including aerial surveillance photos and other intelligence matter—that Iraq was indeed developing and concealing weapons of mass destruction, and that it had ties to al-Qaeda.

Mr. President,
Mr. Secretary-General,
Ministers,
Ambassadors,

I wish to reiterate here the condolences of France to the American people for the terrible Columbia space shuttle tragedy.

I also wish to congratulate the German Presidency for organizing this meeting, and to thank Secretary of State Colin Powell for his initiative in convening this meeting. I listened very carefully to the elements he gave us. They contain information, indications, questions that deserve to be explored. It will be up to the inspectors to assess the facts in accordance with resolution 1441. Already his report brings a new justification to the path chosen by the United Nations; it must strengthen our common determination.

In unanimously adopting resolution 1441, we chose to act through inspections. This policy rests on three fundamental points: A clear objective on which we cannot compromise: the disarmament of Iraq; A method: a rigorous system of inspections which demands Iraq's active cooperation and affirms the central role of the Security Council at each stage.

A requirement: our unity. This gave the message we unanimously addressed to Baghdad its full force. I hope that our meeting today will strengthen this unity.

Significant results have already been seen: UNMOVIC and the AIEA are at work: more than a hundred inspectors are deployed on the ground and they are making 300 visits a month on average; the number of sites inspected has increased; complete access to the presidential sites in particular is a major gain; in the nuclear domain, the first two months allowed the IAEA to make "good progress" in its knowledge of Iraq's capacity as Dr. El Baradei has stated. This is a key element; in the areas covered by UNMOVIC, the inspections have provided us with useful information.

Mr. Blix has confirmed, for example, that no trace of biological or chemical agents has so far been detected by the inspectors: not through analyses of samples taken from inspected sites nor on the 12 empty warheads discovered at Ukhaider on January 16.

Nonetheless, there are still gray areas in Iraq's cooperation: The inspectors have reported real difficulties. In his January 27 report, Mr. Blix gave several examples of unresolved questions in the ballistic, chemical and biological domains. These uncertainties are not acceptable. France will continue to pass on all the information it has so they can be better defined; Right now, our attention has to be focused as a priority on the biological and chemical domains. It is there that our presumptions about Iraq are the most significant: regarding the chemical domain, we have evidence of its capacity to produce VX and yperite; in the biological domain, the evidence suggests the possible possession of significant stocks of anthrax and botulism toxin, and possibly a production capability; Today the absence of long-range delivery systems reduces the potential threat of these weapons. But we have disturbing signs of Iraq's continued determination to acquire ballistic missiles beyond the authorized 150-km range; In the nuclear domain, we must clarify in particular any attempt by Iraq to acquire aluminum tubes.

So it is a demanding *démarche*, anchored in resolution 1441, that we must take together. If this path were to fail and take us into a dead-end, then we rule out no option, including in the final analysis the recourse to force as we have said all along.

But in such a hypothesis, several answers will have to be clearly provided to all governments and all peoples of the world to limit the risks and uncertainties: To what extent do the nature and scope of the threat justify the recourse to force? How do we make sure that the considerable risks of such intervention are actually kept under control? This obviously requires a collective démarche of responsibility on the part of the world community.

In any case, it must be clear that in the context of such an option, the United Nations will have to be at the center of the action to guarantee Iraq's unity, ensure the region's stability, protect civilians and preserve the unity of the world community.

For now the inspections regime, favored by resolution 1441, must be strengthened since it has not been explored to the end. Use of force can only be a final recourse. Why go to war if there still exists an unused space in resolution 1441?

Consistent with the logic of this resolution, we must therefore move on to a new stage and further strengthen the inspections. With the choice between military intervention and an inspections regime that is inadequate for lack of cooperation on Iraq's part, we must choose to strengthen decisively the means of inspection. This is what France advocates today.

To do this, we must define with Mr. Blix and Dr. El Baradei the requisite tools for increasing their operational capabilities: Let us double or triple the number of inspectors and open up more regional offices. Let us go further: Why not establish a specialized body to keep under surveillance the sites and areas already inspected?

Let us substantially increase the capabilities for monitoring and collecting information on Iraqi territory. France is ready to provide full support: it is ready to deploy Mirage IV observer aircraft.

Let us collectively establish a coordination and information-processing center that would supply Mr. Blix and Dr. El Baradei, in real time and in a coordinated way, with all the intelligence resources they might need.

Let us list the unresolved disarmament questions and rank them by importance;

With the consent of the leaders of the inspection teams, let us define a demanding and realistic time-frame for moving forward in the assessment and elimination of problems. There must be regular follow-up to the progress made in Iraq's disarmament.

This enhanced regime of inspections and monitoring could be usefully complemented by having a permanent UN coordinator for disarmament in Iraq, stationed in Iraq and working under the authority of Mr. Blix and Dr. El Baradei.

But Iraq must cooperate actively. The country must comply immediately with the demands of Mr. Blix and Dr. El Baradei, in particular by: permitting meetings with Iraqi scientists without witnesses; agreeing to the use of U2 observer flights; adopting legislation to prohibit the manufacture of weapons of mass destruction; handing over to the inspectors immediately all relevant documents on unresolved disarmament questions, in particular in the biological and chemical domains; those handed over on January 20 do not constitute a step in the right direction. The 3000 pages of documents discovered at the home of a researcher show that Baghdad must do more. Absent documents, Iraq must be able to present credible testimony.

The Iraqi authorities must also provide the inspectors with answers to the new elements presented by Colin Powell.

Between now and the inspectors' next report, on February 14, Iraq will have to provide new elements. The upcoming visit to Baghdad by the leaders of the inspectors will have to be the occasion for clear results to this end.

Mr. President, this is the demanding *démarche* that we must take together for a new stage. Its success presupposes, today as yesterday, that the international community remains united and mobilized.

It is our moral and political duty first to devote all our energy to Iraq's disarmament, in peace and in compliance with the rule of law and justice. France is convinced that we can succeed on this demanding path so long as we maintain our unity and cohesion. This is the choice of collective responsibility.

Thank you.

ACTIVE COOPERATION

ADDRESS TO THE SECURITY COUNCIL AFTER A REPORT FROM
UN WEAPONS INSPECTORS, FEBRUARY 14, 2003

"No one can assert today that the path of war will be shorter than that of the inspections. No one can claim either that it might lead to a safer, more just and more stable world. For war is always the sanction of failure."

Despite the fact that Colin Powell's February 5th speech failed to win over a majority of the Security Council, President George Bush the next day declared "The game is over," and the United States, along with Great Britain, began drafting a resolution that would allow military intervention against Iraq. France, Germany, and Russia led an effort to persuade a majority of the Security Council of the weakness of American arguments and of the consequences of a military intervention. All three argued for a continued peaceful disarmament of Iraq.

On February 14th 2003, Hans Blix and Mohamed El Baradei delivered a report to the Security Council citing increased cooperation from Iraq, and stating that they still had not found any weapons of mass destruction. Blix also contested some of the "proof" presented by Colin Powell in his presentation.

I would like to thank Mr. Blix and Mr. El Baradei for the information they have just given us on the continuing inspections in Iraq. I would like to express to them again France's confidence and complete support in their mission.

You know the value that France has placed on the unity of the Security Council from the outset of the Iraq crisis. This unity rests on two fundamental elements at this time: we are pursuing together the objective of effectively disarming Iraq. We have an obligation to achieve results. Let us not cast doubt on our common commitment to this goal. We shoulder collectively this onerous responsibility which must leave no room for other agendas or impugning one another's motives. Let us be clear: not one of us feels the least indulgence towards Saddam Hussein and the Iraqi regime.

In unanimously adopting UNSCR 1441, we collectively expressed our agreement with the two-stage approach proposed by France: the choice of disarmament through inspections and, should this strategy fail, consideration by the Security Council of all the options, including the recourse to force. It was clearly in the event of the inspections failing and only in that scenario that a second resolution could be justified.

The question today is simple: do we consider in good conscience that disarmament through inspections is now leading us to a dead end? Or do we consider that the possibilities regarding inspections presented in UNSCR 1441 have still not been fully explored?

In response to this question, France has two convictions: the first is that the option of inspections has not been taken as far as it can go and that it can provide an effective response to the imperative of disarming Iraq; the second is that the use of force would be so fraught with risks for people, for the region and for international stability that it must only be envisioned as a last resort.

So what have we just learned from the report by Mr Blix and Mr El Baradei? That the inspections are producing results. Of course, each of us wants more, and we will continue together to put pressure on Baghdad to obtain more. But the inspections are producing results.

In their previous reports to the Security Council on 27 January, the Executive Chairman of UNMOVIC and the Director General of the IAEA had identified in detail areas in which progress was expected. Significant gains have been made on several of these points:

In the chemical and biological areas, the Iraqis have provided the inspectors with new documentation. They have also announced the establishment of commissions of inquiry led by former officials of weapons programmes, in accordance with Mr Blix's requests; in the ballistic domain, the information provided by Iraq has also enabled the inspectors to make progress. We know exactly the real capabilities of the Al Samoud missile. The unauthorized programmes must now be dismantled, in accordance with Mr Blix's conclusions.

In the nuclear domain, useful information was given to the IAEA on the most important points raised by Mr El Baradei on 27 January: the acquisition of magnets that could be used for enriching uranium and the list of contacts between Iraq and the country likely to have provided her with uranium.

Here we are at the heart of the purpose of UNSCR 1441 which is to ensure the effectiveness of the inspections through precise identification of banned programmes, then their elimination. We all realize that the success of the inspections presupposes that we obtain Iraq's full and complete cooperation. France has consistently demanded this.

Real progress is beginning to be apparent: Iraq has agreed to aerial reconnaissance over her territory; she has allowed Iraqi scientists to be questioned by the inspectors without witnesses; a bill banning all activities linked to weapons of mass destruction programmes is in the process of being adopted, in accordance with a long-standing request of the inspectors; Iraq is to provide a detailed list of experts who witnessed the destruction of military programmes in 1991.

France naturally expects these commitments to be durably verified. Beyond that, we must maintain strong pressure on Iraq so that she goes further in her cooperation.

Progress like this strengthens us in our conviction that inspections can be effective. But we must not shut our eyes to the amount of work that still remains; questions still have to be cleared up, verifications made, and installations and equipment very probably still have to be destroyed. To do this, we must give the inspections every chance of succeeding.

I submitted proposals to the Council on 5 February. Since then we have detailed them in a working document addressed to Mr Blix and Mr El Baradei and distributed to Council members. What is the spirit of these proposals? They are practical, concrete proposals that can be implemented quickly and are designed to enhance the efficiency of inspection operations. They fall within the framework of UNSCR 1441 and consequently do not require a new resolution. They must support the efforts of Mr Blix and Mr El Baradei. They are naturally the best placed to tell us which ones they wish to adopt for the maximum effectiveness of their work. In their report they have already made useful and operational comments. France has already announced that she had additional resources available to Mr Blix and Mr El Baradei, beginning with her Mirage IV reconnaissance aircraft.

Now, yes, I do hear the critics: there are those who think that the inspections, in their principle, cannot be the least effective. But I recall that this is the very foundation of UNSCR 1441 and that the inspections are producing results. One may judge them inadequate but they are there.

There are those who believe that continuing the inspection process is a sort of "delaying tactic" to prevent military intervention. That naturally raises the question of the time allowed Iraq. This brings us to the core of the debates. At stake is our credibility, and our sense of responsibility. Let us have the courage to see things as they are.

There are two options: the option of war might seem a priori to be the swiftest. But let us not forget that after winning the war, one has to build peace. Let us not delude ourselves; this will be long and difficult because it will be necessary to preserve Iraq's unity and restore stability in a lasting way in a country and region harshly affected by the intrusion of force. Faced with such perspectives, there is an alternative in the inspections which allow us to move forward day by day with the effective and peaceful disarmament of Iraq. In the end is that choice not the most sure and most rapid?

No one can assert today that the path of war will be shorter than that of the inspections. No one can claim either that it might lead to a safer, more just and more stable world.

For war is always the sanction of failure. Would this be our sole recourse in the face of the many challenges at this time?

So let us allow the United Nations inspectors the time they need for their mission to succeed. But let us together be vigilant and ask Mr Blix and Mr El Baradei to report regularly to the Council. France, for her part, proposes another meeting on 14 March at ministerial level to assess the situation. We will then be able to judge the progress that has been made and what remains to be done.

Given this context, the use of force is not justified at this time. There is an alternative to war: disarming Iraq through inspections. Furthermore, premature recourse to the military option would be fraught with risks: The authority of our action is based today on the unity of the international community. Premature military intervention would jeopardize this unity, which would detract from its legitimacy and, in the long run, its effectiveness. Such intervention could have incalculable consequences for the stability of this scarred and fragile region. It would compound the sense of injustice, increase tensions and risk paving the way to other conflicts.

We all share the same priority—that of fighting terrorism mercilessly. This fight requires total determination. Since the tragedy of 11 September this has been one of the highest priorities facing our peoples. And France, who has been struck hard by this terrible scourge several times, is wholly mobilized in this fight which concerns us all and which we must pursue together. That was the purpose of the Security Council meeting held on 20 January, at France's initiative.

Ten days ago, the U.S. Secretary of State, Mr Powell, reported the alleged links between al-Qaida and the regime in Baghdad. Given the present state of our research and intelligence, in liaison with our allies, nothing allows us to establish such links. On the other hand, we must assess the impact that currently disputed military action would have on this plan. Would not such intervention today be liable to exacerbate the divisions between societies, cultures and peoples, divisions that nurture terrorism?

France has said all along: we do not exclude the possibility that force may have to be used one day if the inspectors' reports concluded that it was impossible to continue the inspections. The Council would then have to take a decision, and its members would have to face up to all their responsibilities. In such an eventuality, I want to recall here the questions I emphasized at our last debate on 4 February which we must answer: To what extent do the nature and extent of the threat justify the immediate recourse to force? How do we ensure that the considerable risks of such intervention can actually be kept under control? In any case, in such an eventuality, it is indeed the unity of the international community that would guarantee its effectiveness. Similarly, it is the United Nations that will be tomorrow at the centre of the peace to be built whatever happens.

To those who are wondering in anguish when and how we are going to succumb to war, I would like to tell them that nothing, at any time, in this Security Council, will be done in haste, misunderstanding, suspicion or fear.

In this temple of the United Nations, we are the guardians of an ideal, the guardians of a conscience. The onerous responsibility and immense honour we have must lead us to give priority to disarmament in peace.

This message comes to you today from an old country, France, from a continent like mine, Europe, that has known wars, occupation and barbarity. A country that does not forget and knows everything she owes to the freedom-fighters who came from America and elsewhere. And yet has never ceased to stand upright in the face of history and before mankind. She wishes resolutely to act with all the members of the international community. Faithful to her values, she believes in our ability to build together a better world.

TOWARDS A NEW RESOLUTION?

INTERVIEW WITH *LE FIGARO*, FEBRUARY 24, 2003

*"The goal of regime change poses a funda-
mental question: Who, acting on whose
behalf, would determine whether a regime
were good or bad?"*

On February 19th the White House announced that the President was ready to present a second resolution aimed at disarming Iraq, a resolution that authorized the use of force by member nations. In the end it was Britain and Spain that presented the new resolution to the Security Council on February 24th. This, despite the fact that on February 16 French President Jacques Chirac had reiterated France's position that force should be a last resort by saying it was "not necessary today to have a second resolution that France would just have to oppose." France had also proposed boosting the inspection team's man power and equipment in order to accelerate the peaceful disarmament process.

Q.—*The United States is getting ready to table a new draft resolution at the UN to legitimize an operation against Iraq. Is the time for the inspections over?*

THE MINISTER—We are most definitely at the inspections stage. They're producing results and are capable of bringing about the complete disarmament of Iraq. The inspectors are reporting progress. With the Iraq crisis, we have to resolve a serious proliferation crisis. But we shall subsequently have to face up to many other crises of this kind, such as those of North Korea and other countries. The challenge is huge. There's something of an exploratory nature, and of an attempt to find a model for future action in what the international community is trying to do in Iraq.

It's been trying to disarm her for the past twelve years, without great success.

Between 1991 and 1998, inspections were carried out. They resulted in the elimination of more weapons of mass destruction than did the armed operations of the Gulf War. Then, they were halted between 1998 and 2002, creating a black hole which today we need to fill. In Iraq, we have to disarm a country ruled by a dictator. It's the case of many other States. So we need to invent a tool, making use of inspections, which allows the effective disarmament of these States and provides the international community with all the necessary guarantees.

According to what the inspectors are saying, Iraq is still refusing to cooperate actively and fully in her disarmament. Can we beef up the system still further?

We have proposed to the inspectors measures to increase the human and material resources available for the inspections. We are going to propose to the Security Council a second memorandum with the aim of defining, going beyond tougher inspections, some concrete criteria to facilitate and mark specific progress in disarmament. We suggest setting deadlines, programme by programme, to facilitate the inspectors' work and speed up effective disarmament, in accordance with last week's statement by the European heads of State and government. We also want to spell out our demands at every stage of the inspection process. For example, the inspectors must be able to interview Iraqi experts without the meetings being recorded and in places of their choosing. Iraq has submitted a list of 83 names of experts who contributed to the elimination of chemical weapons in 1991. That gives us a solid basis to work on.

The Americans assert that UNSCR 1441 authorizes the international community to use force against Iraq if she omits to declare some weapons and doesn't actively cooperate in her disarmament. So they would seemingly today be justified in moving to military action.

France firmly believes that so long as the inspections are working, we must keep on moving along this route.

It's thought that the American text will note Iraq's blatant violation and move on to the "serious consequences" envisaged by 1441.

It's only if the inspections couldn't make any further progress that a second phase would open, that of considering the other possibilities, including the recourse to force. UNSCR 1441 says that a new Security Council meeting will take place if we have reached a dead end, on the basis of a report by the inspectors. But today we are in exactly the opposite situation. The inspectors confirm that there is progress. This is why, in the present circumstances, we are opposed, as President Chirac has said, to a new resolution.

The deadline for deciding on the use of force will be mid-March?

The international community's timetable is based on the regular reports submitted by the inspectors, every two to three weeks. They are due to submit a new one at the beginning of March. We shall then see if we are in a new situation. Today, this isn't the case. We're keen to help the inspectors work more efficiently, more effectively and more quickly. We want to step up the pressure on Baghdad, strengthen its commitment to disarm rapidly.

How?

We have to verify the information received, sphere by sphere, then eliminate any weapons which may be discovered. A good example is provided by the Al Samoud 2 missiles, whose destruction Hans Blix has ordered to begin by 1 March since their range exceeds the UN authorized limit of 150 km. If the Iraqis destroyed those missiles, that would be a positive step.

We have to move on to concrete action and get Iraq to carry out her obligations, in this instance the destruction of these banned missiles. As soon as we get any proof of the existence of other programmes in the chemical and biological spheres, the same principle would have to be applied: information, verification and destruction. That's the right approach.

Do you have enough votes in the Security Council to stop the U.S. draft resolution?

A large majority of countries in the Security Council expressed support on 14 February for continuing the inspections. The situation hasn't changed since. We are waiting for the next interim report.

Are you confident that you won't have to threaten to use your veto to prevent the resolution from being adopted?

The question doesn't arise as there are many of us who are convinced that UNSCR 1441 offers the requisite framework for the action of the international community. We have resolutely chosen inspections and with us an overwhelming majority of States, particularly European, African and non-aligned countries. It is striking that today the Americans seem not to be taking into account the progress reported by Mr Blix and Mr El Baradei, any more than they are the decisions the Iraqis might take.

UN/U.S. UNILATERAL ACTION

Is the UN at risk of being marginalized if the U.S. decided to act alone?

Whatever happens, the United Nations is indispensable at all stages. The day that peace has to be built, the UN will be needed because it constitutes the heart of international legitimacy.

IRAQ/INTERNATIONAL PRESSURE

Are the 200,000 American soldiers in the Gulf forcing Iraq to cooperate?

Several factors are forcing Iraq to cooperate. First of all, the firmness of the international community expressed in the unanimous UN decision on UNSCR 1441; then diplomatic pressure from the Arab world and from certain countries like Russia and China. There are also the regular reports from the inspectors; before 14 February, the pressure generated by the reports by Mr Blix and Mr El Baradei played a considerable role in encouraging Iraq to open up. Of course, there's the role played by U.S. military pressure. Wouldn't it be a greater success for the Bush administration to withdraw its armada after seeing the inspections right through to the very end, right to the completion of Iraq's disarmament, without firing a shot, without a death!

SADDAM HUSSEIN/REGIME CHANGE

But Saddam Hussein would still be there?

The goal of regime change poses a fundamental question: who, acting on whose behalf, would determine whether a regime were good or bad? There is there a risk for world stability. We've, of course, not the least liking for Saddam Hussein. The goal agreed by the international community is Iraq's disarmament, not regime change or "remodeling" the Middle East.

Aren't you worried about appearing to defend Saddam Hussein?

Not at all. We are adhering in a determined and responsible way to the goals set by the United Nations. We have to know how to stick to our goals. With the best of intentions, we could become embroiled in objectives contrary to those sought. Premature action, especially a military operation, would entail dangers of destabilization and a revival of terrorism. It would risk aggravating certain conflicts and so, in the end, bring disunity to the international community and compound the uncertainty in the world. We would find ourselves in a situation where the concept of developing a model for future action through what we're doing with the inspections would be destroyed. Is the purpose of the second resolution being talked of to sanction the failure of inspections, when we see they are making progress, or is it aimed at getting support from the international community for a scenario which seems to have been written in advance?

WORLD PROBLEM/MILITARY INTERVENTION

If the American forces pulled out leaving Saddam Hussein's regime in place, you could say the proliferators had won.

The central question is: what is the state of the world? There are two visions, two analyses. Through Iraq, some think a military intervention can resolve at the same time a crisis of proliferation, part of the terrorism problem and lastly a regional crisis as big as the crisis in the Middle East. So we would resolve a large part of the world's problems like this. That is definitely not our analysis. The world is in great disorder. There are enormous difficulties in various spheres—whether we're talking of proliferation, terrorism or regional crises. We have to try to move forward on all these fronts at the same time. The battle is a complex one. One has to know how far to take each of the methods used. Now, moving forward at this point, without precaution, in a region that is already highly fractured and culturally and religiously extremely sensitive is certainly not the best way to resolve these various crises. On the contrary, we think there is a risk of misunderstanding, tension and humiliation which will only widen the gap, for example between the Arab world and the rest of the world, even though we wish to avoid this "clash of cultures."

MIDDLE EAST "REMODELING"

You don't believe in the "remodeling" of the Middle East sought by the United States?

We all want democracy to advance in the Middle East. But is the use of force the best way to engage such a mechanism? On the contrary, would it not reinforce hatred and intolerance? We wonder. Given the growing number of splits in the Middle East today, the use of force may not in itself trigger a virtuous spiral. It could even have the opposite effect. So it must remain a last resort.

US/EUROPE

Your comments suggest there's going to be a new clash with the United States at the UN? Is that going to exacerbate transatlantic tensions still further?

We uphold a vision of world organization which is very largely shared by the international community. Given the extent of the threats, we need a world with several poles of stability. The temptation to create a unipolar world, to resort to force cannot contribute to stability. No one country can claim to be able to resolve all the crises by itself. We must see the action chosen by the international community, including the U.S., by adopting UNSCR 1441 through to the very end. We must have the determination and sang-froid to abide by this resolution.

You're endeavouring to mobilize a European pole which doesn't give the impression of wanting to be one. At least half the European countries don't share your vision.

There may be some misunderstanding in the minds of certain Europeans. What is at stake today is not the transatlantic relationship but the way in which we deal with the Iraq crisis, which is a proliferation crisis, while laying the foundations for the world order we wish to build.

If you factor in this confusion, I can understand that some countries might hesitate. But that is not the question. We're certainly not looking to pick a quarrel with the United States. Like President Chirac and President Bush, I have a trustful, ongoing relationship with Colin Powell. Moreover you'll not find anything, not one word spoken by French leaders involved in this crisis which is the least bit aggressive towards the United States.

But you're ready to risk a deterioration in relations with Washington, and that's not the case for most of your European partners.

At a time when you hear too much anti-French sentiment in the U.S., I'm happy to note that there is no anti-American feeling in France, nor any association made between the Iraq crisis and Franco-American relations. There are positions on which we all agree: the choice of inspections, the determination to do everything to enable them to be effective, and to accept the consequences if that were not the case. Things become complicated when you introduce the parameter of transatlantic relations. That is regrettable. We have to focus on the Iraq crisis, knowing that we have other crises of proliferation to resolve, not to mention terrorism and regional crises. The difficulty for the world today is that all these crises are happening at the same time. We must acquire joint collective and peaceful instruments to move forward. As President Chirac keeps on saying, force can only be a last resort.

DISARMAMENT OR WAR?

ADDRESS TO THE SECURITY COUNCIL, MARCH 7, 2003

"The stakes transcend the case of Iraq alone."

As the troop buildup continued, President Bush gave a February 28th speech to the American Enterprise Institute in which he looked beyond questions of disarmament and laid out his broader objectives, associated with a military invention in Iraq, for remodeling the Middle East. Meanwhile, Washington and London redoubled their efforts within the Security Council to rally the necessary support for a new resolution authorizing the use of force. On March 5th, the representatives of Germany, Russia and France announced in a joint statement that their countries "would not pass this resolution."

On March 7th, in another debriefing on the progress of weapons inspections, Hans Blix reported to the Security Council that Iraq had complied with demands to begin destroying its Al Samoud 2 missiles (which had longer ranges than authorized by the Security Council resolution), and Mohamed El Baradei presented evidence refuting allegations that Iraq was involved in prohibited activities (attempting to buy uranium from Nigeria and aluminum tubes for their nuclear program). El Baradei also announced that the IAEA would shortly be able to confirm that the Iraqi nuclear weapons programs had been dismantled.

Mr. President,
Mr. Secretary-General,
Ministers,
Ambassadors,

I would like to begin by telling you how pleased France is, that on this decisive day, the Security Council is being presided over by Guinea, by an African.

I would like to thank Mr. Blix and Mr. El Baradei for the presentation they have just given us. Their reports testify to regular progress in the disarmament of Iraq.

What have the inspectors told us? That for a month, Iraq has been actively cooperating with them. That substantial progress has been made in the area of ballistics with the progressive destruction of Al Samoud 2 missiles and their equipment. That new prospects are opening up with the recent questioning of several scientists. Significant evidence of real disarmament has now been observed. And that indeed is the key to resolution 1441.

With solemnity, therefore, before this body, I would like to ask a question—the very same question being asked by people all over the world: Why should we today engage in a war with Iraq?

And I would also like to ask: Why smash the instruments that have just proven their effectiveness? Why choose division when our unity and our resolve are leading Iraq to get rid of its weapons of mass destruction? Why should we wish to proceed, at any price, by force when we can succeed peacefully?

War is always an acknowledgement of failure. Let us not resign ourselves to the irreparable. Before making our choice, let us weigh the consequences, let us measure the effects of our decision.

We all see it: In Iraq, we are resolutely moving toward completely eliminating programs of weapons of mass destruction. The method that we have chosen works: The information supplied by Baghdad has been verified by the inspectors, and is leading to the elimination of banned ballistic equipment.

We are proceeding the same way with all the other programs: with information, verification, destruction. We already have useful information in the biological and chemical domains. In response to questions by the inspectors, Iraq must give us further information in a timely fashion, so that we may obtain the most precise possible knowledge about any existing inventories or programs. On the basis of this information, we will destroy all the components that are discovered, as we are doing for the missiles, and will determine what the truth is. With regard to nuclear weapons, Mr. El Baradei's statements confirm that we are approaching the time when the IAEA will be able to certify the dismantlement of the Iraq program.

What conclusions can we draw? That Iraq, according to the very terms used by the inspectors, represents less of a danger to the world than it did in 1991. That we can achieve our objective of effectively disarming that country.

Let us keep the pressure on Baghdad. The adoption of resolution 1441, the assumption of converging positions by the vast majority of the world's nations, diplomatic actions by the Organization of African Unity, the League of Arab States, the Organization of the Islamic Conference and the Non-Aligned Movement—all of these common efforts are bearing fruit.

The American and British military presence in the region lends support to our collective resolve. We all recognize the effectiveness of this pressure on the part of the international community. We must use it to go through with our objective of disarmament through inspections. As the European Union noted, these inspections cannot continue indefinitely. The pace must therefore be stepped up.

That is why France wants to make three proposals today.

First, let us ask the inspectors to establish a hierarchy of tasks for disarmament and, on that basis, to present us as quickly as possible with the work program provided for by resolution 1284. We need to know immediately what the priority issues are that could constitute key disarmament tasks to be carried out by Iraq.

Second, we propose that the inspectors give us a progress report every three weeks. That will make the Iraqi authorities understand that in no case may they interrupt their efforts.

Finally, let us establish a schedule for assessing the implementation of the work program. Resolution 1284 provides for a time frame of 120 days. We are willing to shorten it, if the inspectors consider it feasible.

The military agenda must not dictate the calendar of inspections. We agree to timetables and to an accelerated calendar. But we cannot accept an ultimatum as long as the inspectors are reporting cooperation. That would mean war. It would lead the Security Council to relinquish its responsibilities. By imposing a deadline of a few days, would we be reduced to seeking a pretext for war?

As a permanent member of the Security Council, I will say it again: France will not allow a resolution to pass that authorizes the automatic use of force.

Let us consider the anguish and the waiting of people all around the world, in all our countries, from Cairo to Rio, from Algiers to Pretoria, from Rome to Jakarta.

Indeed, the stakes transcend the case of Iraq alone. Let us look at things lucidly: We are defining a method to resolve crises. We are choosing to define the world we want our children to live in. That is true in the case of North Korea, in the case of Southern Asia, where we have not yet found the path toward a lasting resolution of disputes. It is true in the case of the Mideast: Can we continue to wait while acts of violence multiply?

These crises have many roots: They are political, religious, economic. Their origins lie in the tumult of centuries. There may be some who believe that these problems can be resolved by force, thereby creating a new order. That is not France's conviction. On the contrary, we believe that the use of force can arouse rancor and hatred, fuel a clash of identities, of cultures—something that our generation has, precisely, a prime responsibility to avoid.

To those who believe that war would be the quickest way to disarm Iraq, I say it will establish gulfs and create wounds that are long in healing. And how many victims will it bring, how many grieving families?

We do not subscribe to what may be the other objectives of a war. Is it a matter of regime change in Baghdad? No one underestimates the cruelty of this dictatorship and the need to do everything possible to promote human rights. That is not the objective of resolution 1441. And force is certainly not the best way to bring about democracy. It would encourage dangerous instability, there and elsewhere.

Is it a matter of fighting terrorism? War would only increase it, and we could then be faced with a new wave of violence. Let us beware of playing into the hands of those who want a clash of civilizations, a clash of religions.

Or is it, finally, a matter of remolding the political landscape of the Middle East? In that case, we run the risk of exacerbating tensions in a region already marked by great instability. Not to mention that in Iraq itself, the large number of communities and religions already represents the danger of a potential break-up.

We all have the same demands: more security, more democracy. But there is another logic beside that of force, another path, other solutions.

We understand the profound sense of insecurity with which the American people have been living since the tragedy of September 11, 2001. The entire world shared the sorrow of New York and of America, struck in the heart. I say this in the name of our friendship for the American people, in the name of our common values: freedom, justice, tolerance. But there is nothing today that indicates a link between the Iraqi regime and al-Qaeda. And will the world be a safer place after a military intervention in Iraq? I want to tell you what my country's conviction is: No.

Four months ago, we unanimously adopted a system of inspections to eliminate the threat of potential weapons of mass destruction and guarantee our security. Today we cannot accept, without contradicting ourselves, a conflict that might well weaken it.

Yes, we too want more democracy in the world. But we will achieve this objective only within the framework of a true global democracy based on respect, sharing, the awareness of a true community of values and a common destiny. And its heart is the United Nations.

Let us make no mistake: In the face of multiple and complex threats there is no one response, but a single necessity: We must remain united. Today we must invent, together, a new future for the Middle East. Let us not forget the immense hope created by the efforts of the Madrid Conference and the Oslo Agreement. Let us not forget that the Mideast crisis represents our greatest challenge in terms of security and justice. For us, the Mideast, like Iraq, represents a priority commitment.

This calls for great ambition and even greater boldness: We should envision a region transformed through peace; civilizations that, through the courage of the outstretched hand, rediscover their self-confidence and an international prestige equal to their long history and their aspirations.

In a few days, we must solemnly fulfill our responsibility through a vote. We will be facing an essential choice: Disarming Iraq through war or through peace. And this crucial choice implies others: It implies the international community's ability to resolve current or future crises. It implies a vision of the world, a concept of the role of the United Nations.

France believes that to make this choice, to make it in good conscience in this forum of international democracy, before their people and before the world, the heads of state and government must meet again here in New York, at the Security Council.

It is in everyone's interest. We must rediscover the fundamental vocation of the United Nations: to allow each of its members to assume its responsibilities in the face of the Iraqi crisis but also to seize, together, the destiny of a world in crisis and thus recreate the conditions for our future unity.

ON THE VERGE OF WAR

ADDRESS TO THE SECURITY COUNCIL, MARCH 19, 2003

"Make no mistake about it: the choice is indeed between two visions of the world."

After the Security Council's March 7th meeting failed to prompt any of the permanent members to change their positions, the Americans, British, and Spanish presented their resolution authorizing the use of force. The British proposed March 17th as the deadline for Iraq to disarm. Several different proposals seeking compromises (from Pakistan, Mexico, Chili, and Canada) were not seconded.

On March 10th, President Chirac announced that France would vote against any new resolution that triggered the automatic use of force. The public debates taking place in the U.N. on March 11th and 12th confirmed that most countries supported the continuation of weapons inspections.

Within the Security Council, the attempt to reach a compromise with the six undecided nations intensified. The new resolution still faced opposition from France, Russian, China, and Germany. The British, Americans, and Spanish failed to rally the necessary nine votes and ultimately decided to withdrawal their proposal.

On March 17th, the United States issued a unilateral, forty-eight hour ultimatum to Iraq.

Faced with the likelihood of an imminent military intervention, Hans Blix, fulfilling the terms of previous Security Council resolutions, appeared again before the Council to present the work he and his inspectors had done. Blix argued that, given the present circumstances, the inspectors could not possibly carry out their mission. Regardless, the inspectors had already begun to depart.

Mr. President,
Mr. Secretary-General,
Ministers,
Ambassadors,

We are meeting here today a few hours before the weapons sound. To exchange our convictions again in observance of our respective commitments. But also to outline together the paths that must allow us to recover the spirit of unity.

I wish to reiterate here that for France war can only be the exception, and collective responsibility the rule. Whatever our aversion for Saddam Hussein's cruel regime, that holds true for Iraq and for all the crises that we will have to confront together.

To Mr. Blix, who presented his work program to us, and Mr. El Baradei, who was represented today, I want to say thank you for the sustained efforts and for the results achieved. Their program is a reminder that there is still a clear and credible prospect for disarming Iraq peacefully. It proposes and prioritizes the tasks for such disarmament and presents a realistic timetable for their implementation.

In doing so the report confirms what we all know here: Yes, the inspections are producing tangible results. Yes, they offer the prospect of effective disarmament through peaceful means and in shorter time-frames.

The path we mapped out together in the context of resolution 1441 still exists. In spite of the fact that it has been interrupted today, we know that it will have to resume as soon as possible.

The Council took note two days ago of the Secretary-General's decision to withdraw the inspectors and all UN personnel from Iraq. The discharge of their mandates has consequently been suspended. It will be necessary when the time comes to complete our knowledge about Iraq's programs and finish disarming Iraq. The contribution of the inspectors will be decisive at that time.

Make no mistake about it: the choice is indeed between two visions of the world.

To those who choose to use force and think they can resolve the world's complexity through swift and preventive action, we offer in contrast determined action over time. For today, to ensure our security, all the dimensions of the problem must be taken into account: both the manifold crises and their many facets, including cultural and religious. Nothing lasting in international relations can be built therefore without dialogue and without respect for the other, without exigency and abiding by principles, especially for the democracies that must set the example. To ignore this is to run the risk of misunderstanding, radicalization and spiraling violence. This is even more true in the Middle East, an area of fractures and ancient conflicts where stability must be a major objective for us.

To those who hope to eliminate the dangers of proliferation through armed intervention in Iraq, I wish to say that we regret that they are depriving themselves of a key tool for other crises of the same type. The Iraq crisis allowed us craft an instrument, through the inspections regime, which is unprecedented and can serve as an example. Why, on this basis not envision establishing an innovative, permanent structure, a disarmament body under the United Nations?

To those who think that the scourge of terrorism will be eradicated through the case of Iraq, we say they run the risk of failing in their objective. The outbreak of force in this area which is so unstable can only exacerbate the tensions and fractures on which the terrorists feed.

Over and above our division, we have a collective responsibility in the face of these threats, the responsibility to recover the unity of the international community. The United Nations must remain mobilized in Iraq to aid this objective. Together, we have duties to assume in this perspective.

First of all, to staunch the wounds, the wounds of war. As always, war brings with it its share of victims, suffering and displaced people. So it is a matter of urgency to prepare now to provide the requisite humanitarian assistance. This imperative must prevail over our differences. The Secretary-General has already begun to mobilize the various UN agencies to this end. France will take its full part in the collective effort to assist the Iraqi people. The oil-for-food program must be continued under the authority of the Security Council with the necessary adjustments. We are waiting for the Secretary-General's proposals.

Next, it is necessary to build peace. No country by itself has the means to build Iraq's future. In particular, no state can claim the necessary legitimacy. It is from the United Nations alone that the legal and moral authority can come for such an undertaking. Two principles must guide our action: respect for the unity and territorial integrity of Iraq; and the preservation of its sovereignty.

By the same token, it is for the United Nations to set out the framework for the country's economic reconstruction. A framework that will have to affirm the two complementary principles of transparency and development of the country's resources for the benefit of the Iraqis themselves.

Our mobilization must also extend to the other threats that we have to address together. Given the very nature of these threats, it is no longer possible today to address them in any old order. By way of example, terrorism is fueled by organized crime networks; it cleaves to the contours of lawless areas; it thrives on regional crises; it garners support from the divisions in the world; it utilizes all available resources, from the most rudimentary to the most sophisticated, from the knife to the weapons of mass destruction it is trying to acquire.

To deal with this reality, we must act in a united way and on all fronts at the same time. So we must remain constantly mobilized.

In this spirit France renews its call for the heads of state and government to meet here in the Security Council in New York, to respond to the major challenges confronting us.

Let us intensify our fight against terrorism. Let us fight mercilessly against its networks with all the economic, juridical and political weapons available to us.

Let us give new impetus to the fight against the proliferation of weapons of mass destruction. France has already proposed that our heads of state and government meet on the sidelines of the next General Assembly to define the new priorities for our action.

Let us recover the initiative in the regional conflicts that are destabilizing entire regions. I am thinking in particular of the Israeli–Palestinian conflict. How much suffering must the peoples of the region still endure for us to force the doors to peace? Let us not resign ourselves to the irreparable.

In a world where the threat is asymmetrical, where the weak defy the strong, the power of conviction, the capacity to convince, the ability to sway opinion count as much as the number of divisions. They do not replace them. But they are the indispensable aids of a state's influence.

Faced with this new world, it is imperative that the action of the international community should be guided by principles.

First of all, respect for law. The keystone of international order, it must apply in all circumstances, but even more so when the gravest decision is to be made: to use force. Only on this condition can force be legitimate. Only on this condition can it restore order and peace.

Next, the defense of freedom and justice. We must not compromise with what is central to our values. We will be listened to and heeded only if we are inspired by the very ideals of the United Nations.

Lastly, the spirit of dialogue and tolerance. Never have the peoples of the world aspired so forcefully to its respect. We must listen to their appeal.

Mr. President, as we see clearly, the United Nations has never been so necessary. It is up to this body to harness all the resolve to meet these challenges. Because the United Nations is the place where international rules and legitimacy are founded. Because it speaks in the name of peoples.

In response to the clash of arms there must be a single upwelling of the spirit of responsibility, voice and gesture from the international community that is gathered here in New York, in the Security Council. This is in the interest of all: the countries engaged in the conflict, the states and peoples in the region, the international community as a whole. Confronted with a world in crisis, we have a moral and political obligation to restore the threads of hope and unity.

The judgment of future generations will depend on our capacity to meet this great challenge—in furtherance of our values, our common destiny and peace.

Thank you Mr. President.

THE TEST

*" It is with great emotion that I speak to
you at the moment when the first military operations are beginning in Iraq...."*

On March 20, George Bush's forty-eight hour ultimatum expired and the American military launched its attack on Iraq. The French Foreign Minister appeared before the French Senate to discuss the consequences of events.

FRANCE/MILITARY ACTION

It is with great emotion that I speak to you at the moment when the first military operations are beginning in Iraq. Throughout the past few months, with all her partners, with the vast majority of the international community, with the hope and support of the world's peoples, France has relentlessly striven for peaceful disarmament to succeed in Iraq, collective responsibility to guide our action, and the law to prevail over force.

This is why France, as President Chirac said this morning, regrets this action. We regret it because it doesn't have United Nations backing. We regret it because another method was possible. The will of the majority of the Security Council members was to pursue the inspections which were producing results; it wasn't heeded.

France wants to reiterate her conviction: war is not the solution. We know it will exacerbate the difficulties of an already vulnerable region; we fear it may intensify the feeling of injustice. The use of force has to be only a last resort. So, must we resign ourselves to what's happened? France can't be fatalistic, she can't reconcile herself to the division of the international community. Confronted with the threats of terrorism, proliferation, regional crises, unity must be our prime objective. This is the sine qua non we defended yesterday in New York with our Russian, German and Chinese partners at the Security Council's ministerial meeting. Together, we reaffirmed our confidence in the United Nations. Here as elsewhere, today like tomorrow, it will have a key role to play.

It is now time for responsible action. France, through the voice of President Chirac, has proposed a Security Council meeting at head of State and government level. This is our collective responsibility, we must accept it, face up to the urgency of the situation.

HUMANITARIAN ISSUE

The first challenge we have to take up, as you have all said, is the humanitarian one. We are calling on everyone to do all they can so that human lives are spared. We must consider the suffering of civilians, all the victims, the refugees and displaced persons, and we hope that the war will be limited and brief.

We welcome the mobilization, by the Secretary-General, of the relevant humanitarian agencies: including the World Food Programme, UNHCR, UNICEF, and WHO. We hope they will also put forward proposals so that the Oil-for-Food Programme, established by UNSCR 986, can resume as quickly as possible, with the necessary adjustments, under the Security Council's authority.

France intends to take her full place in this international action, liaising with the host countries and working in coordination with the United Nations agencies, particularly on Iraq's borders where several hundreds of thousands of refugees could soon find themselves in distress.

We are also keen for this mobilization to take place in close cooperation with the European Union which must resolutely contribute to the establishment of emergency humanitarian assistance. (...)

IRAQ'S POLITICAL AND ECONOMIC FUTURE

The second challenge is Iraq's political and economic future. Only the United Nations has the legitimacy to see through the reconstruction, on the international community's behalf, with the prime concern of ensuring Iraq's unity, integrity and sovereignty. That country's destiny has to be solely in the hands of the Iraqis themselves.

REGIONAL STABILITY/MIDDLE EAST

The third challenge is that of the region's stability. We must avoid anything which widens the gulf between cultures and societies. Force cannot be the main means of settling crises. (...) It is urgent to open up a new political way forward to allay the Israeli people's security concerns and address the Palestinian people's need for justice.

(...) We want to bring the Quartet's roadmap into the public domain. The French proposal for an international conference for the Middle East is now more relevant than ever.

TERRORISM/PROLIFERATION

Concurrently, the United Nations must retake the initiative on all the other crises. (....) To combat terrorism (...) political, police and judicial coordination in the intelligence sphere is more necessary than ever.

On the proliferation front, the issue of North Korea is a daily reminder of the urgent need to develop a comprehensive approach. There's a need to develop or strengthen, in the United Nations framework, the indispensable tools to combat this threat. With this in mind, France has proposed a meeting of heads of State and government in the margins of the next General Assembly. She has also proposed the creation of an international disarmament body in order to take full advantage of the experience gained by the inspectors in Iraq.

DEVELOPMENT/G8 EVIAN SUMMIT

To promote development and solidarity which, as you know, is a priority of France: in Monterrey, Kananaskis and Johannesburg, President Chirac constantly argued the need for the countries of the North to shoulder all their responsibilities vis-à-vis the South. That will again be the major item on the Evian Summit agenda.

IRAQ/EUROPE

Faced with this crisis, Europe has revealed its divisions, but it remains at the heart of our vision, at the heart of our ambition for the world. Europe must pull itself together, and the European Council beginning this afternoon in Brussels offers the opportunity to reaffirm the principles and values which unite us. Everywhere, Europe must be in a position to shoulder its responsibilities, be it under the common foreign and security policy or the defence policy. (...)

FRANCE/NATIONALS' SECURITY

Finally, you can be sure that the government is fully committed, under President Chirac's authority, to ensuring the security of our nationals in France and abroad.

LAW, FORCE, AND JUSTICE

SPEECH GIVEN AT THE INTERNATIONAL INSTITUTE FOR
STRATEGIC STUDIES IN LONDON, MARCH 27, 2003

*"The alternative is not between force
and law. Force must serve law."*

With the war in Iraq still raging, the Foreign Minister was invited to the International Institute of Strategic Studies to discuss the crisis that has divided the international community over Iraq. He discussed the successes and failures of the multilateral institutions implemented under the "new world order" that emerged after the Cold War to balance law and force. This led to a consideration of the concept of humanitarian intervention and the very specific conditions under which it can be used legitimately. He also considered how the disagreements that had arisen during the Iraq crisis revealed two distinct visions of the world. Finally, he took the opportunity to reaffirm the importance of the Atlantic relationship for dealing with regional crises, of stemming the proliferation of weapons of mass destruction, and of fighting terrorism.

It is an honor for me to be here today to deliver the annual lecture given in memory of Alastair Buchan, the founder of your institute.

In these moments of crisis, a place of intellect and reflection such as yours shows its real importance. It is a forum for exchange and debate vital to thought, an essential laboratory for action.

I am speaking to you at a decisive moment in our history. At a serious moment, when the United Kingdom is engaged in the military operations in Iraq. I naturally wish that this conflict finds a swift conclusion with the minimum possible number of casualties.

And in this time of trial, I come to you in a spirit of respect, friendship and dialogue. With the clear awareness that your country is at war and your soldiers at risk, I come here to look to the future, beyond the current differences between our two countries. I believe that we will only overcome the current obstacles if we take a clear and frank measure of our divisions. I am certain that, in the troubled world in which we live, we need unity more than ever before. And I hope to show you a French vision that aims to build and re-establish dialogue.

France and the United Kingdom have particular responsibilities as permanent members of the UN Security Council. They should exercise these responsibilities in pursuit of the same goal: international stability, security and peace. This implies working together to define the balance required for any international action: law, force and justice.

Where were we ten years ago?

The end of the Cold War changed our world. Law was placed at the centre of international concerns. Its relationship with force was profoundly changed.

For nearly fifty years, nuclear deterrence had guaranteed order. Both the West and the Communist world knew that the use of force would result in untold devastation on both sides. War would have meant the failure of deterrence and the unthinkable apocalypse.

Yet, with the end of the Cold War, force came back as a policy option. It could be envisaged again, because its cost was no longer disproportionate.

Yet it was rarely used. Because the assertion of Western values met with little opposition. Because the United States was moderate in its use of force. Indeed, it has always been true that only moderation makes power acceptable. As Thucydides remarked in ancient times: "We should be praised for being more just than our available power would normally imply."

However, no international order can be based solely on what the powers-that-be want it to be based. Collective norms were hence defined to contain the use of force within the bounds of collective responsibility.

This new order met with considerable success.

It curbed territorial aggression. In 1991, respect for the rule of law and the use of force drove Saddam Hussein out of Kuwait. Any similar invasion would surely be met today with an immediate and forceful reaction from the international community.

This order also brought assistance to the populations who fell victim to civil war, authoritarian regimes and natural disasters. Following the Gulf War, operation Provide Comfort stopped the flow of Kurdish refugees into Turkey and helped them to return to Northern Iraq. It paved the way for the right of humanitarian intervention and major UN operations: in Somalia, Haiti, Rwanda, Bosnia, East Timor, and Sierra Leone.

And not least, the new order helped define a set of standards that made force available to a law based on humanist values. Respect for the individual, the defence of freedoms, and the fight against poverty and epidemics were all given the force of law.

Yet this balance between law and force did not solve all security problems. Firstly, it did not solve the question of Iraq's disarmament, other than with a policy of sanctions that hit primarily the Iraqi people. Secondly, it did not open up prospects for solving the regional crises threatening the world's stability: first and foremost the Middle East, which remains a prisoner of a spiral of violence and retaliation; but also the disputes in Cyprus and Western Sahara, and the crisis in Kashmir. In these regions, the promises of the new world order ran up against the complexity of religious and ethnic relations, the weight of history and geographic constraints.

Moreover, the international community's support for this order gradually waned. The results obtained demanded considerable UN resources: in Sierra Leone, a country with 4 million inhabitants covering 71,000 square kilometres, 16,000 UN troops are needed to maintain what remains a fragile order.

The limits of the humanitarian intervention concept have gradually started to show. It makes it possible to take action against a government's will when an imminent humanitarian catastrophe demands it. But it has also prompted concern among the emerging powers and could be criticized for being partial. Why take action here rather than elsewhere? Who makes the decision to intervene, and based on what legitimate authority?

The case of Kosovo reflects the complexity of these issues. We were faced with some disturbing realities in this crisis. The concept of humanitarian intervention was questioned for the first time. Some powers in the South feared it would allow the Western democracies to unduly encroach on their sovereignty. And Kosovo prompted contradictory criticisms from these same democracies: some objected to a premature use of force, or the interference of political leaders in the conduct of military operations.

At the end of the day, the operation in Kosovo was a legitimate enterprise and a political success. But it was also a source of divisions. Some saw it as the first instance of a customary right to intervene on humanitarian grounds without a UN mandate. We, however, saw it as an exception, justified by wide support and the threat of an imminent humanitarian disaster.

September 11 put an end to the emergence of a new world order.

Firstly, the world entered the age of mass terrorism. We now know that the terrorist organizations will stop at nothing to spread their message of hate.

Secondly, it changed the meaning of power: in a world where the weak can destabilize the strong, where ideologies flout the most fundamental rights, the use of force is not a sufficient answer. When the blade unites with new technologies, it side-steps the classic rules of power.

Thirdly, it revealed the vulnerability of the United States, triggered a feeling of anger and injustice and led this country to change its view of the world. Attacked in the heart, America refocused its priorities on its own security, its own soil and its own population.

These times of great changes call for a renewed close and trusting relationship with the United States. France is ready.

We understand the immense trauma that this country has suffered. We showed unwavering solidarity with the Americans after 11 September and we share their utmost determination to tirelessly fight terrorism worldwide. Our military commitment in Afghanistan and especially our intelligence input illustrate this. Lastly, we will continue to work together on the major proliferation challenges facing us, especially in North Korea.

Because they share common values, the United States and France will re-establish close cooperation in complete solidarity. We owe it to the friendship between our peoples, for the international order that we wish to build together.

Over the last few months, some have wondered about France's reasons for its ways of going about settling the Iraq crisis. I would like to say loud and clear that our choices were not made against one country or another, but in the name of a certain idea of collective responsibility and of a world vision.

We shouldn't underestimate the stakes here. We need to know by which rules we would like to live together: only consensus and respect for law can give force the legitimacy it needs. If we overstep this mark, could the use of force become a destabilizing element?

We also need to know how to manage the many crises throughout the world. Iraq is not an isolated case. North Korea and other countries are raising new threats of proliferation. We must therefore give ourselves the means to deal with them. We had started defining a disarmament method together and this method was giving results.

Lastly, we have a fundamental concern: how could we neglect the risk of increased misunderstanding between peoples? A misunderstanding that could lead to a clash of cultures. Isn't that the major challenge of the day? Is it unavoidable? We must find the right answers and fuel the spirit of dialogue and respect amongst peoples.

In this respect we noted two elements that lie at the heart of UNSCR 1441: the international community is most effective only hen it is united; the international community is truly legitimate only when it shoulders all its responsibilities.

Responsibility meant that the Council had to strive relentlessly to improve inspections in order to make the most of UNSCR 1441. We proposed reinforcing the inspectors' resources, adopting a stringent timetable for inspections, a speedy and focused work programme, and a short deadline for the interim report to be presented.

Responsibility also meant that Security Council members should decide together what must be done. And that they should keep control of the process at every stage. That is why the Council could not endorse an ultimatum including an automatic use of force. Indeed it would have been outside the framework unanimously agreed on in UNSCR 1441. And it would not have been in keeping with the spirit of our work. Those are the simple reasons for the impasse in the Security Council during the last round of negotiations. In this context, France was continuously searching for a compromise. Throughout this process, France kept its options open, including the use of force, should inspections fail.

The situation in the Council did not change even by one vote because most members felt the peaceful option had not been pursued to the full. Because the military timetable seemed to overtake the diplomatic agenda from January onwards. Because the very principle of inspections soon seemed to be called into question. Because the sense of a gradual shift in objectives from the disarmament of Iraq to regime change, or even the reshaping of the Middle East, no doubt increased the misunderstandings.

Through the Iraq crisis, two different understandings of the world are coming head to head. They reflect different relationships between law and force, between international legitimacy and the defence of national security interests.

According to one such understanding, democracy can be imposed from the outside. Having faith in the power of the law is therefore something of a delusion. International legal tools become constraints more than safeguards of international security. Some even say that the U.S. would assume its responsibilities alone and thereby show its strength while Europe's position reflects its weakness. It also means that some governments might decide of their own accord to strike first given the scope of the threats. Self-defence then knows no bounds or constraints.

But the limits of the use of force in Iraq and unclear political prospects for the country fuel many questions on the relevance of such an analysis.

We live in a complex world. It can no longer be explained by series of alliances, as was the case in the nineteenth century or the Cold War. Today's world is about new threats— terrorism and the proliferation of weapons of mass destruction; about extremely volatile regional crises; about extremist and fundamentalist ideologies active across the world; about organized crime becoming a new means of financing and implementing these threats. Using force in this context will not solve the real issues. It may reveal new fault lines.

We believe in democracy, just as the British and the Americans do. With the Magna Carta, the 1789 Declaration of the Rights of Man and the U.S. Constitution, our countries headed the democratic revolution. We are convinced that democracy needs resolve, conviction and a long learning period.

We do not oppose the use of force. We are only warning against the risks of pre-emptive strikes as a doctrine. What example are we setting for other countries? How legitimate would we feel such an action to be? What are our limits to the use of such might? In endorsing this doctrine, we would risk introducing the principle of constant instability and uncertainty. We risk not controlling situations and rushing headlong into action. Let us not open a Pandora's box.

How, then, can we act? Our own view is underpinned by a number of requirements.

Unity: it is necessary given the complexity of our world. We can only uproot terrorism if we increase our police, judicial and intelligence cooperation. We can only respond to proliferation if we develop together an effective method. We must build on what we started doing in Iraq. We can only resolve regional crises if we start a constructive dialogue with all parties involved.

Responsibility: all the countries are collectively responsible for increasing the security and stability of our world. Force is not a privilege some enjoy and law the alibi of others. We are all bound by the law.

Legitimacy: it is the key to the effectiveness of international action. If we want to develop the right answers to the challenges of the modern world and to take appropriate measures—including the use of force—we must do so with the authority of collective decisions.

We must now find once again the path to European unity and reassert transatlantic solidarity on the basis of those requirements. We must rebuild the world order shattered by the Iraq crisis.

This is a goal for all Europeans—the fifteen current members of the EU and the soon-to-be members. However, it is a particular challenge for France and the United Kingdom, which have developed over time a different relationship with the U.S. Yet we are both concerned about the quality and strength of the transatlantic relationship, which we acknowledge as a stabilizing force in our world.

The alternative is not between force and law. Force must serve law. Force must be contained by the law to reverse Pascal's words: "unable to make what is just strong, we have made what is strong just." Asserting the primacy of the law is not an admission of weakness. It is a moral and political obligation, the prerequisite not only for justice but also for effectiveness. Indeed, only justice can guarantee lasting security.

Conversely, if the international system is still seen as unjust, if force always seems to prevail over the law, if the opinions of the peoples are disregarded, then destabilizing factors will grow stronger, proliferation programmes will develop, power play will go on needlessly, and hostility towards Western democracies will be increasingly manipulated.

We must now define our common goals.

Firstly, we must fully disarm Iraq. A unanimous international community rallied around this goal. It must now be carried through by the inspectors. The UN must steer the process. More importantly, the UN must be at the heart of the reconstruction and administration of Iraq. The legitimacy of our action depends on it. We must come together to build peace together in a region rife with a sense of insecurity and deep fault lines.

The fight against terrorism must remain our priority. We must pursue our cooperation, strengthen our exchange of intelligence and develop new tools to fight against the financing of terrorist networks.

We continue to have a rich and ongoing partnership with the U.S. and the United Kingdom on proliferation. This partnership must go hand in hand with the work we will conduct in the UN at the summit [of heads of State and Government] proposed by France. We also suggest that European countries consult closely and develop a common analysis of proliferation risks so as to assess together the means to respond. We have started developing disarmament tools. They are based on a balance between force and law. Establishing a standing group of UN inspectors would give flesh to our hopes.

All these challenges demand that we work together more than ever before to find a political settlement to the Middle East crisis. Because it is a fundamental crisis, because it is fuelled by a deep sense of injustice, we can only have lasting peace if it is justice-based. Such justice must meet the expectations of the Palestinian people and guarantee the security of Israel. Only justice can strengthen peace and law.

All these goals can only be met if the UN gives the impetus. But they can be implemented within major regional poles.

To be truly stable, this new world must be based on a number of regional poles, structured to face current threats. These poles should not compete against one another, but complement each other. They are the cornerstones of an international community built on solidarity and unity in the face of new challenges.

The determination of European countries to develop a common foreign and security policy must reflect that. This determination shows our will to bring about a true European identity. An identity that all the peoples of our continent are yearning for. We wish to go resolutely down this path with the support and involvement of the United Kingdom. We have already covered much ground together in the field of defence. After the decision in Macedonia, we must pursue our projects: taking over from NATO in Bosnia and establishing a European armaments agency. A strong Europe will be in everyone's interest. It will strengthen the security of our world.

France and the United Kingdom must overcome the current difficulties and remain united.

I am convinced that what brings us together goes to the heart of the identity of our peoples. We have the same sense of independence. We have the same sense of our countries' global role. I cannot forget that, at the bleakest time in our history, the United Kingdom welcomed the man who personified the honour and spirit of resistance of our country. At the same time, Winston Churchill and the British people embodied the hopes of the free peoples.

Strengthened by our mutual respect and friendship, France and the United Kingdom want to be present and active when Europe comes together, to contribute to a world that fulfils our shared yearning for peace and justice.

THE POLITICAL PROCESS
MUST BE ACCELERATED

INTERVIEW WITH *LE FIGARO*, JULY 10, 2003

*"What we said was that winning the peace
would be much more difficult."*

On May 1, 2003, President Bush announced the end of military operations in Iraq.

On May 22, the Security Council adopted Resolution 1483, lifting all of the international sanctions placed on Iraq since 1990, with the exception of those concerning arms. France voted for the resolution even though it reflected American policy in Iraq because, as de Villepin put it, "it does not legitimize the war, it opens the way to the peace that we want to help build together."

On May 30, Hans Blix presented a final report to the Security Council on the inspections that took place between January 27 and March 18, immediately prior to the opening of hostilities. The inspectors, he said, as subsequently with the U.S. military, had not found any weapons of mass destruction.

On July 22, 2003 UN Secretary General Kofi Annan and the UN Special Representative in Iraq, Sergio Vieira de Mello presented a report that was highly critical of conditions in Iraq. Anan cited a growing climate of violence and requested that coalition forces implement a rapid transfer of sovereignty to the Iraqi people.

Iraqi dictator Saddam Hussein, meanwhile, was still at large.

T hree months after the fall of Baghdad, the Americans still have not found weapons of mass destruction in Iraq. They are meeting with what seems to be an organized resistance. Do you feel this shows that you were right when, in the name of France, you opposed the war in Iraq?

DV—The problem should not be posed in those terms. The war happened. We were very happy to see Saddam Hussein's regime fall. We had always been aware that winning the war was something that one country could accomplish by itself. What we said was that winning the peace would be much more difficult. And we see from day to day how difficult the situation is. The instability that currently plagues Iraq is a source of concern for all of us, especially for the coalition forces, who are suffering daily casualties from a growing number of attacks. We share the emotion and the pain of the families of the dead and wounded soldiers. Then the Iraqi people are concerned because they are now living in a very precarious situation. Finally, both neighboring countries and the international community are concerned that a new pole of instability is developing in the Middle East.

How can stability be reestablished in Iraq?

DV—Will simply increasing the number of troops in the region solve the problem? Our belief is that the real solution is political rather than military. It thus seems essential to us that full sovereignty be returned to the Iraqis as soon as possible. I am very pleased with the decision to create a provisional government in Iraq. In this context, Mr. Vieira de Mello, the UN Special Representative in Iraq, and the American administrator, Paul Bremer, are working in the same spirit. That's moving in the right direction.

Will France send troops to Iraq to join the stabilization force?

DV—I don't think that the problem is one of military strength. What seems essential to me is the restoration of full Iraqi sovereignty. What steps are required here? The political process must be accelerated, and tighter, precise deadlines must be set for each step, whether it's a question of creating a provisional government or of holding the general elections that can lead to the formation of a legitimate government. Economic reconstruction also needs to get underway; investor confidence must be created through transparent management of the country's resources. Finally, the military and security structures must be reorganized under the framework of a political process defined by the UN.

Under what conditions would France send troops?

DV—We would like the political transition to be placed under the responsibility of the United Nations. Right now, that's a condition for effectiveness. Participation of French troops could only be considered in the context of a United Nations peacekeeping force with a precise mandate from the Security Council and thus benefiting from the support of the international community.

So a new resolution would be necessary in addition to Resolution 1483?

DV—Resolution 1483 marked a positive step toward a solution. But is it what the situation calls for? That remains to be seen. It sets out a plan for the occupation period, but makes no provision for a peacekeeping force. It would be rather incoherent for France to participate in a coalition force when it did not support the war in Iraq and indeed, had been defending a solution based on the peaceful disarmament of the country. France is arguing that it should be the United Nations that assume responsibility for security and organize the political process for restoring sovereignty to the Iraqi people.

AVOIDING THE SPIRAL OF VIOLENCE

INTERVIEW WITH *LE MONDE*, AUGUST 23, 2003

"There is a temptation to reinforce security measures without reclaiming the political field."

In addition to attacks and ambushes continuing against British and American forces, terrorism against civilians made its appearance in Iraq on August 7 with an attack on the Jordanian Embassy in Baghdad that left 17 dead. No one took credit for the attack, but it was thought to be perpetrated either by followers of the fallen dictator or by fundamentalist elements filtering through Iraq's ill-defended borders.

On August 14, the adoption of Resolution 1500 established a UN aid mission to Iraq to coordinate humanitarian efforts and provide political advice. But on August 19, the mission's offices in Baghdad's Canal Hotel were struck by a car bomb. Twenty-one people were killed, including Sergio Vieira de Mello, UN High Commissioner for Human Rights and its Special Representative in Iraq. In the aftermath, criticism mounts over the poor security conditions in which UN personnel are forced to work. At UN Headquarters in New York, officials consider reducing staff in Iraq to a minimum.

What are your thoughts on the situation in Iraq the day after the attack on the UN Headquarters in Baghdad?

DV—My feeling is that we are threatened by a double spiral. First, a spiral of increasing confrontation, for under the logic of force that prevails today, we are seeing terrorist acts multiply, causing more and more casualties and provoking strong emotions everywhere in France. Then we face a spiral of disengagement. It is alarming to see how the Iraqi people are increasingly being cut out of the reconstruction process as the coalition pursues its work. Each day this continues, the chances for a successful reconstruction are diminished.

This situation is fraught with dangers for the country and the entire region. We thus have to ask what the most effective response is. I am convinced that focusing solely on security is not the best way to get Iraq back on track. We have to move from an occupation footing to a political approach that has the restoration of Iraq's sovereignty as its objective. We need to begin implementing this new approach immediately; it should provide a beneficial kind of shock treatment for everyone.

What do you mean in concrete terms?

DV—There is a temptation to reinforce security measures without reclaiming the political field. We must be clearheaded. I do not think that merely by declaring war on terrorism and redoubling security efforts—even if, obviously, we should do all we can in that regard—we're going to succeed. What needs to be done, I believe, is to give priority to a political process that will eventually let the Iraqis take control of their future.

This also implies the involvement of the entire international community. Through the United Nations, its presence will reinforce the process and confer legitimacy upon it.

We must have the courage to take the measures the situation requires. We know there is no easy solution, but we cannot afford to remain in an ambiguous position. The path of collective responsibility is the only one that can lead us out of the trap we find ourselves in today.

How?

DV—First, the Iraqi Governing Council must be transformed into a real provisional government, capable of acting independently and making decisions concerning the restoration of order in its country. The reestablishment of essential public services is, in particular, the main priority.

This provisional government should be in charge of preparing the elections, and if possible, these should take place by the end of the year, so that a constituent assembly can be elected. A special representative of the UN Secretary-General should be named alongside the government to supervise the transition process.

So there would be no American chief administrator?

DV—It is important that responsibility be exercised by the Iraqis themselves. It's with the Iraqis and through the Iraqis that we will leave this impasse. It's not enough to be merely moving towards this goal: we must speed up the timetable for the transition because we're in a serious, urgent situation. Once more, what is essential is moving from a security focus to a sovereignty focus. To ensure the legitimacy of the provisional government, we must have the presence of the United Nations and the support of the countries of the region, through organizations like the Arab League and the Organization of the Islamic Conference.

You make a point that collective action and a UN mandate are necessary in Iraq, yet in Afghanistan, where we have both, the postwar situation is a failure...

DV—What we see in Afghanistan does indeed illustrate the difficulties international action must face. That does not mean, however, that if we redouble our efforts over time we won't do any better in that country. The main challenge in Afghanistan is the reinforcement of the Karzai government. If on the other hand the international community attempts to substitute itself purely and simply for the will of the people, whether in Afghanistan or in Iraq, then it risks being seen as an adversary.

But where do you draw the line between assistance to a country in difficulty and an intervention that violates the principles of sovereignty and respect for the other?

DV—Admittedly, it's a very fine line. The art lies in how the action is undertaken. Time is a major constraint: One must move quickly because there is a race against the clock in these situations. The conditions for reconstruction must be put in place before the forces of destabilization and disengagement can gain the upper hand. And when I say that we need to move quickly in Iraq, I mean that we need to move much more quickly. Generally speaking, I think that the international community needs a better appreciation of the situation's urgency.

EXIT STRATEGY

COMMENTARY FOR *LE MONDE*, SEPTEMBER 13, 2003

"...we are courting a vicious circle from which there is no exit."

Resistance to the occupation forces continued through August and into September, taking on the character of a full-blown guerilla war. There was regular sabotage of the electricity grid and water mains, and oil pipelines to Mediterranean ports were set on fire, holding back economic recovery. An August 29 attack in the holy city of Najaf, an killed over 100 people, including the spiritual leader of the Shiite community, Ayatollah Muhammed Baqir Al-Hakim, providing a striking indication of the explosive potential of religious divisions inside Iraq.

On September 13, at the initiative of Secretary-General Kori Anan, the five permanent members of the Security Council met in Geneva to discuss the UN's role in the reconstruction of Iraq, and an American draft resolution for creating a multinational force.

With the fall of Saddam Hussein's dictatorship, Iraq has turned a page of its history and can now hope for a better future.

Yet, a tragic cycle of disorder and violence has set in. Attacks have multiplied. Fanaticism and hatred have struck throughout the country: at the Jordanian Embassy, at the United Nations and at the Mausoleum of the Imam Ali in Najaf.

We now risk moving inexorably towards failure, a risk aggravated by the absence of a tangible political perspective. The situation has thrown international organizations into confusion and is creating deep anxieties among all present on the ground. The most serious danger, however, lies in the growing despair and apathy of the Iraqi people. Only a major new gesture, backed up by the international community, will allow us jump-start the reconstruction process and tackle the challenges confronting us.

Everyone's responsibility is quite clear.

President Bush has demonstrated his desire for openness, and this is most welcome. Yet the draft resolution put before the Security Council expands the United Nations' role in a very limited way, and places us in an ever more paradoxical situation. For how can one ask the United Nations to intervene more broadly on the ground without giving it the capacity to act and without providing the security conditions indispensable to its work? The draft resolution merely continues along the lines of what has already been done. Is this adequate to the situation? Is it likely to keep the problems we see from deteriorating further? We do not think so.

We have no wish to minimize the scale of the task and its complexity. We don't want to fall victim to the illusion that solutions are simple. But we are convinced of one thing, and that is that by continuing with the current approach, we are courting a vicious circle from which there is no exit. The clock is running. Immediately following the war, and in spite of sustained efforts, the direct administration of Iraq by the occupation forces produced an abiding malaise in the general population. The resumption of essential public services and infrastructure reconstruction were delayed. The legitimate expectations of the Iraqis were not met.

Another approach is still possible—placing the Iraqi people at the heart of the reconstruction process and appealing to the responsibility of the international community.

We share the same objective: establishing stability and the conditions for reconstruction in Iraq. France is ready to work in the Security Council with the United States and the other countries with forces aiding Iraq on the ground. But we must leave any ambiguity as to our purpose behind, for this will lead to failure for the Iraqi people and will risk discrediting the international community. This requires taking a radically new approach.

This is all the more necessary because the stability of the whole region is threatened. We are all aware that the problem goes far beyond Iraq—the stability of the entire Arab-Islamic World is at stake. In the Middle East, an approach devoid of political perspectives and solely concerned with security will only end up maintaining the cycle of violence and reprisals. This strategy—let's have the courage to admit it—is a dead end. Far from promoting stability, it stirs up rancor, feeds misunderstandings and multiplies frustrations. And wherever terrorist organizations exist, they exploit the slightest weakness to improve their implantation and foster violence that affects us all.

How do we get out of this impasse and create the conditions for stability in Iraq?

Before all else, let's agree that the foreign presence is a magnet for contention all by itself. Despite the goodwill of its members, it crystallizes frustration, focuses discontent and distorts the political landscape. All parties concerned must define themselves in relation to it, rather than being able to work directly for the benefit of Iraq. The reconstruction effort demands that we operate from clear bases, and thus that we fix a deadline for the current transition period. That's the key to all progress.

It is thus above all important to respect the Iraqi national feeling, which draws its force from thousands of years of history and bears the country's future stability within it. In contrast, we must avoid reinforcing particularist or ethnic mentalities.

Iraq is a country with a long memory. Its attachment to its traditions and its identity have led it to reject external models before. The result, over the past century, has been a series of upheavals that have profoundly shaken the country, a series of revolutions and coups from which the peace so ardently sought by the Iraqis has yet to emerge.

The pressing task today is to transfer sovereignty to the Iraqi people so that they can assume full responsibility for themselves. This is how the different groups will find the strength to work together. This is a simple matter of justice: it ought to be up to the Iraqis to make the decisions that will determine the future of their country. But it's also a question of effectiveness: only a politically sovereign Iraq will restore dialogue and a constructive spirit to the different Iraqi communities and to neighboring countries.

Does this mean that the coalition forces should immediately withdraw from Iraq? Certainly not, and many have pointed out that such a withdrawal would create a political vacuum that would be worse than the current situation. These forces can remain under the command of the main contributor of troops. Should the coalition be enlarged? We think that what is essential is not increasing the number of troops but defining the coalition's mission through a precise UN mandate that limits its duration and requires regular, detailed reports to the Security Council. One of today's priorities is securing Iraq's borders and stopping the infiltration of terrorists. A redeployment of coalition forces, in consultation with the Iraqis, could address this threat.

We should use Afghanistan as a model and speed up the creation of an Iraqi national army. This partly means calling on demobilized Iraqi troops, whose skills will be indispensable for reestablishing lasting security. The same task should be accomplished with the police. Over time, we should be able to arrive at a division of responsibility that would be more in keeping with a sovereign Iraq and likely also more efficient: external security would be a priority for United Nations forces, while maintaining order inside the country would be the responsibility of the Iraqi authorities.

In this context, and as negotiations over a new resolution begin in New York, we propose the following timetable.

The UN Security Council would make the current Iraqi institutions, namely the Governing Council and the recently appointed ministers, the depositaries of Iraqi sovereignty for the transition period. After a very short period, for example, one month, a provisional Iraqi government could be established on the basis of these institutions, and executive power would gradually be handed over to it, including economic and budgetary authority.

A personal envoy of the United Nations Secretary-General would be mandated to organize consultations with the existing Iraqi institutions and the Coalition authorities and marshal support from neighboring countries. This envoy would report to the Security Council and would propose a timetable for gradually transferring power to the provisional government and would define the modalities to achieve this political transition.

The timetable should anticipate the stages of a constitutional process, with the goal of finalizing a draft text before the end of the year. General elections would be planned for the earliest possible date between now and next spring.

France is ready to take on all of its responsibilities. As soon as sovereignty is reestablished in Iraq, an international conference will be organized to address all of the elements of the reconstruction. The conference will attempt to ensure the effectiveness of international action in Iraq. In the area of security, the composition of the future United Nations forces and the support for the national army and police forces must be determined. Similarly, commitments for economic aid and other assistance to help restore the Iraqi administrative structure must be decided.

This is the nature of the proposals we are putting before the Security Council. We do it in a spirit of dialogue with the United States and our other partners. Tomorrow we will be meeting in Geneva with the other permanent members of the Security Council and the Secretary-General, Kofi Annan, convinced that the international community can come together for an ambitious and rigorous plan for Iraq.

It is an unprecedented challenge, requiring our understanding and adaptation to the realities on the ground. It demands that we move beyond ideology and polemic. What we need most of all are clear principles and a common political strategy. Only these will open the way to a successful reconstruction.

FOR A SPIRIT OF RESPONSIBILITY

INTERVIEW WITH *LE MONDE*, OCTOBER 18, 2003

"An occupying power is always going to be tempted to decide that the country they are occupying is not quite ready to take charge of their own destiny. We need the courage to learn from history, which has so often taken a tragic turn when action has come too late."

On October 16, the Security Council unanimously passed Resolution 1511, redefining the role of the United Nations in the reconstruction process. The new resolution gave a larger role to the UN, and charged the Secretary General with determining the form this commitment should take. It also authorized the creation of a multinational force under the command of the United States. Finally, 1511 requested the transitional Governing Council to present, before December 15, a timetable for drafting a constitution and holding elections.

The new multilateral effort, however, did not stop the violence from mounting. On October 27, a wave of attacks killed 43, and left over 200 wounded. One of these attacks struck the building of the International Committee of the Red Cross, killing twelve people. The Red Cross had actively participated in humanitarian tasks and water and electricity maintenance in the country since the beginning of the economic sanctions in Iraq.

France wanted a clear text that set binding requirements and a rapid timetable for the handover of power to the Iraqis, now it has adopted a resolution that contains none of this. How is this consistent with France's position?

DV—From the beginning, we wanted to come at this with a responsible, clearheaded attitude. Responsible because faced with the worsening spiral of violence and terrorism—which is taking place in a context of extreme tension in the Middle East—it is important to make the unity of the international community stand out clearly. Clearheaded, because the negotiations completed in New York are a step in the right direction. Several improvements were made relative to the previous draft, for example, the principle of the transfer of sovereignty, the recognition of the importance of the constitutional process, the increased role of the interim Governing Council and the supervision of the future multinational force by the Security Council.

At the beginning of the week, you were saying the main weakness of the text was that there was no timetable for handing over political power to the Iraqis. Well, there's no timetable...

DV—That's true. There's not a precise timetable. The American representative in Iraq will retain his prerogatives until a government has emerged from general elections, and this could take quite a while. From that point of view, the resolution did not go far enough. The role of the United Nations, which should be central, will also remain limited so long as the occupation is maintained. Why did we overcome our reservations here? Because, in a context that has been growing more and more difficult, we are trying to be constructive and move forward. We don't want to create a deadlock in the process. This unanimous vote puts the Americans before their responsibilities. Our own conviction is that action should have been more ambitious and more rapid.

After this, aren't the Americans likely to draw the conclusion that they have been handed a blank check to go on with what France has been calling the "occupation" of Iraq?

DV—No one should become complacent or self-congratulatory because of a single Security Council vote. Since the end of the war, all of the Council votes have been unanimous. That shows to what extent we are aware of how much is at stake. However, and I'll say it again, this resolution is still too timid. It is not adequate for Iraq's needs. At the moment, the Americans don't feel that they are in a position to do any better. We say to them: this is not sufficient to create the conditions of a real reconstruction in the country, but we dare to believe that the dynamic that's being created is eventually going to allow us to move forward. So we are not going to block the process. However, at the same time, we're saying to the Americans that it is up to them to improve the situation. That is our role as friend and ally, our duty as French and as Europeans. An occupying power is always going to be tempted to decide that the country they are occupying is not quite ready to take charge of their own destiny. We need the courage to learn from history, which has so often taken a tragic turn when action has come too late.

PART TWO

THE E.U.
AND
A NEW ERA
FOR EUROPE

FOR A EUROPEAN CONSTITUTION

SPEECH GIVEN DURING THE PLENARY SESSION OF
THE EUROPEAN CONVENTION IN BRUSSELS, JUNE 5, 2003

"Let us... refuse the status quo. Let us reject excessive caution and the temptation to withdraw into our national interests.... Let us not resign ourselves to a powerless Europe reduced to the role of spectator of the world."

Crisis was looming when the European Convention held its penultimate session on June 5 and 6, 2003, in preparation for a report to the European Council in Thessaloníki later that month. The governing body of the Convention, known as the Presidium, had proposed an ambitious constitutional amendment a few days before that was meant to address problems within the laborious and defensive compromise reached two and a half years earlier at the European Council in Nice. The amendment proposed to restrict the size of the European Commission, to calculate the voting rights of the states in the Council according to their population, and to reduce the number of representatives in the European Parliament.

But the amendment provoked a rebellion among the states attached to the status quo, and a number of Convention members were prepared to back, by default, a consensus involving a minimal compromise. In debates on June 4, a large majority of governmental representatives refused the proposed advances and insisted that the Convention remain within the terms of the Nice agreement.

On June 5, de Villepin left the French National Assembly to join the plenary session, where he was scheduled to speak the next day. But when he arrived and was informed by Convention chairman Valéry Giscard d'Estaing of the course taken by the debates, he decided to speak immediately.

W e have another week of work before Thessaloníki. Some might agree to a minimal compromise. We will not accept it. It would be better not to have a constitution than to settle on a bad compromise.

For the challenges to be overcome are immense. The world has changed: it is dangerous, disorganized, and dehumanized; everywhere nations are waiting for Europe to assume its responsibilities. Europe has changed: the increase from fifteen to twenty-five members represents a transformation whose true magnitude must be appreciated. Europeans have changed: they want more from Europe, they expect security, prosperity, and solidarity. The European ideal is mobilizing our people. If we do not respond, they will recall us to our duties.

Our Convention must rise to the level of the important issues at stake here. This is our responsibility. Let us not look to the past for solutions; let us refuse the status quo. Let us reject excessive caution and the temptation to withdraw into our national interests.

Let us escape from shortsighted compromises and from the mirage of "options." Let us not resign ourselves to a powerless Europe reduced to the role of spectator of the world. Let us go beyond our differences and use the dynamic energy of the

Convention to demonstrate our inventiveness and to reach an agreement. For we know that where the Convention has failed, the Intergovernmental Conference will not be able to succeed. Let us be prepared, then, for a very long IGC, for it can only reach a conclusion with an ambitious result that will mark a real step forward for Europe.

The Praesidium has the courage to defend a vision and an ambition: a stable presidency for the European Council; a more politic and collegial Commission; a larger qualified majority for more effective decisions; a European Minister of Foreign Affairs, for a unified European voice on the international scene, which all the recent events have shown to be sadly lacking.

These propositions will provide a way out of this institutional impasse. Consider the example of the General Affairs Council: it doesn't work. We meet each month, but to what end? What is decided? As for the Commission, who can seriously believe that there is a risk of conflict with the Council? Who could question the general European interest that it embodies?

But let us not limit our debates to institutions alone. Let us not forget where the strength of the European project lies: in its policies and in its actions. Let us continue to make advances in research, education, public services, employment, economic policy, foreign policy and defense…. That is what our citizens are expecting, and it is an urgent matter.

Today, there are countries who are not resigned to powerlessness, who are resolved to rise up to meet these challenges, and who are convinced that Europe must and will succeed in its transformation. And I want in particular to salute the president of the Convention for his determination and his demanding rigor, he who was the first to recognize the historic importance of our meeting.

How could we be satisfied with a third rate Europe? We must defend a vision, a set of values and common interests... and we will defend them! The real question is rather: Will we do it all together within a common space, or must some in this space take the initiative and the responsibility for clearing the path? In one way or another, I want to communicate to you my firm belief: Europe will go forward.

It is quite clear to all of us that we are faced with an imminent crisis, and our Convention must find common ground and come together. We still have a few days to do this, and France, through its representatives, wants to contribute. Let us never forget that we are not making Europe for the next decade, but for our children, our grandchildren, and for many generations.

THE FUTURE OF
FRANCO-BRITISH RELATIONS

SPEECH GIVEN IN LONDON AS PART OF THE BBC'S
"DIMBLEBY LECTURE" SERIES, OCTOBER 15, 2003

*"Power means an ability to listen to others
and understand their concerns."*

This speech was given on a BBC television show hosted by Richard Dimbleby, a famous British television and radio reporter best known for his coverage of the Belsen Camp liberation. Former guests of the show included the Archbishop of Canterbury, Prince Philipp, as well as foreign political figures such as Bill Clinton or the German Chancellor Helmut Schmidt. The French Foreign Minister was its first French guest.

Thank you David for your kind words.

I'd like to thank the BBC: It is a real privilege and a moving experience for me to be able to speak on your channel. I'd also like to pay tribute to your temerity: inviting a Frenchman could be risky. Just a few weeks ago, the writer Julian Barnes said: "If you were God and you were trying to create a nation which would most get up the British nostril, it would probably be the French." And that's a Francophile speaking! We French love giving lectures, with the sense of humility and modesty which... we share with you. But rest assured; this evening I don't intend to give another French lecture.

At a time when the world seems to be spinning out of control, when it is split over the painful ordeals of Iraq and the Middle East, we need greater clarity, determination and boldness to find our way back to the path of unity and action.

Britain and France can be proud of our record. For most of our history, we were the "best of enemies." A hundred years ago, the *Entente Cordiale* brought us closer together. And since then, after the tragedies and the sufferings of the two world wars, we have been united in the same European destiny.

For several centuries, we went through the same ordeals. Democracy prevailed over absolute monarchy. Decolonization restored peoples' freedom and replaced our dreams of empires with new forms of solidarity. The Second World War brought the resistance to the Nazis. And I haven't forgotten that the man whose memory we are honouring today, Richard Dimbleby, was the first reporter to describe the horrors of the Nazi concentration camps on BBC radio. Out of all this shared hardship, we have forged a common heritage. We have the same love of justice and liberty, the same fierce sense of independence; we each have pride in our country, and an absolute refusal to surrender.

This is the spirit which inspired the French officer shouting on the battlefield at Fontenoy: "*Messieurs les Anglais, tirez les premiers*": which means, "Englishmen, please shoot first." And Nelson's dying words at the Battle of Trafalgar: "Thank God I have done my duty."

When I think of that spirit, I see it embodied in the imposing silhouette of Churchill standing amidst the ruins, rekindling with his gruff voice the flame of hope. I see it again in General de Gaulle's refusal to surrender and in his call to resistance, issued on your airwaves, on the eighteenth of June nineteen forty. London was then the last bastion of freedom; and the BBC, the voice of hope.

On this bedrock, our two peoples have built a singular relationship, made up of a mixture of irritation and fascination.

In daily life, there are so many differences between us! Your passion for talking about the weather, our love of political games; your art of brevity and pregnant pauses, our liking for theoretical debate. It's a pity we can't resolve these differences on the cricket field, but rugby and football provide us with plenty of opportunities. However, there is one area where the referee has blown the final whistle: cuisine.... Although I am told by my sources, there are one or two pockets of resistance.

And yet there's still, and always will be, the magic of our mutual fascination. About a quarter of a million French people have made their homes here. On your side, many Britons believe they have found in Normandy or in Dordogne a corner of "Paradise Lost." Many of you have turned your "year in Provence" into a second life. Doesn't Dickens' novel *A Tale of Two Cities* tell of the cross destinies, between Paris and London, of one family at the time of the French Revolution?

In France we have a profound respect for your acute awareness of your identity. Since Victor Hugo nourished himself on the work of Shakespeare, and Dickens inspired Zola, Graham Greene invoked Péguy and Mauriac, or more recently, David Lodge explored Roland Barthes and Jacques Derrida, our writers have read and responded to each other. Our poets, from Artur Rimbaud to Dylan Thomas, sounded the same cry of revolt. The rage of the "angry young men" in England and the tumult of the "new wave" in France, brought home, at the beginning of the 1960s, the same images of a cinema breaking with the past.

Our two peoples are curious about each other. They know they can find, on the other side of the Channel, a mere 35 kilometres away, pardon my French—22 miles! that otherness which helps them discover something new in themselves. By remaining true to ourselves, we shall best be able to cope with an uncertain future.

Our world today needs security. But it also needs justice and stability. I believe that, together, France and the UK have the tools to achieve these goals. The path to a new world is one we can truly map out together.

With the fall of the Berlin wall, the world of 1989 was full of hope. The confrontation between the Cold War blocs had ended. Peoples were asserting their right to self-determination.

Europe was regaining its unity. New democracies were burgeoning. The dream of a new world order seemed within our grasp.

And yet what do we see today? Everywhere, tensions are causing havoc, and threatening the creation of terrible ruptures. Everyday violence rears its ugly head. A violence that erupts as a result of a clash of ideologies, religious fanaticism or nationalism. It scars the Middle East, India and Pakistan, the Balkans. But there is also a blind and senseless violence that grows in the areas of crisis and lawlessness, in Africa, Latin America or Asia. Violence which sends child soldiers to die on landmines or drunk gunmen to decimate a village.

September eleventh has shown us a third kind of violence: one seemingly intent on hijacking all the others. I remember that fateful day in September two years ago as New York, the town where I had lived, this tall, proud city on the Atlantic, was being defaced. This violence—the violence of al-Qaeda and the terrorist networks—tries to set the world against itself. It fuses all grounds for resentment and hatred. It strikes everywhere blindly and without mercy. Opportunistic, calculating, it takes advantage of disorder to spread its influence and establish its networks.

This violence must be fought by all the means at our disposal. Let us also beware of the possible connections between terrorism and the proliferation of weapons of mass destruction. Such a combination can be a destabilizing factor for whole regions. More grave still, it could result in blackmail or even a direct threat to our security interests. Here we are facing a major global risk: from North Korea to the Middle East, an arc of proliferation has taken shape, with its trafficking in technology and materials, and the underground activities of scientists.

Against this background, one of the first tests of our determination will be the settlement of the Iranian crisis. Here we share the same analysis: the Iranian nuclear programme is raising concerns, which must be allayed. We won't compromise on the strict adherence to the Non-Proliferation Treaty, nor on the mandate given to the International Atomic Energy Agency. Nothing less than full transparency on the different aspects of the Iranian programme will make the restoration of confidence possible. First and foremost, we are asking Iran to sign and implement immediately the strengthened accord which all the European countries have already signed. Once confidence has been established, we would be ready to discuss ways of ensuring that the Iranian people get legitimate access to civilian nuclear technology, with all the necessary safeguards and precautions.

This will not be easy. So it's essential for our two countries, along with Germany, to find the way to break the deadlock. To do this, we also need to work closely with our European partners, the United States and Russia.

At the same time, we must however keep open the possibility of a political approach to these issues.

Not backed by force, law is powerless. But force alone is futile. A strategy focusing solely on the use of force cannot destroy the roots of terrorism. It would risk giving political legitimacy to individuals acting in the shadows. In the area of proliferation, it could incite States to acquire the most destructive military capabilities. It would then soon reveal its flaws: who today would contemplate military action against North Korea?

Indeed our idea of the nature of power has undergone a complete revolution. Pen knives, explosive belts, suicide cars can today spread horror and death. Today the weak can threaten the strong. An armed group can, in an instant, shatter all our previous certainties. Power is no longer a mere matter of military and technological might. Power also means an ability to listen to others and understand their concerns. At the heart of this revolution in our concept of power, there is, in fact, the assertion of identity. Religions, societies, individuals want to be respected for what they are. They refuse to bow to the pressure of military, technological or economic dominance.

So we must be vigilant. If we wound those identities, we run the risk of provoking an allergic reaction. At a time when we have just emerged from a trial of strength between two ideological blocs that took the world to the edge of the abyss, let us be careful not to recreate the conditions for a new clash between North and South, East and West, Christianity and Islam.

How can we respond to these global threats without locking ourselves into a spiral of violence? We must start by trying to resolve the current crises. They are like a wound, always liable to fester and spread the infection. To be effective, a commitment to justice has to be at the heart of everything we do.

Justice in the Middle East first of all.

We cannot accept the status quo. If we go on procrastinating, the situation will deteriorate even further. We share the grief of the Israeli people facing the ever more deadly and unacceptable violence of terrorist actions. We share the despair of the Palestinian people who see no future. But we cannot resign ourselves to a policy solely driven by security. The time has come for us to ask ourselves the right questions. Is it constructive to blame all the difficulties on Yasser Arafat? Is the building of the present security fence acceptable? Does all this strengthen Israel's security?

The answer is no. For a simple reason: the security of Israel and the sovereignty of the Palestinians cannot be dissociated. We have to realise this: we won't put an end to the present spiral of violence unless we get recognition of Israel's absolute right to security and that of the Palestinian people to a State within the 1967 borders.

We must all, and I mean all of us, take the initiative: the Quartett, Europe, America, Russia, the UN. This time, let's do it together, not separately. As the region's leading economic partner and the Palestinians' main supplier of aid, Europe has a special responsibility. And France and the UK, which share the same beliefs, have a duty to take action.

Let us speed up the implementation of the road map by convening a peace conference. Let us guarantee the process by means of a collective monitoring mechanism and the deployment of an interposition force. In any case, there is no place for preconditions. We must map out a path towards peace, persuade Israel and the Palestinians resolutely to embark on it. And there must be no turning back.

In Iraq too, justice must prevail.

Judging by the debate here, which I have followed from afar, I am under the impression that our position may have sometimes have been very slightly misunderstood. So, perhaps, you will allow me to come back to it briefly.

Last winter, France advocated Iraq's complete, immediate and verifiable disarmament on the basis of Security Council Resolution 1441. Along with the UK, France was one of the major architects of the consensus achieved on this text. France made proposal after proposal throughout the first months of 2003 to increase the effectiveness of the disarmament efforts. There was absolutely no idea of condoning the existing regime or its behaviour. On the contrary, France's constant aim was to achieve, as fast as possible, the objectives we had set together.

Quite obviously, Saddam Hussein's regime inspired only disgust and horror. But we must think seriously about the conditions required for such regime change. Can the use of force without a UN mandate serve as a universal method of settling crises? France didn't believe so then; and we do not believe it any more today. Let's face it: unless we all act together with due regard for international law, there will be no acceptance for regime-change by force.

We too were concerned by the security threat of Iraq. But what were we talking about? Was it weapons of mass destruction? At that time, there was an inspection system which we had consistently adapted and was working. Was it terrorism? At that time, there was no established link between Iraq and the al-Qaeda network. Today, in Iraq, terrorist groups, which hadn't been there before, are taking advantage of the inadequate border controls to infiltrate. Was it remodeling the Middle-East region? Today we can all clearly see the concern of the neighboring countries. Is the region more stable? Are we on the way to peace? Have no doubt about it: despite the difficulties, despite our differences, France will spare no effort to achieve stability and security.

Coalition soldiers are dying in Iraq, among them Britons. My thoughts are with the victims' families. I pay tribute to the memory of the fallen. I share your grief. Every day civilians are dying. The number of terrorist acts is increasing. An outrageous attack has taken a heavy toll on the local UN mission. In the face of so much suffering and pain, there has to be another way forward. This, my country feels, is to allow the Iraqis to take control of their destiny. They must regain their sovereignty as soon as possible.

It's by asserting this principle that we shall bring home to everyone the fact that Iraq is no longer an occupied country, but, on the contrary, a nation supported by the whole international community. The hand-over of sovereignty must take place as soon as possible. Once that's done, the actual responsibilities will have to be transferred gradually to a provisional Iraqi government set up with the support of the Security Council. Similarly, a multinational force under UN auspices can then be organised. Momentum will be created, supported by all the parties, including Iraq's neighbours, with the full backing of the international community, at last reunited. Let us not underestimate the ability of the Iraqi people to take responsibility for their destiny. Let us not repeat the mistakes made in the past. Let us not consider, as all occupying forces have always done, that an occupied country is never ready to recover its sovereignty. We, ourselves, made this mistake and paid the price in our decolonisation wars.

In Iraq just like in the whole of the Middle-East, we must embark on the road to democracy. In a world where peoples must be able to assert their identities, reform is indispensable. It has to come from within, it mustn't be dictated from outside. We would be seriously mistaken if we were to think that democracy can be exported as if it were a mere set of formal rules. Democracy has to be nurtured. It requires an apprenticeship. It is our duty to foster dialogue, freedom and respect in these countries.

But we must go further still. To gain the support of the peoples and adapt to a new world situation, we have a duty to share.

Without barriers or borders our world is rich with promise for the future. Globalization encourages technological progress and the expansion of trade. But it accentuates also prosperity gaps, speeds up the spread of viruses, damages our environment.

I was born in Morocco, on the other side of the Mediterranean, and raised in Latin America. For me, those inequalities are shocking. They are also dangerous. They create a feeling of injustice and fuel resentment. Can we really pay no heed to the lack of development in some African countries because the fight against terrorism is taking up so much of our energy? Can we turn a deaf ear when social divisions grow and threaten to turn limited tensions into fully-fledged civil wars?

At the Cancún summit, the failure of the World Trade Organization to agree on further trade liberalisation was a wake-up call for all of us. The South, driven by countries like Brazil, India and South Africa, to mention but a few, is clamouring for its place in the international institutions. We must make room for them. We have to recognise that all countries have equal rights.

We must realize that, in a radically changing world, we won't regain peace and security if we deal only with emergencies. We can build a new balanced world order only if we forge the conditions for it. Two major trends are emerging today.

Firstly, several new groups are emerging and demanding their say: we saw this not just in Cancún, but also at the time of the Iraqi crisis, when the countries of the South made up their own minds. Strong and dynamic regional organisations are providing these players with new structures.

Secondly, the destinies of these major groupings are now linked. All the barriers have been shattered. There used to be protective borders. Modern means of communication have removed them. There used to be legal and technological barriers to prohibit the movement of weapons. Now trafficking prospers. Twenty years ago, no one paid attention to China's economic growth. Today it is the focus of the whole world. Finally, there were conflicts then considered to be peripheral, not seen as affecting the balance of the major powers. When the war broke out in Afghanistan in 1979 who could seriously have feared their security was threatened by the toppling of a regime in Kabul? Many thought, to use Neville Chamberlain's words, that Afghanistan was another of those "far-away countries of which we know little." It wasn't right in nineteen-thirty eight, it wasn't right in nineteen seventy nine, and it isn't right now. Today, interdependence is the norm. No State can turn its back on the Afghan situation. On the success of that country's reconstruction hangs the success of our battle against terrorism, our efforts to stop drug trafficking, and maintaining the main balances in southern Asia and beyond.

No international order can be built upon the power of a single country. So what path must we take?

To go the unilateral route is utopia. It is also, more importantly, obsolete. We all know that no one State is in a position to respond on its own to the challenge of security, economic growth and social development. People everywhere in the world are no longer prepared to accept solutions imposed on them from outside. The times when a minority decided and a majority obeyed are over. What is true in our own societies is also true at the international level. Only negotiated decisions, only decisions agreed between all partners command support. If we want to be effective, we must have legitimacy.

So the multilateral route is the only realistic one. This choice is in our interest. If we all share the same risks, we must share decision-making. And it is up to all of us to define the ways and means to achieve genuine collective responsibility.

My country isn't naive. Every day the constraints on multilateral action are clear to everyone.

Far from discouraging us, all this must prompt all of us to mobilise. Let us not forget: it took two world wars before the international community, at long last, established the UN. This is a legacy we must enrich, expand, and enhance. For, without world democracy, there will be no stability.

France and the United Kingdom are key players in this remodeling process.

In building this new international order, another priority is obvious: transatlantic relations.

For the links between Europe and the U.S. are paramount. It is obviously another area in which it is in our countries' clear interest to cooperate. There is no contradiction between our determination to see Europe play a world role and strengthening the transatlantic link. Only a Europe capable of speaking with one voice, will be a credible partner for the U.S. and respected as such. This is in the interest of the U.S., our common closest ally. How can we, for example, cooperate with the U.S. in the area of intelligence, if Europe hasn't got its own strategic analysis? How can we fight proliferation together, if Europe hasn't got its own assessment of the relevant programmes and a determined policy to put an end to them?

By a strange paradox, the relationship with the United States too often acts as a brake on Franco-British ambitions when it should, on the contrary, speed up their realisation. The UK and France are both firm and reliable allies of the U.S. There are many ways the two shores of the Atlantic can complement each other. We must exploit them. Take NATO: It's our countries which are today making the most active contribution to the modernisation of the Alliance. They are putting forward proposals, ideas and, most of all, providing troops.

Let us keep this fact in mind: far from vindicating prejudices, it lays the foundations for fruitful and constructive cooperation.

Europe has to be one of the pillars of this new world! It is a continent open to the world. The North Sea, the Mediterranean, the Atlantic look to every corner of the globe. Europe carries the flame handed on from the Age of Enlightenment. It embodies the universal values which must underpin a legitimate world order. But this is not all. In the last century, the European continent, our common land, experienced absolute evil. This evil, vanquished and put behind us, has transformed us. It imposes upon us a duty to remember. It imposes upon us a duty clear-sighted. But the flame of hope still burns as brightly as ever. The wisdom we have gained at the price of blood must lead to action. That wisdom leads to strength, it is the exact opposite of the weakness which some would like to attribute to the Europeans. This is the point I was stressing in my speech to the Security Council in New York on the 14 of February this year. And nothing since has led me to change this message.

As holder of its share of the conscience of the world, Europe has the duty to assist in the birth of a new international order. This is a responsibility our two countries must share.

Today a new era is dawning in Europe. As it confronts the challenges and the changes of the world, Europe faces three tasks.

First, Europe's enlargement and deepening. As every one can sense, European integration will be undergoing far-reaching changes in the years to come. To make Europe more democratic, more efficient and closer to the citizens, its institutions will have to be reformed. This is what the draft Constitution is about. European economies will also have to change. They will have to be stronger, healthier and more competitive at world level, in all areas, research and development, the cutting-edge industries and education.

Second, Europe's role in the world. If they want to be able to hold their own on the world stage, Europe must have its own foreign policy and be able to fight for its principles. This is what the current draft Constitution provides for. The appointment of a European Foreign Minister, together with the creation of a European Defence policy, backed by credible assets, will enable Europe to defend its vision and shoulder its responsibilities.

Third, Europe's new frontiers. For tomorrow's Europe, with its thirty or so members, relations with its neighbours will take on new and greater significance. New partnerships will need to be devised with the Mediterranean countries, Russia and other nations. To do this will require dialogue and solidarity.

France wants a strong Europe. We believe that Europe, by pooling together our sovereignties, increases, not reduces, each of our nation's influence. Ours must be a political Union. Were we to confine Europe to a mere free-trade area, we would be betraying the spirit of the Founding fathers and failing to seize the opportunity Europe offers to each of us.

With our strong will to preserve our identities, the British as well as the French people have, at times, expressed reservations on one or other aspect of European integration. But believe me we know that, in order to exert influence on the course of history, Europe represents a key asset. Unity is the essential condition if we want Europe to take its future into its own hands.

This is especially true in an area where Britain and France can make a major contribution: defence.

There can be no Europe without European defence and no European defence without Britain. And indeed it was your

Prime Minister who paved the way for the agreement reached at the Saint-Malo Summit in 1998, which gave a decisive boost to the European security and defence policy. This initiative allowed us both to clarify relations with NATO and to establish the first elements of an autonomous European defence. The operations conducted in Macedonia and very recently in Congo flow directly from our joint initiative.

In the wake of the Second World War, France developed an unparalleled partnership with Germany. This cooperation has made a major contribution to the success of the European venture. This success has spurred France and Germany to be ever more ambitious for Europe. This drive has stood the test of time. Today, more than ever before, it is very much alive. As Europe enlarges, French and Germans know that the UK's contribution is key to its future progress. The individuality of each of our three nations is a strength. And we must take European unity forward by bringing together the different views across Europe. It is for us to convince people that our old continent has a bright future ahead of it.

On my way to London today, I was pondering the heritage of our two countries which has inspired our common values and principles. This heritage will serve us well, helping us to give a new lease of life to our cultures, our languages, our experience as we confront the world. What unites us is stronger than what separates us. This is what we must carry forward into the future. This is what we must now make a reality.

Together with Germany, our three countries have the political will, the economic significance and the military capabilities that can shape our continent. At a time when some Europeans are apprehensive, together we can make a real difference. At a time when the world is dithering between unity and division, we have a duty to posterity: to find the path which will lead to a new world. A fairer, more stable, and more peaceful world.

How far we have come since that fateful day in 1815 when, before boarding the ship Bellerophon, Napoleon pleaded in vain with the Prince Regent: "I come, like Themistocles to appeal to the hospitality of the British people." Several years later, he died, on the remote island of Saint Helena, after being confined to a diabolical tête-à-tête with the island's governor Hudson Lowe. An encounter, which has still not surrendered all its secrets.

Today, the forces of land and sea, the spirit of fire and water are at last reconciled. And I have come to you this evening as a Frenchman, as a European, as a member of our family. Nothing, neither tea or the Channel will ever be able to separate us. I beg you, stay British. I promise: we shall stay French. Together let us be Europeans because as Europeans, we are strong.

Thank you.

A NEW ERA FOR EUROPE

ARTICLE WRITTEN FOR *LES ECHOS*, NOVEMBER 7, 2003

*"Power means an ability to listen to others
and understand their concerns."*

On 4 October 2003, the Inter-Governmental Conference in Rome took up the plan for a Constitution that had been prepared by the Convention presided over by Valéry Giscard d'Estaing. The main innovations proposed were: replacing the rotating presidency of the Union with a president to be elected by the Council; creating the position of a European Minister of Foreign Affairs; modifying the composition of the Commission and broadening the areas governed by the vote of the qualified majority.

Europe is returning to the political stage. The future European Constitution gives rise to an extensive debate. We should be glad about this: we are entering a new era in Europe. In the face of the upheavals in recent history, the vision of the fathers of the Treaty of Rome should be enriched and broadened. And France, faithful to her calling, wishes to be in the vanguard.

With the fall of the Berlin Wall and the end of the logic of being divided into blocks, a different Europe is emerging. Yesterday, it was a question of establishing a vast economic market. Today, the European plan needs to be developed on the scale of the entire continent and inscribed at the very center of a globalized world. The Union must, at one and the same time, invent new rules to organize a collection of twenty-five nations, which will be more than thirty countries tomorrow; assign new objectives to its internal policies; establish its role on the international stage as well as with its closest neighbors.

This difficult task is well within the capabilities of the genius that is one of Europe's attributes. Since the beginning, the "communal method" has allowed for the building of an original institutional architecture, halfway between a federal model and a union of States. We must go further by imagining ways that will allow a greater number of States to deepen the construction of Europe without denying them any of their distinctions.

Indeed, the profound originality of our approach lies here, in the ever-closer union of nations with confirmed identities, the ever stronger cohesion of a mosaic of peoples, languages, and cultures. Europe combines unity and diversity. It even makes the recognition of the diversity into the source of its unity in order to better thwart the demons of the past.

While the world hesitates between an aspiration toward the universal and the call of specific identities, the European venture shows its capacity to force destiny. As Michelet noted, "what is least simple, least natural, most artificial, that is to say least fatal, most human and most free in the world, is Europe."

The ambition is as enormous as the challenges are: proposing a new model founded on law, demanding dialogue and sharing, paying careful attention to those who are weakest; exercising the new responsibilities that both the management of the world economy and collective security call for.

As opposed to the vision of a Europe that lacks a true will to act, we must assert our capacity to confront regional crises and to participate in the settling of the great strategic problems. Under the aegis of the High Representative, an evaluation of threats was introduced so as to establish a security strategy: this is an important step toward the awareness of our responsibilities. Furthermore, four European countries have formulated proposals that are open to all in order to reinforce the methods of European defense. Together with the tasks of the Inter-governmental Conference, this is the base for a true affirmation of Europe on the international stage.

Two examples attest to this evolution: in the area of maintaining peace, the autonomous operation led by the

European Union in Ituri allowed the stability of that region to be guaranteed and a solid transition to be arranged with the mission of the United Nations. In the area of nonproliferation, Germany, the United Kingdom, and France are working to make an agreement with the Iranian authorities. The method implemented deserves to be continued: action is a requirement, but so is an ability to listen that goes hand in hand with the necessary resolve when defending principles, and finally there must be the flexibility which led to putting the best placed European capitals forward in order to convince Teheran. London, Berlin, and Paris are mobilizing around the Iranian issue. Nothing prevents the same thing from happening around other issues tomorrow with, for example, Madrid or Lisbon around Latin America, Brussels and London around Africa, taking into account the bonds justified by history and culture.

Peace, so dearly won by Europe, must be effected beyond our common borders, in Afghanistan, in the Middle East, as well as in Asia or Latin America, for threats no longer recognize any frontiers. As for our ambition for prosperity, it can no longer be limited to the abolishment of barriers or restrictions of exchange: in order to prepare for the future, we must integrate our economies more, put true industrial strategies in place, tackle the delays in our scientific research and our educational systems, and invent new forms of solidarity for the benefit of the new member nations.

Together with Germany our country has offered proposals for a significant boost for growth through concrete projects, especially in the realm of transportation and research. For a long time, it has been pleading that the rules of competition not prevent European industries from emerging, being able to confront their competitors from a standpoint of industrial development and job protection.

This lies at the core of our discussions with the European Commission. First on the stability pact: far from wanting to shirk our commitments, we ask that the respect for budgetary discipline take the situation into account and be accompanied by an indispensable flexibility so as not to curb the economy's renewal. Then on the Alstom project, where the objective must be that of safeguarding the future of a great European enterprise and of its jobs that are spread all over Europe: is it not time to mobilize the public power and private partners in order to prepare the terrain for new industrial strategies?

Europe must have its foothold in everyday life. To this end, it is essential that it develop policies that are more relevant to our fellow citizens.

There is no shortage of examples: we have the issue of security, whether it is a question of the struggle against unauthorized immigration or the public health's protection against the risk of epidemics; we have the fight against unemployment through reforms and investments that should create a new environment of growth; we have the defense of social rights, henceforth inscribed in the European Charter as fundamental rights; we have education where a great deal remains to be done in order to ensure the authentication of any study program and the recognition of diplomas. For the environment to benefit from a high level of protection, for nutritional safety to be confirmed, and for the rights of the consumer to be defended, protective devices must be fully in line with the European level.

Europe must forge the path for the new candidates. And beyond that, it will have to elevate its relationships with its neighbors in the East and the South: Russia, the Ukraine, the countries of North Africa or of the rest of the Mediterranean.

It should suggest a new perspective to them all, that of Europe as a more generous and more open partner, able to promote a common space for exchange, prosperity, and peace. This will be a particularly helpful contribution to the stability of the region and of the world.

There are many dimensions that contribute to the promotion of a European model of economic development, attentive to equilibrium and justice. But we must also allow the traditions of each country and each people to continue to flourish on the cultural level and in everyday life, everywhere that supplemental support can be applied. Europe must be there, each time, so that we can become stronger together.

The European Union must guide these necessary evolutions through new institutions. All the credit goes to the Convention over which Mr. Giscard d'Estaing presided for having developed an ambitious project that provides our Union with a unique chance: a direction of affairs that is better centered around the president of the European Council, the Commission, and the European Minister of Foreign Affairs, and more votes for the majority in accordance with a formula that is understood by all. So these new innovations give a new *élan* to our institutions.

The adoption of this future Constitution is a prerequisite for any future progress of Europe. That is the reason why the French authorities hope and pray for a rapid conclusion to the current negotiations: we need a new pact between the states and the peoples of the continent. The importance of the challenge justifies our ambitiousness. Who could understand that we might be satisfied with a compromise that would be no more than the smallest common denominator of the states participating in the negotiation?

This mechanism, however, cannot remain stationary, as we all know; it will have to evolve. In which direction? Probably in the direction of a better definition of the different areas of intervention. First there is that which must constitute the base of our communal organization, that is to say the great interior market. Each of the Union's members must be an integral part of this and participate loyally by respecting all the rules. Added to this are the accompanying policies directly linked to this vast market: as soon as they are inspired by a concern for solidarity, following the example of the common agricultural policy or that of regional aid, they, too, must be shared by all.

Beyond this, should greater ambitions in matters of research or leading industries, a true autonomy in the area of defense, be necessary for all the members at the risk of leading to impediments and delays? If certain members are hesitant, nothing should force them to take part in such actions; but nothing should force those who wish to engage in these actions to have to wait. We need an efficient, mobile, and dynamic Europe today, a Europe that is capable of responding quickly to the pressures of its international competitors and of acting with determination in the areas of defense or diplomacy. Consequently, it is essential that, beyond the European market, our working methods show sufficient flexibility to allow those that are most energetic to move forward. In the absence of such flexibility, those who are most enterprising would have no other choice but to move ahead alone.

France intends to bring a European project that is best adapted to the world's realities to a good conclusion together with all the Union members who so desire. First of all with Germany: for more than a year our cooperation has found a new vigor and effectiveness unprecedented since the end of the war. Conscious of the ambition that inspires them, our two countries must preserve their spirit of permanent dialogue and urge European integration further along. With Great Britain, too, where a spirit of responsibility must incite us to cooperate increasingly. We see it in Africa, the Balkans, and the Middle East. We see it especially in the realm of defense, where we are inspired by the same desire to have efficient and credible means available.

On the foundation of the new Constitution, an in-depth debate on Europe's future will have to be initiated, both in France and the other European countries. To the French people I would like to say that this new era in Europe offers the chance for unity, a new space, and new initiatives. To our friends who are coming into the Union, I would like to express France's pleasure and hope in the face of this shared venture. Our Europe has a mission, a vocation, namely that of setting an example of democracy and of social and economic progress; of participating in the world's peace, stability, and development. Let us be aware of our European duty: without an audacious, generous, and fraternal Europe there will not be a more just, more stable, and more peaceful world.

PART THREE

FRANCE
AND
ISRAEL

FRANCE AND ISRAEL:
A PASSIONATE RELATIONSHIP

SPEECH DELIVERED AT THE KING DAVID HOTEL, JERUSALEM, MAY 25, 2003

"Between France and Israel, between the French and the Jewish people, it is an affair of the heart."

The crisis in Iraq had a considerable impact on the region's ongoing conflict between Israelis and Palestinians, making it increasingly urgent for the major powers to renew their efforts to end the conflict. On December 22, the United States, the European Union, Russia and the United Nations met agreed on a peace plan—the roadmap. The plan had been accepted by the Palestinians but not yet by Israel when the French Foreign Minister arrived in Jerusalem. His visit there was aimed at improving bilateral relations with the country. On his last visit, in June 2002, the Minister had stressed his desire to develop these relations beyond differences of opinion on regional questions. A work group was set up in July 2002 in order to make propositions toward this end. The Foreign Minister was there to address the final meeting of this group when the government of Ariel Sharon announced its approval of the "road map." The Foreign Minister took the occasion to discuss the impact of the Iraqi conflict and the Israeli-Palestinian crises on the people of the Middle East, the links between France and Judaism, and the relationship between France and Israel.

I am pleased to be with you here in Jerusalem, a city I return to with great emotion. And I wish to thank you for your welcome.

A land steeped in history, Israel is a modern country that shows its creativity, its victory over adversity, but also its capacity to transmit the values that its people have always carried inside them. A living democracy, a mosaic of cultures, it can pride itself on its economic and technological capacities of the first order, and the greatest density of scientists in the world.

The cradle of the Jewish people, Israel has become their refuge and their homeland after centuries of dispersion marked by intense suffering. From those years you have retained, and rightly so, the duty to be vigilant and alert. Those who built the state of Israel took an oath that never again would Jews be delivered up to the blind forces of hatred and barbarity. Today your country is a living testimony to that commitment. In the words of André Malraux: *Israel bears on its face the oldest past in the world and the state of Israel is only the most recent chapter in the history of Israel.*

I came here in June 2002 on one of my first trips as Minister for Foreign Affairs. I return to you today with two objectives: to inject new dynamism into Franco-Israeli relations and to stress my conviction that a new possibility for peace can, and must be, seized.

France has a passionate, sometimes even an impassioned relationship, with your country. It is based on deep bonds, marked by intense experiences, some of them joyful, others tragic, and illuminated by so many of our fellow citizens. Finally, it is enriched by the multiple links that exist between our peoples today. Here we are talking about more than two centuries of universal history, beginning with the a twin encounter: the Jewish Haskala and the European Enlightenment, particularly the French Enlightenment of 1789 and the emancipation from which modern Jewishness was forged. Léon Blum pointed out: *The emancipation of the Jews was one of the pillars of the real and immediate application of the ideals of the French Revolution. We owe the birth of the modern Jew—with the dignity of the citizen and the integrity of the free man—to that great midwife of freedom, the French Revolution.*

Individual emancipation, for which *abbé* Grégoire was the intellectual architect, but also collective emancipation with the creation of the first *Consistoire* by Napoleon Bonaparte. An era opened up with the *Declaration of the Rights of Man*, which called for the recognition of all citizens and united them in the same universality. Proclaimed by the French Revolution, these principles were delivered around the Mediterranean by the first international francophone association in history, the Universal Israelite Alliance, bringing a message of openness and sharing, and teaching from its very creation the values of the republic to the future citizens of the Jewish state.

Today, schooled by this history, we must think together about how to construct the future. Israelis arouse lively sentiments in the heart of every French man and woman: sentiments of tragedy, creativity and the duty of a shared peace. The Shoah is part of your history, of our history, the history of all humanity. When I went to visit the Yad Vashem memorial a year ago I bowed my head before the immensity of the suffering and the horror.

In his Vél'd'hiv speech in 1995 the French President acknowledged the responsibility of the French state in the horrors of the deportation of French Jews. He referred to it again only a few days ago: France is *forever inconsolable for this inexpiable transgression.*

Our country's desire to see justice done has led the French government to create the Study Mission into the Looting of Jewish Assets in France and to apply its recommendations, particularly the creation of the Commission for the Compensation of Victims of Spoliation and the Foundation for the Memory of the Shoah.

The moral prejudice remains beyond imagining. All those names, all those martyred souls, remind us every day of the dark part that lies in every man. They remind France and Europe of their duty to peace and tolerance, their duty to remember a crime whose memory must never be taken for granted. And although France and Europe have always born within them the creative mark of the Jewish people and identity, today they have not forgotten, after fifty years of efforts to construct a space for peace and sharing, that to a large degree they derived the energy to accomplish that duty from the absolute rejection of the horror and barbarity suffered by the Jewish people.

Between France and Israel, between the French and the Jewish people, it is an affair of the heart. In the middle of the Dreyfus affaire father Emmanuel Lévinas pointed out, paradoxically, that *a country that is divided over the fate of a Jewish captain is a country worth living in.*

France was very quick to understand the vigor of the movement that brought about the immigration of Jews from all over Europe toward Palestine. It was very quick to recognize the miracle of the rebirth of the Hebrew language after twenty centuries of absence. In a certain sense it was even its cradle, as Eliezer Ben Yehouda, the founder of modern Hebrew says: *It was in one of the streets of Paris, in a café on the Boulevard Montmartre, that I started speaking Hebrew for the first time, with one of my friends, sitting at a round table with two cups of black coffee.* It was indeed in the heart of Paris that your language reemerged from its long years of sleep. Beyond its anecdotal interest, how can we fail to see this as the sign of a future for us to build together?

France and the Jewish people constitute two histories that interweave and echo each other. On the one hand we have the first great monotheism establishing the rules of a universal morality. On the other, the land of the Rights of Man, the ideals of the Enlightenment, a France that recognized the spiritual vocation of the Jewish people from the very beginning. These two modes of universal thought are now indissociable, so deeply are they indebted to each other. I carry the memory of all the French Jews who walked to their deaths; we also remember the just French people who joined forces to save so many lives. Marked by the memory of the dark years, the French people joined together to support the creation of the state of Israel. France was fully committed to defending your position in the community of nations. She was one of the first to recognize the state of Israel and to give its unstinting support during the most difficult years of that renaissance.

We share immense advantages that we should put to more use.

Firstly, the Francophone community in Israel, which weaves strong links between our two societies. Israel, the second Francophone country of the Middle East, wishes to join the International Organization of Francophones. As President Chirac stressed to President Weizmann when he was here in October 1996, we hope more than ever that Israel will be admitted to the Organization as soon as possible.

Next, the Jewish community in France, a blessing for France. It is the second largest in the world outside of Israel and plays a major role in our country. France would not be what it is today without Marcel Proust, Léon Blum, René Cassin, Albert Cohen and many more, both today and yesterday. These French people, having a great attachment to the genius of Judaism and to Israel, weave privileged links between our two countries. I wish to acknowledge our debt to them and to reassert my attentive commitment in the face of unacceptable provocations from certain quarters in order that they may live and flourish to the full in our Republic. Anti-Semitism is intolerable. The French people and government have joined together to fight it in all its forms.

It is up to us to breathe new life into our relations. Together, and convinced that we must not let the relations between our two countries become tattered and worn, we have set our hearts on restoring them. France is one of Israel's leading providers, a partner on a scientific level and the only European country to have a cultural presence in your country with our centers at Haifa, Beer Sheva and Nazareth. Our country is also your second tourist destination. And today Europe is your first trading partner.

Our links are intense and are only waiting to flourish and diversify. On the French side we have appointed Professor David Khayat, an eminent cancer specialist who is present with us here, to make daring suggestions. I am delighted that you have appointed Mr. Yéhuda Lancry, the ex-ambassador to

France and a man with a considerable cultural profile, as Israeli co-chairman. You can trust me to make sure the conclusions of the group's work will be implemented.

In this context ambitious projects have been prepared on all sides and in all domains ranging from political dialogue to cooperation on scientific, commercial, cultural and academic levels. And allow me to inform you that as a token of our commitment and confidence France is going to build a new *Institut Français* in Tel Aviv, one of the world's great centers for contemporary creation, an institute that will be on a par with the cultural vitality of our two countries. The institute will act as a meeting place, a place where French and Israeli intellectuals, artists and scientists can come together to debate and exchange ideas. It is destined to become a hub from which the French culture and language can radiate.

Let us also renew our political dialogue in every domain: security, the struggle against proliferation and terrorism, and conflict management. Faced with new threats, we have the duty to work together, with the whole international community. The Israeli people, who suffer greatly from terrorism, understand this need. We understand what the Israelis have been feeling for all too long, for all too many years. The threat of terrorism haunts each family here. The feeling of insecurity kindles a permanent anxiety. The horror of the attacks revolts us, just as it revolts you. France condemns all terrorist acts. It is fighting a merciless battle against this scourge, with the help of all its partners.

France has always been adamant about the security of your country. Israel is entitled to full and complete security. This can be achieved by building a peace that is based on justice. That is the meaning of the French commitment to the Middle East.

We understand that for Israel the security of its citizens ranks among its primary preoccupations, and we shall always stand beside it in its struggle against fanaticism, hatred and violence. It is precisely for this reason that we must not let the logic of confrontation overcome our desire for reconciliation at a time when the perspective of a new opportunity may be taking shape.

Peace will be built on respect for the identities and rights of the peoples in the region: The right of the Israeli people to live in total security within safe and recognized frontiers, the right to integrate into the regional environment and be accepted by all. Little by little your neighbors are coming to recognize this, following the example of the Egyptians, brave pioneers of peace in 1978, and then the Jordanians in 1994.

This absolute right is now recognized as a vital necessity in the region. With the Beirut summit in 2002 all the Arab states proposed to normalize relations with Israel as soon as the Occupied Territories are vacated. That means that today no one really contests Israel's right to exist within its internationally recognized frontiers. And if anyone did contest it, they would meet with firm opposition from France.

Today the *status quo* is no longer possible. The Israeli-Palestinian conflict has become a symbol of division in the world. The impasse feeds frustrations that are converted by international terrorism which radicalizes the fears of all. It strengthens the feeling of injustice that we have to fight against. Because justice is one; it does not divide.

How can we break away from this logic? The very idea of a peace process seems to have disappeared over nearly three years. Rendered desperate by the attacks, a growing number of Israelis seems to be convinced that any peace negotiated with the Palestinians is an impossibility. The legitimate security to which the people of Israel are entitled appears to be an absolute priority that is always beyond reach.

In its own right the objective of security is insufficient to ensure peace. Without a political perspective it kindles violence. Can the reoccupying of the West Bank, the curfew, "target" operations that quite often make victims of the innocent, the destruction of dwellings, as well as expropriations, be a guarantee of security for the Israelis? Let us also question the meaning of history. Only by providing political answers, by seeking a fair and sustainable peace can we cross the threshold. I understand your doubts. Indeed, how is it possible to imagine concessions when bombs are exploding in your buses and before your schools?

But we can also find the response in the strength of our democracies, in the wisdom of our cultures and in the demands of our peoples. What people could possibly understand the sentiments of the Palestinians better than your people, you who have experienced so much injustice, repression and exclusion?

We must wrench this region out of the grips of the fever that is strangling it. France wants to see an Israeli state that is fully integrated into its environment, living in peace and total security and maintaining relations of exchange with its neighbors. I tell you this with friendship and conviction: such a thing will not be possible without brave choices, compromises and openness.

After fifty years of wars and hostility, your state is beginning to see its neighbors acknowledge its legitimacy. There is one more step to take and it is because you are strong that you can take it. That step is to respect the principle of exchanging territories in return for peace. And you can make that peace with the Palestinians, as you can make it with the Syrians and the Lebanese. Once you have accomplished this step, with all the necessary international guarantees, including that of France, you will finally be able to live in peace and security, to forget the anxiety that goes with violence and receive full acknowledgement of your presence in the Middle East.

There is a new opportunity for peace today: a plan proposed by the Quartet comprising Europe, the United States, Russian and the United Nations. It lays down a calendar leading over three years to the creation of a Palestinian state with a state of Israel that is fully recognized by its neighbors and integrated into the region. The Quartet's plan must be implemented in good faith by all parties. The Palestinians have accepted it. No one can force you to commit yourselves if you do not decide to do so: not France, not Europe, not the United States. In this respect Israel is making an historic decision today. Let us consolidate the movement. Let us make peace an irreversible path.

We cannot resign ourselves to another failure, that would turn the roadmap into a sort of bloodbath and would deprive the region of all hope, abandoning it to ever more violence, repression and sacrifice. Abandoning the roadmap leads not to war but to the abyss.

France and the European Union are ready to commit themselves and to work with the parties in order to restore trust, to back up the implementation of the roadmap day after day. That is why I made a speech in Cairo presenting five stages to support and follow through the implementation of this roadmap. I particularly urged that the international conference it recommends should be held from the beginning of the process, and that there should be an immediate and simultaneous stop to the violence. All the fathers of the roadmap must accept their responsibility for its implementation. Together we must set up the supervision mechanism as outlined by the Quartet in order to follow through the implementation of this plan.

Why wait any longer, fearing the ineluctable or irreparable with each passing moment, when peace can be built every day both in us and around us? For peace, like justice, does not divide. Let's think about what it would mean: would it not be the return of hope and horizons for all? Everyday life restored in all its lightness, its carelessness, its thousands of ordinary and extraordinary projects, the future etched into our consciousness? Israel would first of all benefit from dynamic development of the region. New perspectives are already opening up with the Euromediterranean process in Barcelona. This dialogue, in which Israel has played a part from the beginning, will give me the occasion to renew acquaintance with my Israeli colleague in Crete the day after tomorrow. It is precious because today it is the only framework that brings together Israel and the countries from around the Mediterranean.

Let's not hide our faces. Choosing peace is always difficult in a tragic context. We all know that: people who are fighting for their rights never give up. You know it better than anyone else. Let's be daring in our search for a global peace. France would like to see the resumption of the negotiations that were interrupted when just beginning.

Here in Jerusalem in 1805 Chateaubriand was gripped with admiration for the Jewish community, still living, still true to its history when so many great civilizations, from Persia to the Greece of Alexander the Great and the Roman Empire, had all been swallowed up. He wrote. *If there is something among the nations that has the character of a miracle, we believe it is this character we find here.* This miracle belongs to you. Each day you make a point of renewing it and France will always be by your side to nurture this light that comes to us from the dawn of time, to remain true to this demanding goal in the great convolutions of history.

Today the goal is peace with the Palestinian people. Together we must open up a new page of history. Israel, a much dreamed of land, a lost land now recovered, is still experiencing disturbance and disquiet. The veritable victory of your people will be to win peace in a region that aspires to tranquility, to bring to it the humanism that you have always carried in the depths of your own identity.

PART FOUR

CONFRONTING TERRORISM

THE CHALLENGE OF TERRORISM

SPEECH DELIVERED DURING THE MINISTERIAL-LEVEL MEETING OF
THE UN SECURITY COUNCIL ON THE FIGHT AGAINST TERRORISM,
JANUARY 20, 2003

"Let's take an honest look at things: Where there is injustice, terrorism thrives."

At the request of France, a meeting of the United Nations Security Council was convened on January 20, 2003 on the subject of the fight against terrorism. In this forum, in the midst of the Iraqi crisis, this address by, the Foreign Minister emphasized the necessity of deepening the thinking on terrorism by linking it to the strategies and tools used to combat proliferation. The speech also reiterated the importance of the international community's unity in confronting these new threats.

The world today is at a turning point. Its crises have global consequences. In this context, the Security Council, the supreme expression of the will of the international community, has a special responsibility. This is why France has taken the initiative to call this meeting. I thank you, your excellency, the Secretary-General, dear colleagues, to have responded in such numbers to my invitation.

I would not like to speak on the subject of terrorism in New York without recalling with great feeling the victims of the September 11 attacks. Their memory should inspire in us the greatest determination in the fight against terrorism.

New attacks, in Karachi, in Bali or in Mombasa, have confirmed that the terrorists are more than ever bent on destroying lives and sowing destruction. They have also confirmed that terrorism threatens all countries and all peoples. It thus cannot be fought in an isolated manner. Confronted with terrorism, it is our duty to mobilize collectively. And it is duty to achieve results.

Much has been done. I think of the United Nations, the essential role of the Security Council, the adoption of Resolution 1373, the sanctions imposed on al-Qaeda and the work of the UN Counterterrorism Committee, which I would like to commend. I think also of the G8 and its work on non-proliferation or in the fight against the financial networks that fund terrorism. But there is much left to do, for terrorism is constantly transforming itself. It is skilled at adapting its methods and its networks, and it is affirming its global character. It is imperative that we do more and that we do it better.

How? First of all in enlisting, to an even greater degree, the efforts of the entire international community. The United Nations can and should play a major role in this new impetus. Because it has a universal mission, the United Nations should be at the center of our efforts and focus us in a programmatic way on those areas in which it can make a contribution more effectively than others.

The UN has already played a decisive role in the development of international juridical tools against terrorism. But we should go still further in this area, not only to finish the negotiations around central texts, like the draft General Convention on terrorism or the draft Convention on nuclear terrorism, but also to speed the implementation of documents that have already been signed. Let us give a new impetus to the United Nations institutions charged with this task.

Because it has a universal mission, the United Nations can also do much more to help countries—in particular, the countries of the South—to reinforce their national programs for fighting terrorism. In this perspective, I suggest that we consider setting up a cooperation and assistance fund within the United Nations that would be endowed with its own resources and that would have close ties with the other international financial institutions.

But we should also continue with the work begun in other forums. We will only be effective against the financing of terrorism if we marshal all the tools at our disposal, from the G8 to the FATF [FinancialAcion Task Force on Money Laundering] and beyond, and we must also get the IMF [International Monetary Fund] and the World Bank fully involved.

While it holds the presidency of the G8, France intends to give a decisive push to the Global Partnership Against the Spread of Weapons and Materials of Mass Destruction launched at the Kananaskis Summit. It is high time to address the rapprochement of terrorism with other threats such as the proliferation of weapons of mass destruction, arms smuggling and illegal financial activity.

France intends to make it harder for terrorists to acquire and use the radioactive sources that are scattered throughout the world to make so-called "dirty bombs." It will make specific recommendations towards the drafting of an international convention tightening controls on the use and transfer of these radioactive materials.

Let's take an honest looks at things: where there is injustice, terrorism thrives. An equitable model for development is thus necessary if we are to stamp out terrorism definitively. This is why we are working nonstop to resolve the crises in Iraq, in Korea, and particularly in the Middle East, the core of crises in the region and in the world. This is why it is imperative to put development at the heart of our agendas, to step up our activity and to use our imagination. This is why, finally, we should privilege dialogue between cultures rather than highlighting their differences. The United Nations' role in this endeavor is indispensable.

We all recognize the urgency here. On each of these points, we must act. Our fate is in our hands. Let's begin this process without delay and fix timetables for action. I suggest that we meet at on the occasion of the next General Assembly, perhaps even as part of a special session of that event, to adopt new measures that will give concrete form to the new impetus we would like to give to our mobilization.

The fight against terrorism is a universal cause, because terrorism is a universal evil. It is only through our unity, our imagination and our action that we will overcome it.

THE MENACE OF PROLIFERATION

COMMENTARY PUBLISHED IN *LE FIGARO*, SEPTEMBER 23, 2003

*"Proliferation is a match on a powder keg.
It's time we put it out."*

During 2003, the development of Iran's nuclear program became a growing preoccupation for the international community. The countries of the G8 and the European Union expressed their concern and requested Iran to make its program completely transparent. Toward this end, on August 6th the Foreign Ministers of France, Germany and the United Kingdom addressed a letter to their Iranian counterpart reminding Iran of the demands of the international community. On September 21, the three ministers visited Tehran, where they obtained commitments from the Iranian authorities, thus avoiding a new proliferation crisis.

Proliferation has become one of the major threats of our times. The black market for materials, technologies or means to acquire them is growing larger. Scientists cross borders, bringing their expertise to secret programs. We see the result: countries once lacking weapons of mass destruction are on the verge of possessing them today.

Proliferation takes advantage of globalization's weak points—the fluidity of transactions, access to confidential information, opaque financial networks. Yesterday, it was based on known and more structured transactions. Today it relies on secret and diverse pathways, and is much more difficult to fight. For now it is not merely arms sales that must be supervised, but also the circulation of sensitive information, the delivery of electronic components and technical cooperation between countries.

Why does this phenomenon create such deep concerns in the international community? First of all because it forms around regions in crisis, from North Korea to the Middle East. It can thus only contribute further to the instability of these regions, multiply the risks of confrontation and engender dangerous imbalances. Proliferation is a match on a powder keg. It is time we put it out.

International accords have been created, and for decades, they have proven their effectiveness. The twenty nuclear states

President Kennedy feared at the beginning of the 1960s did not materialize. The Nuclear Non-Proliferation Treaty ensured that such predictions did not come true. But we have no illusions: countries have maneuvered around these accords in the past, and they threaten to do so to a greater extent in the future. Their value today depends on our capacity to see that they are respected and that they are fully implemented.

Iran has the value of a test.

For decades, this country has sought to acquire the capacity to generate nuclear power. This is a legitimate ambition. But it will not remain so unless Iran proves that its program is destined for strictly civil ends. Recently, the reports of the International Atomic Energy Agency have raised doubts throughout the international community. Faced with the ambitions of the Iranians, concern is growing.

The alternative is clear: either we allow this country to go forward with its clandestine activities, with the assurance of creating an atmosphere of confrontation that will lead to a deadlock, or we begin a rigorous dialogue to define an exit strategy that is in the interest of all parties. By going to Tehran on October 21, my British and German colleagues and myself have resolutely opted for the second path.

We did it for Iran, with the strong conviction that this country should have major responsibilities in the region. Trust, once reestablished, should allow Iran to become a real pole of development and stability in the region. Its history, its geographical location and its natural resources all predispose it to this role.

We do it for Europe. Out ties to Iran's culture and its people are profound and go back many years. Europe cannot be indifferent to a country with which for years it has discussed every one of its preoccupations: human rights, terrorism, regional security.... And it is just as impossible to ignore the unacceptable risks to its interests that a nuclear Iran would pose. In taking the initiative, we are reaffirming that Europe has the prerogative to define and defend its own strategic interests.

We do it for the Near East and Middle East regions, whose peoples deeply want security, peace and development.

Finally, we do it for the international community, which is animated by the challenge of finding a new method of resolving proliferation crises. All of us are aware that whether the case concerns Iraq, North Korea or Iran, we need effective oversight procedures and appropriate ways to respond. We should be in a position to weigh the risks, secure the transparency of the programs in question and dismantle prohibited installations.

Over the last several months, we have heard an increasing number of warnings: European conclusions, the declaration of the G8 countries on non-proliferation and the resolution of the Board of Governors of the International Atomic Energy Agency among them. These texts set out the requirements Iran needs to address. These requirements were the impetus for our action, and they were accepted by the Iranian authorities during our October 21 visit. The Iranians agreed to cooperate unreservedly with the IAEA, to sign and immediately implement a stricter verification accord, and to suspend uranium enrichment activities.

The effort undertaken by the Europeans should be long-term, for our initiative goes beyond the present case of Iran.

It is first of all evidence of what Europeans can do when they have the capacity to evaluate threats themselves, develop responses and implement them. A strong Europe is in everyone's interest. It is in the interest of our fellow citizens, who thus benefit from greater security, and also in the interest of the United States, who can only be pleased to have this additional support in efforts to achieve security and peace. It is in the interest of Russia, whose ties with Iran will develop more easily in a climate of trust, and finally, also benefits multilateral organizations, whose resolutions stand more of a chance of being respected thanks to this support.

Our initiative also expresses a principle which is at the heart of French diplomacy: collective responsibility. In the area of proliferation, the international community will only achieve lasting success if it demonstrates that it is unified and determined. The strict observance of international commitments should be guaranteed. This would require setting up effective means for verification, for example, by creating a permanent corps of inspectors at the United Nations. New instruments should also be developed, in the context of current international law. France's active participation in the American antiproliferation initiative is one example. Tomorrow, the commitments made under this framework will allow suspicious vessels to be boarded and will help shut down the most important conduits of illicit arms.

This principle of collective responsibility has allowed us to make progress in Iran. It should allow us to take more important steps in the Middle East. Before this crisis, which remains a breeding ground for violence and extremism, no one can be indifferent. How many more days of grief and hatred must this region go through? It is time for us to get together and work to force the doors of peace. It is possible. The principles that we have put to work in the Iranian case—unity of the European countries, respect but frankness in the dialogue with our partner, awareness of the larger stakes, firmness on the objectives—should continue to be an inspiration for Europe and its allies across the entire region. They will not lead to an immediate solution. But they will allow us to move from a climate of crisis to a climate of trust, and from silence to dialogue. And as it has been with Iran, that will be a decisive step.

ISLAM AND THE WEST

SPEECH DELIVERED IN THE FRENCH SENATE, JUNE 14, 2003

"Let's sidestep the game that consists of taking quotations from the holy books of each religion. Bellicose phrases taken from the Torah, the Evangelists and the Koran conceal the message of peace that every religion transmits. Today, there is more to be feared from a clash of ignorances than from the clash of cultures."

On the occasion of History Book Day, the Foreign Minister was invited to address the French Senate as it gave special focus to the West's relationship with Islam.

I am very happy to be here in the Senate taking part in this History Book Day. Happy to participate with you in this focus on Islam and the West, in which Europe and France have a particular responsibility.

The fear of a clash of civilizations had invaded the sphere of ideas well before the September 11 attacks. Of course lots of things separate the two worlds. On the one hand we have a group of populations and countries sharing a religion that is often considered to be indissociable from politics, countries that have achieved the wealth of the industrialized world; on the other, a geographical area whose unity lies in a series of common heritages ranging from Ancient Greece through Christianity to the Enlightenment: a pole that now consists of democracies that are attached to a certain idea of secularism.

History may give us the impression of there being an antagonism between these two worlds, with numerous confrontations, from the Arab invasions to the Crusades, from the Ottoman expansion to European colonization. The twentieth century was often dependant on tensions and conflicts between Muslim countries and western nations, from wars of independence to the Suez crisis and the Iranian revolution. The fact that a triangle between Palestine, Iran, and Arabia contains the most sacred holy places of Sunni and Shiite Islam, Judaism and Christianity today only serves to exacerbate passions.

New fears have appeared in recent years. All peoples are affected by the increasing tensions and anxiety about a future that seems to be out of their control. The Muslim and Western worlds are uneasy: are they condemned to fight tomorrow or can they live together? We all bear an immense responsibility in this time of change when, on both sides, there is a growing temptation to forge straight ahead. In our "disorientated" world, a world that has in fact lost its Orient, we must find the path that leads us toward each other.

Confronted with these fears, we owe a debt to truth. As Merleau-Ponty stressed, *our relation to the truth goes through others. Either we go to the truth with them, or we are not going to the truth.* Islam is the religion of more than a billion people who live their faith in peace. How can Islam and the West, far from opposing each other, respond together to the real questions posed by our world?

Let's begin by avoiding false truths. First of all, imprecise geopolitical perspectives: neither the West nor Islam represents homogeneous realities. The western world is varied. Democracy sometimes arrived there very late: we only have to think of Spain, Portugal and Greece, who freed themselves from the yoke of dictatorship only in the mid 1970s. Let's also think about the central European countries, today members of the European Union, yesterday oppressed by the Soviet system.

The Muslim world is also marked by diversity. A diversity of continents, from the Maghreb to sub-Saharan Africa, from the Middle East to Eastern Europe and Asia. Let's not forget this: Asian Islam represents the majority of Muslims in the world today and Indonesia constitutes the leading Muslim country in terms of the number of its inhabitants. In other words, a diversity of peoples, histories, languages, and cultures, but also a diversity of religious currents: Islam constitutes a tree with two main boughs—Sunnism and Shiaism—with a variety of branches, with Hanafite, Malakite, Chafeite and Hanbalite rites, as well as the many nuances of Shiaism.

The worlds of Islam and the West intermingle and are all the richer for this diversity. The five million Muslims in France are an illustration of this: the Islamic dimension is an integral part of Europe. European Muslims are anxious to fully assume their national identity and participate actively in the future of their country. As veritable transmitters of culture they represent an opportunity that our societies must seize in order to project themselves into the future. Let's not forget the bonds established in the course of history by European peoples, and by our country, particularly with the Lebanon, Syria, Egypt, and of course the Maghreb and sub-Saharan Africa.

Yes, Europe has a vocation to build links between civilizations by virtue of its experience, the multiplicity that inspires it, and its geography. Yes, Islam already has a well-established place in Europe, and this will increase in times to come. Let's look at Turkey, or Bosnia, countries that have managed to keep alive their double European and Muslim heritage through the worst of trials.

Let's also avoid false historical perspectives. Islam generated a whole spectrum of intellectual and cultural currents ranging from the most conservative to the most progressive, the most dogmatic to the most open.

The history of our relations is punctuated by intense periods of exchange and sharing. Our culture bears the traces of this, from Saladin, the hero of medieval literary works, to Racine's Bajazet. And although *Candide* retires to a Turkish dervish, the sultan of Mozart's *The Abduction from the Seraglio* is the archetype of a magnanimous sovereign.

And lastly, let us avoid false political perspectives. The recent conflicts and crises are not wars of religion. And although al-Qaeda terrorism involves Islamic fundamentalist groups, their ideology is no more than a warped form of Islam.

Today it is time to unravel the threads of history. As early as the eighth century, while the Arab Orient was still dominant, a civilization based on Christianity and Roman civilization began to emerge in Western Europe. The end of the fifteenth century marked a major turning point: this occidental civilization took the flame that was offered by the oriental world. With the discovery of the Americas and Spanish and Portuguese expansion, the Occident spread across the Atlantic Ocean and enlarged its sphere of influence while simultaneously opening itself up to a new awareness of other peoples and places.

Successive conquests and discoveries amplified the initial movement. The occidental ideology and values spread throughout the world, traveling with missionaries and functionaries, sailors and poets who set out in search of adventure and knowledge. Western thought spread to the four points of the compass rose and formed a new frame of reference that was often hegemonic.

This model imploded with the two World Wars. History then came to be written in terms of the confrontation between East and West. Political, social and economic competition seemed to relegate all cultural and religious questions into the background. But this period came to an end in its turn: witnessing the fall of the Berlin wall with a sense of triumph. Little by little the West developed an awareness of the profound upheaval that was taking place. Germany was reunited; old configurations from the ex-USSR to Yugoslavia were fissured under the pressure of cultural and religious identities. The end of the last century witnessed the large-scale return of spiritual and cultural dimensions in opposition to state boundaries and the ideologies based on the concept of the "block."

In order to restore trust between people we must now make our way through the labyrinth of the wounds and bitternesses accumulated in the course of history. It is essential to avoid one major pitfall: ignorance, which leads men to claim that they can reduce the essence of a religion to a few words. With regard to Islam, let's exclude the clichés that feed the imagination: it makes no distinction between temporal and spiritual; it is incompatible with all forms of critical thought. Let's sidestep the game that consists of taking quotations from the holy books of each religion. Bellicose phrases taken from the Torah, the Evangelists and the Koran conceal the message of peace that every religion transmits. Today, there is more to be feared from a clash of ignorances than from the clash of cultures.

Ignorance sometimes finds a refuge among the believers themselves. Literalism, which advocates a single eternally valid reading of the sacred texts, contains the seeds of all divisions and all wars. This runs the risk of reducing believers to fixed attitudes in relation to the sources of spirituality: the letter of the text can sometimes cloud its spirit.

The quest for internal perfection, which dates back toward the source of human existence, must not be perverted into a feeling of superiority and mistrust. What are we to think of those who read a sacred text as if it were a map? Those who incite people to hatred and death, beyond all teachings, all heritages, all of humanity's most elementary duties?

It is sometimes said that Islam lends itself more easily to a dogmatic reading of its texts than other religions. This is forgetting that the tradition of the *ijtihad*, the personal effort to interpret the law, is as ancient as the Koran. It is also forgetting that literalist tendencies have affected and continue to affect all religious practices, including Christianity. Let's not forget that the Reformation was in born in part out of a fight for the right to interpret texts.

For the mystic Ibn Arabi, each belief is a mirror of a unique and invisible God. According to the great theologian of the Middle Ages, although God is unique, the "God of beliefs" is nevertheless as diverse as the world of men: all the religions of the book thus deserve the same respect. This reading of the Koran leads to a principle of tolerance and openness that nurture the quest for a mystery that it is our duty to explore together. The mystery of God and the ignorance of men, which the emir Abd-el-Kader evoked magnificently in writing: *If you think and believe what the various communities believe—whether Muslim, Christian, Jewish, Mazdean, polytheistic or anything else— bear in mind that God is that, and something other than that.*

At the start of the twentieth century the Egyptian Ali Abderraziq placed the principle of separating the religious from the political at the heart of his thinking. Today, many thinkers from Mohammed Talbi to Burhan Ghalioun and Yadh Ben Achour have focused on the necessity of enabling religious interpretations to advance without perverting their bases, and adapting them to a constantly evolving world. The existence of this debate at the heart of the Muslim world is a testimony to the quality of the dialogue, which is very far removed from the caricature of Islam that we often see.

The Muslim and Western worlds have always been accessible to each other and have never been separated by any insurmountable barriers. Only nine years after the taking of Constantinople, in 1462, the Ottoman Sultan Mehmet II on his way to Lesbos and passing close to the site of Troy, cried out: *God reserved it for me to avenge this city and its inhabitants.* An observation that testifies to the importance of the Homeric myth in the oriental world and shows that Islam was always a part of the great dialogue between cultures.

If we wish to renew this dialogue we must be able to question ourselves and to put ourselves in the place of others. Let's remember Montesquieu and his *Lettres persanes* in which he says that we are blind to our own society until we have been enriched by another's vision.

With regard to the tensions in the world, peoples are today confronted with the question of their identity in a particularly violent fashion. The Muslim world must face up to many challenges.

Firstly, that of social and economic development. Today only 0.5% of international investment is channeled toward the Arab world. Rapid urbanization, the absence of a strong middle class, and inequality, particularly in terms of education, all feed a rejection of an economic system that seems to give its profits essentially to other regions of the world.

Next, there are political problems: hesitations in the march toward democracy, feelings of bad governance, and the difficulties encountered in the struggle against corruption, all nourish frustrations. We are aware of the dysfunctions that affect some countries in the Muslim world, as they affect other regions of the world. These trends should encourage us every day to demand unconditionally the necessary changes, both in a bilateral and multilateral framework.

Lastly, we must take into account the feeling that the Western world is exercising a form of cultural domination through the growth of globalization. Doesn't the West often give the impression that it wants to impose a single mode of life all over, thus jeopardizing cultures and identities?

This risk is no doubt inherent in all relations between two worlds. In his account of the events of the year 1213 of the Hegira, the Egyptian historian Al Gabarti wrote: *This year thus comes to its end. Among all the unprecedented events that it numbers, the most deadly was the cessation of the Egyptian pilgrimages.* The year in question was 1798, the year when Bonaparte entered Egypt! Recounted by Arnold Toynbee, this astonishing reading of history shows that the heart of a civilization cannot simply be reduced to techniques but must accord full importance to the cultural and spiritual life Elsewhere Al Gabarit recounts the presence of the French in Egypt but, being sensitive to the deep movements of history, he proves to be worried most of all by the interruption of a pilgrimage that linked believers to Islam and to each other.

The resistance of the Muslim world is organized around this question of identity: let's be careful not to create a veritable rift, not to give the impression that modernity and religion are opposed to each other. By adopting a position of technological superiority the West would run the risk of creating new forms of opposition and clouding the true face of modernity, which finds its true expression in education, progress, tolerance and openness. Chateaubriand wrote: It is time for European man to recede into the background in order to discover another planet. In a world in which identity is the key to relations between peoples, let's make sure that, without allowing modernity to recede into the background, it does not come to be seen as the rival of traditions and religions.

We must be all the more careful because, in a world where societies can easily become hidebound, fundamentalism presents itself as a seductive remedy. It is not specific to Islam, and constitutes an extreme form of entrenchment in identity and its exacerbated crystallization. Today, neither Islam nor Christianity is a violent religion: but fanatics everywhere can find pretexts in religion for drifting into intolerance.

It is important to highlight certain recent developments at the source of terrorist movements. The liberation of Afghanistan by Muslim combatants fighting the USSR of yesterday opened up the path for fundamentalist claims that were able, in the wake of the first Gulf War, to exploit the presence of western troops in Saudi Arabia and to develop opposition to the Saudi regime and its western supporters. This quickly translated into violence, with the anti-American attacks of 1995 and 1996 at Riyadh and Al Khobar.

Wherever they spring from, these terrorist movements are obviously inexcusable. There is no question of there being good and bad terrorists. They threaten the Western world, but also the Muslim world, with the greatest barbarity. However, we must be vigilant. Everything that increases the feeling of humiliation opens the door to fundamentalist propaganda. Let's not allow the much-bandied image of suburban Islam to force us to resort to the nineteenth century bogeyman of "dangerous classes".

By rejecting the other we would be sounding the waking call for wounded identities within our own societies. Is it an accident that the leading actors in Al-Qaeda were all reared in an Western environment? Sweden for Bin Laden and the United Kingdom for Omar Sheikh, the kidnapper of Daniel Pearl. Let's make sure that a failed encounter of two worlds does not produce other individuals bent on the most radical forms of violence.

Today, given the social difficulties that are appearing inside the Muslim world, the fundamentalists are confident that they can offer a different model: strict religious education in the *madrasas* instead of nondenominational schools, loans based on trust instead of bank loans, religious charity instead of the welfare state. This propaganda also feeds on two geopolitical factors:

Firstly, the regional conflicts that create zones of disorder and non-law favorable to recruiting and training terrorists, like in Afghanistan yesterday. These crises are eating away at the world. For nearly half a century the Israelo-Palestinian conflict in the Middle East has torn asunder two peoples, each of whom is entitled to live in dignity and safety. Israelis and Palestinians, Jews, Muslims, and Christians must find the way to reconciliation. Given the new escalation of violence that is affecting the region, the international community must be more united and determined than ever before. It is imperative to put a stop to the logic that is capable of crushing the hope that is born from the adoption of the roadmap by all parties. There is no question of resigning ourselves, but we also realize that the conflict cannot be resolved except through respect for law and justice: only a commitment by the international community standing side by side with the parties involved can confer the legitimacy that is indispensable for any sustainable solution.

Open confrontations with the Western world constitute the other great risk. In the Iraq crisis the positions adopted by France, Germany, and Russia clearly showed that the conflict cannot be reduced to confrontation between two blocks— Islam and West. Today we must follow the situation in Iraq with particular attention, with its population aspiring to recovering its full sovereignty. And it is the duty of the international community to favor the emergence of a free Iraq that is independent and democratic, and capable of contributing to the stabilization of the region.

All attempts to settle crises by purely security or military means cannot fail to lead to resistance that will be amplified by the accelerating changes in the world and the multiplication of tensions. Today, we must therefore trace another path together. We cannot allow disorder to gain ground in a world that is becoming more unstable by the day.

How do we get out of this impasse? How can we stabilize a world that is today given over to doubts and fear? We are now faced with brutal facts that no one can deny.

Firstly, let's agree that there's no magic solution, any more than it is fate that would reduce us either to unilateral action or impotence. All action, in order to be effective, presupposes the unity of the international community. The same unity that led us to vote unanimously in favor of resolution 1441 in order to face up to the risk of proliferation in Iraq; the same unity that led us to vote unanimously in favor of resolution 1483 in order to engage the reconstruction of the country. Today the international community is ready to mobilize its energies, perhaps more so than ever. It is important to be able to use such an advantage.

Next, all action must reflect the complexity of the world with a triple objective: freedom, of course, which democracy alone can give. Development also: there will be no lasting peace without a more equitable distribution of prosperity. This leaves respect for identities, which must be based on exchange and dialogue between the cultures. If we omit one of these objectives, the West would only be deepening the distrust and doubts of the Muslim world and other parts of the international community. It would strengthen the positions of those, on all sides, who try to impose blind violence.

Lastly, let's assess the urgency and choose to act against the *status quo* by renewing the international system, in order to place the principles of respect and dialogue at the heart of international relations. This choice presupposes the confirmation of a multilateral order. We are ready to commit ourselves to an in-depth reform of the United Nations, which has to channel wishes more effectively. Let's invent the tools to enable us to act: for example, why not set up a disarmament corps and a "rights of man" corps? An overhauled international system would probably mean a more representative Security Council, principles for more voluntary action and more numerous means of intervention. The multilateral choice must be a choice in favor of responsibility and efficiency.

Within the framework of a new international architecture, regional groups today have an essential responsibility to combat identity tensions. Europe is an original example and opens up new hope. Firstly, because it can confer increased stability all around *Mare Nostrum*. That is the purpose of the Euromediterranean dialogue, which takes into account the three essential aspects of any realistic partnership: political, economic and social. Next, because the debate about Turkey joining the European Union provides the framework for a focus of attention that has never been seen before: what is the reality of Islam? What kind of relationship should exist between Europe and the religious, Muslim world in particular? It is urgent, today, to provide innovative responses that look toward the future. That is one of the great challenges facing each of us today.

Can we speak of Islam and the West and accord to Judaism the place it deserves? I will therefore borrow an idea from Martin Buber, one of the great Jewish philosophers of the modern era. He stresses how those who live side by side must learn to live together, otherwise they inexorably end up opposed to each other and plunge the world into war. It is our responsibility to combat this spiral and to patiently weave the strands of a dialogue that is driven by respect and curiosity with regard to the other.

We all have our references, our ideal cities and our golden ages; our revolutions and our fears, our heady conquests and our secret hopes. Today, in a world that is heir to ancient forms but new by virtue of the proximities it establishes, the time has come to enrich our awareness with the other's vision.

At the heart of the debate, France and Europe have a special vocation. Because of their geographical disposition, turned toward all regions and all peoples. Because of their culture, enriched by centuries of exchange and discovery. Because of their history, rich in glory and sometimes painful lessons stretching from the wars of religion to the conflicts of the twentieth century. But also because of their incredible will, born out of the Enlightenment, to share their great ideals with others.

Yes, France has made a choice to which we intend to remain faithful.

Given the divisions and uncertainties, we resolutely reject the confrontation of cultures and seek to grasp the opportunity for a world that yields neither to the pitfall of power nor to that of immobilism. And the idea we have of ourselves is indeed one of a Occident with several voices, the voice of diversity, debate and democracy. It is up to us together to live this demand that is rooted in the heart of our history, and thus build a safer and more just world.

PART FIVE

TOWARD A NEW WORLD

FOR A NEW GLOBAL ETHICS

SPEECH GIVEN AT THE CONFERENCE "PARTAGER LES FRUITS DE LA
MONDIALISATION" (SHARING THE FRUITS OF GLOBALIZATION),
ORGANIZED BY THE *JOURNAL LES DÉBATS DE L'UNION*,
AT THE INSTITUT DU MONDE ARABE, IN PARIS ON NOVEMBER 4, 2003

"In the twenty-first century, it is impossible to accept a fate of powerlessness and ignorance."

The fifth meeting of the World Trade Organization, which took place in Cancun from September 10 to 14, 2003, ended in failure: the one hundred and forty-six member countries did not reach a final agreement. What remains from this decisive episode of the Doha talks is the refusal—on the part of the Southern countries, emergent countries and the least advanced countries united within the Group of 21—to open negotiations on the so-called "Singapore" subjects: investment, competition, and public markets. Once again, the Southern countries accused the wealthiest countries of maintaining export subsidies that skew the terms of trade. A Korean farmer killed himself in front of the building where the negotiations were taking place.

Since Seattle, the emergence of an antiglobalist or "alterglobalist" movement has been reflected by a critical tendency in public attitudes toward globalization, in the North as well as in the South, a tendency in which many growing concerns are taking shape. Here it is a matter of understanding this inflection within a tense and difficult international context marked by a resurgence of violence in the Middle East.

With the new century we are seeing the repetition of a strange paradox: just as the dawn of the Renaissance was darkened by the Wars of Religion, and just as the hopes inspired by the French Revolution were drowned in the blood of the Terror, it is at the very moment when civilization is entering a decisive phase, when it is undergoing the most tremendous changes and is the bearer of the greatest hopes for peace—it is precisely then that it is burdened by the deepest anxieties concerning its future. The fall of the Berlin Wall opened a new era. The wind of freedom has helped to spread hopes for democracy in every direction. The freeing up of trade and the revolution in information technologies have given birth to a more prosperous and integrated world. And yet the world is suffering: far from the radiant serenity of the end of history, again the crises are multiplying; many people have the sense that they are losing their bearings, in the North as in the South, in the East as in the West.

As with every significant turn it has taken, humanity is seeking a path between the certainties of yesterday and the hesitations of the future. Globalization is being impelled by uncontrolled economic, social and technological forces on which the will seems to have no hold. What then must be done? Simply let the ship drift headlong toward possible destruction? Brace ourselves against all movement and remain complacently nostalgic for a Golden Age? Or, on the contrary, must we not base ourselves in the present as it is and join forces in constructing the future?

France refuses nostalgia as well as fatalism. And, in the situation that is currently being played out, it is not alone. Europe has a particular responsibility: as an economic giant located at the heart of all the great international networks of circulation, it has a duty to remain tirelessly vigilant against the excesses and perversions that are always possible, the tragedies of history in which, unfortunately, we are all too experienced. As the birthplace of humanist values, Europe must fully assume this role as guardian, but also as a bringer of enlightenment, alongside the other great areas of the world. How could it be that, in a world of rapid transformations, the watchman of Argos would not find a new mission in the service of man?

For a long time, nations strove to protect themselves from an often threatening external world. Cities, states, and empires sought—in the image of the quintessential empire, the Roman—to hide behind solid lines of fortification. An opposition was asserted between the citizen invested with the rights of the city and the foreigner, the barbarian.

Gradually, however, a new aspiration developed. Men recognized that they all share a single nature, that they belong to a single species, and that consequently they have duties toward one another. This new conception was one of the bases of Christianity, which, beginning in the Middle Ages, spread throughout all of Europe: Romanesque and Gothic architecture traveled across borders, Latin became the language of scholarship and knowledge. Soon, the House of

Habsburg dreamt of a universal monarchy, and the Renaissance, with the discovery of the New World, mapped a new global space; already trade was being emancipated, and the same bankers lent gold to different states at war with one another; the humanists declared themselves citizens of the world. Under the name of reason, the Enlightenment advanced a new principle of unity for humankind and established a freedom that would be both political and economic. Voltaire and Diderot proclaimed the intangible character of the human person, while Adam Smith maintained that the wealth of nations rests on the wills of individuals, brought into harmony by the invisible hand of the market. The French Revolution proclaimed, before the unsteady monarchies of Europe, the new democratic values that would inspire the Springtime of Nations. A century and a half later, at the end of a devastating world war, attempts were made to lay the groundwork for a system that would banish war from international relations.

Globalization bears the imprint of this long road that we have traveled. On the path toward a unified humanity, it marks a decisive new phase. With an irresistible force, it corresponds to man's deep need to push back every frontier and to broaden the realm of possibilities. Like all great moments in history, it is rich with exceptional opportunities.

There is the opportunity for every person to have access to economic well-being. Consider the evolution of Asia, whose most advanced countries, after only fifty years, have attained standards of living comparable to those of Europe and North America. Consider also the progress made by the countries of Eastern Europe which, like Poland and Hungary, are preparing to rejoin the European Union and its unified market.

There is the opportunity for each person to have access also to information and to knowledge. Through a marriage of telecommunications, computer technology, and television, an immeasurable amount of information is now spreading across the entire planet in a way that is simultaneous and interactive, and for a negligible cost. This is a true liberation of energies.

Finally, there is the opportunity to root democracy more firmly throughout the world. We recall the constant effort made by the dictatorships of the former Soviet bloc to isolate the societies they oppressed. With the fall of the Berlin Wall, the loosening of borders in these countries is everywhere accompanied by a increasing demand for democracy. All these changes are not without certain hesitations: the disappointments on every continent are numerous—in Africa, in Latin America, in Asia, and in Europe too. But the destination is set and the direction is clear.

And yet our age raises many deep concerns, at a time when globalization is transforming the organization of collective life at every level.

First, if the shrinking of space accelerates the circulation of commodities and information, it also multiplies the risks. A financial crisis in Thailand can affect Russia by way of Brazil more rapidly than a traveler, a few centuries ago, could have arrived to announce the news. Epidemics spread with the speed of airliners. And if the long and dense time of history and of cultures seems to be erasing itself, our points of reference become blurred along with it, so greatly has the technological revolution modified the very texture of our world.

Moreover, globalization substitutes a new topology for traditional geography, at a moment when states are no longer the only entities thinking or acting on a global scale. When

General Motors has a sales turnover that exceeds the GDP of Denmark, the restructuring of a corporation can have unforeseeable repercussions. Today, an important decision made anywhere on the planet can affect stock prices and economic life in all the capitals. Thus, certain sensitive regions can suffer layoffs, which leads to broken lives, which in turn brings political and social consequences that can at times threaten to undermine the very authority of states.

Finally, the development of globalization establishes a new dynamic among continents and nations. The poles of activity are multiplying, from Brazil to South Africa, by way of India, now the world's largest exporter of information services. Or China, which, with an economic growth rate around 8 percent, is becoming one of the great motors of economic growth in East Asia and beyond. Recently, in Cancun, we saw the determination of the Southern countries to carry out a coordinated and autonomous collective action. The question is now openly raised by the major international authorities: how to reduce the deficit of democracy that affects the legitimacy of the mechanisms now in place.

The opening of borders and the growth of free trade present an exceptional possibility for spreading the polyphony of cultures. But the circulation of products and the distribution of images create a homogenization of behaviors, a convergence of dreams. The global concentration of production and distribution in the domain of collective representations—particularly in the areas of publishing, cinema and audiovisual work—is endangering the expression of diversity. This risk of erasing specific social contours and textures can actually lead to a resurgence of religious or communitarian allegiances based, at times, on violence. Under the pressure of these identitarian reactions, there is, paradoxically, a greater tendency toward fragmentation the more globalized the world becomes. A trap is waiting for us: that of incomprehension between cultures.

For some ten years now, the warning signals have not been sufficiently heeded—for the question of identity is at the heart of most of the great tensions visible today. An injured, humiliated, and scorned identity can become a source of violence and hatred. From Bosnia to Kosovo, from Afghanistan to Rwanda and to the Ivory Coast, the warnings continue to come. Everywhere the hostility of communities, ethnicities and religions has precipitated conflicts or wars in which entire nations are broken up and recomposed. We must remain an active presence in all these countries.

Faced with these changes, we must not let fear get the better of us. There is the fear of terrorism, which since September 11 is on everyone's mind, for it can strike anyone and anywhere; the fear of the stranger suspected of complicity with these enemies hidden in the shadows. The fear of natural disasters, which seem to be multiplying, even as the very rhythm of the seasons appears to be disintegrating; the fear of our food, poisoned by certain excesses in the mad race to productivity. The fear, in the end, of living in a world dominated by technology and commerce and, through them, by forces which may or may not possess any kind of conscience, any ethics or any true respect for man.

Now that our destinies are linked more than ever, this fear betrays a real power vacuum: no power today is able to assert any order. The planetary malaise is fed by the sense of a world poorly governed, although it needs so badly to be governed well. There is no doubt that our technical resources enable us to transform our environment more than ever. But today the strong reveal their weaknesses; in one instant, a madman can unsettle all our certainties.

Faced with this new ordeal, each country must take up a position according to its own heritage, particularly the United States, a model of democracy and freedom. What an alarming reversal! For a long time this country escaped from the embarrassments of power because it was able to present itself as a modern Babel, the site of an alchemy of cultures. The founding fathers who crossed the ocean in search of a pristine space in which to construct an ideal society, in the long line of those men and women who came from the world over in order to forge their own destinies, America has increased its energy through optimism, enthusiasm, and faith in the future. So many useful assets in understanding the world—and yet doesn't this country's internal miracle obscure its understanding of other lands, which are often beset by identitarian aspirations and are at times even ready to oppose it in order to affirm itself? This risk is all the greater after September 11, when the United States has discovered that it is a vulnerable power, one that, together with other countries, has a duty to rethink the world we live in.

Our European continent, for its part, must draw on all the lessons provided by its painful history. First, in the desire to put an end to the dark pages of the past it has found the strength to lift itself up again. And today Europe has a vocation to work alongside other peoples in order to lay the groundwork for this new world. That is the challenge it intends to take up in order to build a model of its own: it places the Union above competing interests, establishing dialogue as a method for advancing and resolving conflicts, and fervently promoting the universal values of respect and tolerance.

We have reached a point where the very foundations of power are undergoing a undeniable revolution. The United States appears, of course, as the dominant figure in this process, and in that respect, it too is engaged in great debates and experiencing great tensions. There are some neoconservatives who are trying to create oppositions between Americans and Europeans: the Americans, the masters of war and force, are from Mars, and the Europeans, who let themselves be lulled by the facilities of idealism, are from Venus. But today we must say: Mars is not Mars and Venus is not Venus. The United States cannot rely on force alone, whether economic or military. Europe is fully endowed with a defense policy, and it assumes its responsibilities, including military responsibilities, whether in the Balkans, in Afghanistan, or in Africa. We are all of the same earth, made of grandeur and fragility, united by the realities of globalization, confronted by the same threats, attached to the same hopes, dependent on the same phenomena. To find the solutions for taking on our future together, we must look beyond force.

In the face of fear, there is no cure but action. We have a mission: to place man once again at the heart of a new age. How can we do that?

The answer is to be found among the many peoples of the world. Every day they step toward the front of the stage and make their voices heard in the political arena: faced with catastrophic health problems, ecological disasters, and the persistence of extreme poverty, they are demanding an account from their leaders. For a few years now, large scale mobilizations—from Seattle to Pôrto Alegre—have brought together many of the concerns and contradictions inherent to globalization. But it is within each of us that a true global conscience is being born.

First, a global conscience concerning inequities. We have not yet seriously faced the challenge of development, which can be summed up in the fact that a quarter of the world's population lives on less than one dollar a day. Certainly, a long term effort is underway in the international community: beginning in 1961, the United Nations General Assembly introduced the idea of a "decade of development" whose goal was to help the Southern countries enter into modernity. Today, Latin America and Asia are experiencing a general dynamic of growth, since the economies of Southeast Asia, Brazil, and Mexico have taken off, as have those of the two giants of Asia, India and China, together with South Korea. But, for many people, Africa remains excluded from the world's development, and its share of trade continues to diminish. Today the GNP of the entire continent of Africa is one third that of France.

We have a duty of solidarity toward the least advanced countries. We see this today: globalization does not guarantee any convergence in standards of living. That is why France is making efforts to place the Southern countries at the center of international priorities. France decided to increase by one half its public aid for development by 2007, with the goal of reaching 0.7 percent of the GDP in 2012, but it is also essential to favor the insertion of the most impoverished countries into the large networks of international trade. It is with that in mind that we are giving support to NEPAD [The New Partnership for Africa's Development], through which we would like to construct a true politics of partnership with Africa.

In the perspective of the goals of the millennium, France will launch a new initiative to promote the development of African agriculture. We defend the idea of a preferential trade system unique to Africa, in combination with a moratorium on farm subsidies in order to protect local producers. We also propose a privileged commercial treatment, to ensure that Africa has better access to our markets. Finally, we know that the lives of a billion human beings depend on the cost of raw materials, and there is a clear necessity for protecting the prices paid for them when trading with developed countries.

A global conscience with regard to illness, as well. With AIDS, humanity is confronted with one of the greatest health challenges in history: forty-two million people throughout the world have been hit with the virus, almost thirty million of which are in Africa. And the death toll is steadily rising, with five million people dying every year. In certain countries in southern Africa, almost 40 percent of the active population is infected. The social, economic and political equilibrium of entire populations have been damaged by this destruction of their life force.

The struggle against AIDS is a complex one; France intends to show determination in facing it.

It is a complex struggle in its social aspects, particularly for the most affected countries, in which prevention must take cultural factors into account: this prevention has to begin with education and with the schooling of children—with a particular focus on the education of girls, which must become the norm. That is why France is committed to setting up a modern and effective educational system in these countries. In several countries, such as Burkina Faso, France is in the forefront of this type of aid, with the construction of schools, the training of teachers, as well as more specific work on school programs.

It is a complex struggle also because of the very nature of the epidemics. The SARS epidemic—which was able to strike a farmer in a remote province of China and a businessman passing through Toronto—is another recent illustration of this. The entire international community must join forces, in order to make every possible means available for the struggle against disease. France has decided to triple its contribution to the Global Fund to Fight AIDS, Tuberculosis, and Malaria, increasing its aid to 150 million euros a year. Because we can only hope to have success in fighting disease if we act collectively, our goal is a permanent integration of all the actors involved in this work, states as well as corporations and NGOs.

It is a complex struggle also because it means that we must find ways to remove the barriers that make access to care difficult for those who need it, even when cures are available and generic drugs can be manufactured at low prices. But in France's view, access to drugs constitutes a moral duty. The speech by President Chirac Abidjan in 1997 constituted a significant departure the international consensus—a consensus that made it virtually impossible for the sick in poor countries to have access to antiretroviral drugs. The results are beginning to show: the agreement reached on August 30, 2003, within the framework of the WTO is moving in the right direction by facilitating the development of generic drugs. There is still a long road to be traveled, but our determination remains intact.

Indeed, whatever the obstacles, France will act; it will remain faithful to its duty of solidarity and to a tradition of medical assistance that it has shown for a long time, from the tests given for sleeping sickness, to the struggle against river blindness. Today this tradition is being renewed with several hundred French doctors in Africa, technical assistants from the local areas, and the strong presence of associations specializing in health intervention, from Doctors without Borders to Doctors of the World.

A global conscience, finally, regarding the disaster that is taking place with the destruction of the environment. "Our house is burning," warned President Chirac in Johannesburg. Consider the catastrophe that would result from the disappearance of our primary source of oxygen, the forests of the Amazon or of Africa. Imagine the consequences of climate change, responsible for a rising sea level that threatens the densely populated deltas of Bangladesh and Vietnam. Today we are confronted with a series of threats that weigh on our future, from desertification to the impoverishment of biological diversity and the pollution of the oceans.

The problem of water is one of the most troubling: according to the United Nations, thirty-one countries are facing grave water shortages, and more than a billion people do not have access to potable water; three billion people do not have sanitary facilities. Soon the water shortage will affect more than 70 percent of the earth's population.

In order to act we must clearly grasp the mechanisms by which different problems are interconnected, and water is at the center of a whole range of issues. There is the issue of peace: the management of the water in the Niger River basin, for example, risks becoming a source of conflict between neighboring countries. It necessitates political understanding and therefore a regional integration. But there is also the issue of health, for there can be no public health in the region if there is no potable water, and this requires certain kinds of infrastructure. Hence the necessity of an effort on the part of developed countries to help set up these infrastructures. and all the means necessary for improving health in various regions. Finally, the issue of agriculture: a commitment to energy management and climate protection is indispensable in avoiding desertification, particularly for the production of cotton.

The large scale cotton production, which was established with aid from France, provides a living to fifteen million people in the Sahel. It is profitable, and it stabilizes the populations and the social structure. But it must be able to benefit from an equitable organization of markets: that is where the issue of trade comes in. Beyond our support for the cotton initiative, the international community must be organized in order to analyze and deal with interconnected problems. Through its bilateral as well as multilateral commitments, France will not cease pursuing new initiatives, in order to establish the real foundations of a partnership with Africa—for these are the only foundations on which to base adequate solutions that are both global and concrete.

Now that we are aware of the dramatic and serious lack of drinking water on the planet, it is time for the international community to adopt decisive measures to reduce by half the number of people confronted with water shortages, and to do so by the year 2015. At the G8 Summit in Evian, we committed ourselves to a more active role in realizing the objectives of the millennium: we must encourage the effective management of available drinking water and of water purification, but we must also strengthen the programs of international organizations.

Beyond the question of water, we have a collective responsibility to protect our global public goods, a responsibility that we must be able to carry out within an adequate framework: President Chirac suggested the idea of an international environmental governance. In particular, we must rethink the programs of the different organizations currently at work in this sector. Why not give the United Nations Environmental Program the role of initiator and political coordinator it once had?

On this basis, a Global Organization for the Environment could have two primary missions. First, to take up the task of scientific observation, ecological vigilance and heightened awareness of risks, in order, secondly, to establish regulations and environmental codes. Finally, it would be responsible for coordinating the work of different international organizations charged with the protection of the environment.

Strengthened by this shared conscience, we must therefore conclude a true alliance among nations, for we all have global interests to defend. But for that we need rules accepted by all; we need a global ethics based, in every domain, on the respect for human dignity, the spirit of justice, and collective responsibility.

First, some limits should be established in the scientific domain. For example, can we accept the idea that one day people could profoundly transform the nature of the human species? In dealing with this question, which is open to a number of approaches, whether religious, historical, philosophical, or strictly medical, we must preserve the idea of man against all particular interests. Europeans are working together to lay the groundwork for a substantive bioethics, so that scientific progress will not bring harm to humanity in its very nature. At UNESCO a few days ago, President Chirac recalled this imperative and the necessity to have laws with a universal scope, laws that would reconcile scientific progress and the protection of the person in the protocols of investigation.

Next, in the area of human rights, we have a duty to act, to move, to take the initiative. How could we accept that in certain countries human dignity suffers the outrage of torture? Nothing can justify this practice, against which all our values rebel. Our struggle should also confront the death penalty, with the ultimate goal of universal abolition.

France is fighting so that the International Criminal Court can play its full role and make crimes against humanity, massacres, and ethnic barbarisms impossible. We must put an end to the impunity that is a recurrent factor in the violation of human rights. That is why we are asking for the universal ratification of the status of the Court. In addition, we must make the Commission on Human Rights more capable of effective, concrete missions. Why not provide it with a permanent team of human rights inspectors, with the mandate to intervene?

Finally, we must preserve cultural diversity. Globalization is a positive opportunity only if it allows for the mixing and ferment of cultures, the source of a new effervescence: with the cinema, we can travel through the Iranian landscapes of Mohsen Makhmalbaf, understand something of Brazilian society from the films of Walter Salles, enter the exuberant world of the magnificent Indian productions of Bollywood. We can look at Mexico through the great frescoes of Alfaro Siqueiros, read about the transformation of China in Gao Xingjian or the power of ancestral traditions in Nuruddin Farah, cross the wildlands of America with Jim Harrison, pass through its tortured cities with Philip Roth and plumb the depths of urban solitude in the photographs of Cindy Sherman. This cultural richness is the strength and vigor of our new world: it is up to us to protect it from drying up; it is up to us to open the way to a globalization of creativity.

That is why the works of the mind cannot be reduced to mere commodities. The right of states and governments to promote cultural and linguistic policies deserves to be protected, not only in laws, but also in practice, particularly when confronting the circumventions made possible by modern technology. Given the rapid disappearance of cultures and even languages, half of which are now in grave danger, it is more urgent than ever to find ways to protect the specificity of cultural creations on a global scale.

Within the framework of UNESCO, we must put all our efforts into the preparation of an International Convention on Cultural Diversity. France is working to bring together as many countries as possible in this essential struggle for the future, and it is for this purpose that we are also preparing to set up an international news channel enabling the expression of more diverse points of view regarding our planet. For globalization constitutes a tremendous opportunity for transmitting our creations in our language: it is up to us to humanize a process against which it would be vain to want to barricade oneself. But the rules that will govern this process must be established in an equitable fashion.

The Internet is a tremendous tool; it is being used more and more each day for information and communication. It has gained a central role in our societies, transforming the lives of a growing number of users for whom it opens doors to knowledge and dialogue; at times it arouses suspicions and concerns, especially when it is used as a means of disinformation, racist or anti-Semitic propaganda, or even incitement to hatred. Here too, there must be regulations that would enable us to forestall any effort to misuse such a valuable tool. The World Summit on the Information Society that will soon be held in Geneva[6] should provide an occasion for advancing some solutions to the most grievous problems. Presently controlled by private institutions, the Internet should be supervised by a representative and responsible governance at the international level, respectful of the material and immaterial issues at stake in our world.

What we must do, then, is build a true global governance. France proposes the creation of a new political body capable of providing—in the economic, social and environmental domains—the impetus and the leadership that the world needs. Given the range and complexity of the issues, it is indispensable that an Economic and Social Security Council be able to take the general interest into account.

---

[6] The first phase of this summit was held December 10–12, 2003.—Trans.

In the sectors where the collective interest must be defended—whether it is a question of the environment or the food supply, public health or cultural diversity—the specific institutions must be strengthened so that they can establish norms and ensure that they are applied, while taking into account the extent and nature of the challenges: despite the ever greater flow of published written material, one in six children throughout the world is forced to work for his or her own survival or to support a family. At the WTO, procedural rules must be created to facilitate debate and decision-making for almost one hundred fifty nations. To approach a consensus, we might consider prior negotiations on the regional level, as Europe has already done. At stake is the future of multilateralism and its ability to respond to the demands of a complex world.

Every day globalization creates supplementary benefits that should aid those who suffer the most from the current changes. In this regard, let us reflect on the creation of a system that will correct its excesses and free up new resources for financing development. Likewise, the responsibility that corporations have to protect the environment and to aid the development of societies must be approached with new concepts; this question was raised by France during the G8 in Evian. A French observation and research group would be set up to work on all these subjects, in order to define the greatest priorities and propose innovative solutions.

In the twenty-first century, it is impossible to accept a fate of powerlessness and ignorance. Nations must be more involved in the great decisions that matter to them. By means of NGOs, civil societies are claiming a greater place in the international debate. Their voices must be heard along with those of the states.

But let's be careful, for we also have another immediate duty, of which the regional crises that riddle the planet remind us each day: the duty to mobilize for peace. And the duty to struggle against every threat and to deal with every element of a crisis. This role falls to the Security Council of the United Nations, whose authority and representative status must be strengthened. With these necessary changes, the entire international community must bring about a veritable revolution: we must transform minds, but also adapt our responses.

We must transform minds because the world is being transformed. A number of mechanisms are now being put into place which are creating veritable synergies of destruction.

There is a synergy between factors of destabilization: terrorism, proliferation, and regional crises. There are no longer any completely independent problems or isolated cases. We are witnessing the development of a new model of violence, with mass terrorism now in search of new alliances, whether with small local groups, with mercenaries or with nationalist or ethnic movements. Is this dark scenario not in the process of becoming a reality, at a time when Iraq—in the wake of Afghanistan and Chechnya—is forming a new laboratory for terrorist networks, which are taking advantage of the current disorder, of porous borders, of the absence of a strong central state, and all the interethnic rivalries?

Every crisis situation creates a call to arms for the elements of violence and disorder. All the more so since, beyond this immediate link, there is reason to fear that terrorist groups will play on the proliferation of traffic in prohibited materials and military equipment to pursue their own ends: more dead, more suffering, more fear. The illicit cargo circulating from one country to another, particularly in the Middle East, continues to elude every effort to intercept it. The trade in sensitive technologies is facilitated by greater access to information, and by more rapid transmission. It used to be that the acquisition of weapons of mass destruction was virtually impossible. Now, despite a number of barriers that have been put into place, it is becoming potentially much easier. How could one not be worried about a possible intersection of this reality and the development of mass terrorism?

The old methods are being exhausted, as we watch the threats growing and mutating, like an opportunistic virus, and as terrorism follows the crises and moves from one theater of operation to another, or from one base to another—from Afghanistan to Iraq, for example. Or as armed groups in Africa take advantage of every lapse in a state's authority to plunder and to spread hatred, as in Sierra Leone or in the Great Lakes region.

But there is also a synergy between regional crises, with phenomena of contagion between crises which are themselves aggravated by vicious circles. In Iraq, the attacks are greatly disrupting the current situation, sowing chaos and making efforts to reconstruct the unity and peace of this country much more difficult. The terrible wave of violence that shook Baghdad only a few days ago underscores the scale of the difficulties. The coalition troops believe—no doubt justifiably—that these difficulties point to the presence of outside military groups. The vacuum created by the absence of Iraqi sovereignty and security along the borders can only aggravate this crisis as it spirals ever deeper.

In Afghanistan the Taliban are attempting to regroup, and they are taking advantage of the shock waves coming from the Middle East. The poppy production is underway again, and it now represents almost 50 percent of the country's GNP. There is the risk that all the efforts of the international community will be called into doubt in a very short period of time.

In the Near East, peace efforts are becoming more and more bogged down week after week, creating greater insecurity for everyone, Palestinians and Israelis alike. Israel is faced with a terrorist threat that is growing every day. And the construction of a security barrier whose path contradicts international law, as well as the continued development of settlements, only intensify the frustrations of the Palestinians and needlessly fan the flames of hatred. The implementation of the road map is being continually thwarted by dramatic events.

Today, all the crises are related. How is it possible to reestablish calm in Baghdad without showing that one is capable of taking the risk of peace and justice in Jerusalem? The coming months will be decisive for the future of the Middle East and the world: never before has there been so great an urgency. The entire international community must join forces: we must overtake the contagion of violence.

It is important for us now to adapt our responses. It used to be that the logic of blocs was enough to immobilize the conflicts, for the most part, and to contain them within a structure that made it possible to avoid direct confrontation. But the present situation is reflected by many uncertainties that must be taken into account. Today it is necessary to be able to respond throughout the world to the shocks caused by ethnic or religious divisions, or to the communitarian clashes: the stability of the world is at stake.

We are shifting from a Cold War dialectic to a logic of asymmetrical risks. It therefore becomes essential to maintain very circumspect relations with weaker states that may be tempted by the rupture with the international community. Let us try to understand the calculations of a state like North Korea: using its own security as a pretext, it has engaged in a headlong rush toward nuclear armament. Rather than responding to the injunctions of the international community, it has preferred to play at blackmail and verbal aggression while propping itself up with its ballistic capabilities and a clandestine nuclear program. Faced with this defiance, an entire region finds itself in great danger.

It is imperative that this game of terror not be reproduced in other parts of the globe. This is what the European Union is attempting to do in Iran, by engaging in a firm dialogue with the authorities in Tehran. Beginning with the assertion that the Iranian nuclear program raises legitimate concerns for the international community, we have posed a demand: the refusal of all military nuclear ambition, which would have effects reaching as far as the European Union. But we also recognized Iran's right to have access to civil nuclear energy, in conformity with the Nuclear Non-Proliferation Treaty. This strategic choice made it possible for us to initiate a process capable of building trust, based on Iran's willingness to respond immediately to the demands of the international community. While vigilance is of the utmost importance, we also want to give ourselves the means for avoiding a major crisis, which could have led to Iran's withdrawal from the NPT and to the emergence of a new zone of disorder in a region that is already very destabilized.

At such a juncture, with the risks of instability it involves, there is only one protection: the engagement of a political multilateralism, founded on collective responsibility and on the imperative to act.

To be sure, the possible recourse to the use of force remains indispensable, and France knows how to pay the price for it: faithful to its principles, it is engaged in the service of peace in operations in the Balkans, in Afghanistan, and in the Ivory Coast, with a total of twelve thousand troops on the ground. We are one of the largest contributors of troops to interventions outside of NATO, and one of the first partners of the United States in the struggle against terrorism, particularly with our Special Forces in Afghanistan.

But the response of mere force can only be a last recourse. By itself, it is incapable of resolving the world's problems. The logic of security only spreads the crisis, worsens the ills, deepens the lines of fracture. In confronting terrorism, direct military confrontation is impossible when the enemy is hidden in the grey zones and is only encouraged by the force exerted against it. And above all it constitutes no defense against blind violence. Yes, military means can be employed when the international community authorizes it, and with a legitimate political objective. Terrorists must be pursued using police, judicial, and informational techniques. But the only solution is in the mobilization of the international community, which, after September 11, revealed its ability to unite in the face of this scourge. This assumes that together, in a spirit of responsibility, in any crisis or conflict, in any situation apt to deteriorate, we will make the choice of engaging a political will.

There must be a choice of political will in Afghanistan where, faced with the deteriorating situation on the ground, we have to organize elections as quickly as possible. We see how urgent it is to place the progress toward democracy on an irreversible path. That is why we want to make sure that the dates set for elections are respected, and that the presidential and legislative consultations take place within a specified time period. We cannot regard the persistent pockets of disorder or the outbreak of violence in certain zones as a pretext for giving up. On the contrary, it is only by engaging the direct responsibility of the Afghan people that we will consolidate the first results obtained.

And there must be a choice of political will in Iraq where, through the quickest possible transfer of sovereignty, the Iraqis must regain control over their own destiny, with the full support of the international community.

In the Near East, we must go beyond the preconditions having to do with security. Initiatives such as the Geneva peace plan, which serves as a complement to the approach initiated by the road map, gives us new perspectives; they show that an agreement is possible. Let us be realistic: there will be no lasting peace in the world without a lasting peace in the Near East.

Likewise in Africa: the world will not be secure as long as there is no relief on this continent, which today concentrates all forms of trafficking and every kind of risk.

A global strategy is needed. We need adequate tools and appropriate rules for dealing with different threats and different crises. We must strengthen the United Nations so that it can truly deal with problems of efficacy and open a new horizon and a new goal: the construction of a global democracy, in which the principle of responsibility will help to assure the stability of the world and to organize the cooperation of all nations. It is up to us to map out the road into the future, and it will be a difficult one. But we must begin now to lay out its main features.

From now on, the world forms a whole; but a whole yet to be imagined and built. It must be organized politically, supported by an ethics, and grounded in a certain idea of man. This assumes the establishment of new balances between states, peoples, and a global governance yet to be constructed.

Today the Humanist is being recalled to his tasks and his duties. We have known for quite some time what goals must be reached. From Voltaire, who dreamt of an understanding among nations, to Hugo, who shouted in the name of humanity: Down with arms! Alliance! Unity! From Jaurès, who gave his life for his commitment to peace, to Briand, who brought a message of union to the Court of the League of Nations, or to de Gaulle, who called for the cooperation of all peoples, France has always been guided by a certain idea of the world, and by an ideal.

How many opportunities to realize this alliance have been glimpsed and yet missed! How many hopes have been disappointed because we did not find the means to seal the pact of nations and of peace! It is up to us to do this. After the terrible dramas of the twentieth century, after the warnings that already surround us everywhere, let us not wait until we have to undergo another apprenticeship in the abyss. It belongs to each of us to work, within himself and in the world, for the awakening of a new humanism.

COMMENTARY
AND DEBATE

LIGHTHOUSE, NOT STEAMER:
FRANCE'S FOREIGN POLICY SHINES BUT FAILS TO MOVE EUROPE FORWARD

BY CHRISTOPH BERTRAM

"France likes to provide the recipes but shuns the cooking."

Christoph BERTRAM (Germany)

Since 1998, Bertram has been the director of Stiffung Wissenschaft und Politik, the principal German think tank in matters of defense and foreign policy, similar to the American Rand Corporation. He is the author of many publications devoted to international and strategic questions. In 2003, he published Rousseau and the Social Contract.

When Dominique de Villepin, sitting behind the proud place-name of FRANCE in the UN Security Council on February 14, 2003, delivered what has been the most elegant and persuasive condemnation of America's rush to war in Iraq, I was among the millions around the world watching him with agreement, admiration and gratitude. Finally here was the representative of a major European power skillfully and mercifully taking all the arguments apart which a war-eager U.S. Administration had concocted against giving the UN inspectors under Hans Blix another chance.

Events since then have provided additional, now irrefutable evidence that the course pushed by the United States was void of justification. There was no clear and present danger brewing in Iraq, there was no link to international terrorism, and—even more ominous—the overthrow of the Saddam regime has not meant the beginning of more stability in the troubled Middle East but instead more conflict, more killing, more instability. Yes, a nasty tyrant has been removed. But the grounds advanced for doing so have turned out, predictably, to be spurious.

France, a lighthouse sending beacons of reason and good sense out into the dark world of prejudice and ideological fervor. Indeed, that is how the French diplomatic class has presented itself and has wanted to be seen by others. But as sailors know, beacons provide the light for other ships to steer a safe course. They are indicators, perhaps even inspirers. But they depend on others to act. France's foreign policy, not for the first time, has preferred to look good as opposed to doing good. And the Iraqi crisis is no exception.

This is even more obvious in retrospect. Since 1998 when the Iraqi regimes had told the UN inspectors to leave the country, most members of the Security Council, France included, seemed not to mind. Together with Russia, France even sought a rapid lifting of sanctions against Iraq, as if the expulsion of the inspectors did not really matter. It was not until early in 2002 that the issue of inspection came back on to the agenda—as a result of American, not French of European pressure.

Perhaps there was a chance then of forming a European coalition on how best to proceed. If there was, nobody tried. Neither the Nato nor the EU Council had much patience for the issue. The German government flatly declared, in August 2002, that it would not be part of any military pressure on Iraq to allow the inspectors in, France left her decision open, and both supported UN Security Council Resolution 1441 merely as an intermediate step. Neither tried to build a consensus within the European Union and the countries eager to get in. Instead, they were castigated on the steps of the palace of Versailles as unruly and ungrateful children. Perhaps it would have been futile to bring Europe together, given the strong pressure from the Bush Administration. But the effort was never seriously undertaken, except early on by the British Prime Minister in the vain attempt to bring other European governments along in support of the U.S. When that failed, no other major EU country, France included, seemed to care much for Europe's disarray.

There was a last chance, however small, in March 2003. Tony Blair's government, fighting for political support in the country and in the House of Commons, had committed itself not to join the U.S. in an invasion of Iraq without a second UN Security Council resolution. That resolution would have given a few weeks more time to Hand Blix and his inspectors and would have involved an ultimatum: should Iraq not come clean by the indicated time, the UN Security Council would authorize the use of force against Baghdad. More important, it would have made it impossible for Britain to join the U.S. if the latter were to move regardless. Europe would, miraculously, stay out of the war, once again united.

As usual in politics, alternatives to what happened are inevitably hypothetical. In the absence of certainty, we depend on plausibility. Yet plausibility suggests there was a real chance in these fateful weeks of March 2003 if not to prevent the war at least to prevent Britain from joining the U.S., and to re-unite Europe. The Bush Administration refused all delays, U.S. forces were already being deployed in large number and the onset of the summer heat gave a premium to immediate action. Perhaps a further delay imposed by a second UN resolution would have forced America, as some expected, to postpone action to the autumn. Most probably it would have been vetoed by the U.S. and the invasion would have gone ahead as planned.

But Britain would have found it extremely difficult to join that invasion in he absence of a second resolution or a U.S. veto against it. Tony Blair had committed himself to that effect. Most probably, the U.S. would have had to proceed on their own. The rift would have been an Atlantic, not an intra-European one.

The sad fact: France never even tried to bring about

this outcome. Her leaders refused to support an ultimatum and thus to extend the time for Blix to inspect. They were content with being right as opposed to getting things right, a lighthouse, not a steamer.

Unfortunately, the Iraq episode is no exception, it has been true to style, French style. France likes to provide the recipes but shuns the cooking. Take the increasingly pressing issue of giving the European Union a major say in our fragile world—France prefers to have her own say, even at the expense of European unity, and spends precious little effort to build a European consensus. Take the need to organize European defence without constantly arousing U.S. suspicions and attempts to frustrate European moves: the best way to avoid both would be for France to rejoin Nato's military integration, a move which anyway has lost much of its military significance with the end of the Cold War. Yet the mere suggestion is quickly derided in Paris. Why give up on self-rightousness in exchange for getting things right?

Getting things right—for European unity, for Atlantic trust, for an effective foreign policy—is not, it seems the primary concern of France's foreign policy. Her ambition is that of the lighthouse, not the steamer; the fact that most if not all European governments are no better is no excuse. While sailors lost at sea in the dark are grateful for the beacon's beam, that alone will not get them into port. Foreign affairs would be poorer without a French ambition to shine. But Europe would be better off with a French commitment to results, not just to applause.

SUDDENLY FROM HIGH IN HIS TOWER

BY RÉGIS DEBRAY

"Rare are the bureaucrats who still take time to spend with Eluard, Bashô or Kerouac."

Régis DEBRAY (France)

President of the Scientific Council of the École Nationale Supérieure des Sciences de l'Informaiton et des Bibliothèques as well as president of the European Institute of Religious Sciences, he has just published Le Feu sacré, fonctions du religieux [Sacred Fire, the Functions of the Religious] *and* L'Honneur des funambules, réponse à Jean Clair sur le surréalisme [The Honor of the Tightrope Walker, a Response to Jean Clair on Surrealism]. *In 2003, he received the Combourg Prize for his book* Dieu, un itinéraire (God: An Itinerary).

There is in each one of us an instinctive calculation of probabilities that doesn't like to be flouted. That is why mysteries repel us. The Villepin mystery is an exception: instead of provoking disquiet, it restores serenity, even to those who have screamed their lungs out in the desert for so long they've lost all faith (nothing more to expect from this depressed protectorate—make way for the mice). And just when it seemed that everything was played out, there was still room for the improbable. When it comes to this enthusiast in the corridors of power, the observer is faced with two riddles in one: in the inner voice and in the public vote. One mystery in the darkroom, another in the spotlights. To avoid disappointing anyone, I will admit from the start: I do not have the key to either one. Since I am neither a private detective nor a political pundit (God forbid), I give up, and will content myself, as an astonished onlooker, with a simple summary of my position.

The first puzzle: the anachronism of a lyric sensibility in power. A precedent was set by Aimé Césaire? But that was the post-war period, and the Fort-de-France city hall lies in latitudes quite unlike those of the Quai d'Orsay. A man haunted by poems and paintings sitting in Vergennes' seat is surprising all the same. The model of the *enchanteur* in the style of Chateaubriand isn't exactly the norm. To be sure, the diplomat who makes a habit of pestering the Muses is a familiar figure, and, beyond mere pastimes, the Quai has many titles of glory in its genealogical tree. But—without comparing—Saint-John Perse, the secretary general, was a fake, Paul Morand was a dilettante, and Paul Claudel a simple ambassador. Rare are the bureaucrats who still take time to spend with Eluard, Bashô or Kerouac. Pompidou's anthology of French Poetry? That was before the ENA [L'École Nationale d'Administration]—none of whose glassy doors opens onto the marvelous, the magical or the baroque—took up the duty of recruiting for the government offices. And before the passing of the men and women of the Resistance and the old folks of colonial France, those two great reservoirs of originality. Even if quoting René Char at the beginning of exam papers has become obligatory at the Sciences-Po cookie cutter—where *Le Monde* is considered the Bible, Raymond Aron is taken for Moses, and M. Pascal Lamy is a sort of Ezekiel—, it is still an education in platitudes. The original minds that manage to emerge unscathed (there are a few, as it happens) tend rather toward André Siegfried than Henri Michaux or Victor Segalen. So when you have a copy of *Éloge des voleurs de feu* (In praise of the thieves of fire) in hand, you obviously can't help asking: where does he get so many names, images, rhythms? Is it a matter of concentration, physiology, vital discipline? Does he dictate it? Does he take the time to eat? Does he have a family? I would bet that our well-read troublemaker belongs to that enviable species, *homo vigilans*, able to sleep four or five hours a night, an aristocratic branch of the vulgar *sapiens* which, with its eight or nine hours, can only harbor resentment toward the former, as the present writer can attest. Only an investigator, a biographer, a duly licensed shrink would be able to break through the defenses of the private man, force which the kingdom counters the Empire, balance counters excess, complexity counters simplemindedness—we see the emergence of the second mystery. "No individual can overleap his own age," said Hegel, pessimistically. How is it that a high level functionary from a proper family, wholesome and well behaved, with an impeccable career (spokesman for the French embassy in Washington, unobtrusive cabinet director, unobtrusive secretary general), motivated like all his peers by the healthy spirit of competition, that is, by an uncontrollable desire to please ("Don't worry, I'm one of you")—how is it that he could thus overleap his milieu? When we realize 1) the dependence—bordering on servility—of governments with respect to the powers of opinion, 2) the resounding, staggering, and sonorous power—once the Soviet party disappeared—of the American "party" in France (in Cardinal de Retz's sense), and 3) that our official centers of strategic reflection have, like Josephine Baker, two fatherlands, then we can better appreciate the improbability, and its cost. Since the employers, the intelligentsia, and the media are the three pillars of this influence, spreading like an oil stain, slowly and implacably (the integrated system functions in isolation), our great notables consider thought to be inherently neurotic or a sign of ill humor, while the jingoism of the Anglo-Saxon media is touted as a generous globalization—even though, at home, they jeer at the idea of the nation, and the very word *state* reeks of Louis XIV. In this environment, it would have been natural for a dashing fellow located squarely on the Right, and fond of his creature comforts, to stick to the trodden path: "A humanitarian France, flexible and dynamic, far from the vain nostalgias and fevers that burn for another age, loyal ally and worthy emulator of the great American society, a rival in Europe with the United Kingdom for the spot of brilliant first among seconds."

Thus speaks, in our day, the prudent shopkeeper of all times. And no one would have been able to cast a stone at him. We men and women of fine words, we confabulators and day-dreamers, we can obey the flattering logic of ideas (it's free); more exposed to the reality principle, our ministers have to bend before the bitter logic of force (the ideas come later). For one who lives at Court, it is so costly to defy the Money, the Experts, and the Loudspeakers! And so unpleasant to have one-self insulted by one's old friends (*Foreign Policy, The New York Times,* and the local sponsors)! But not only did Villepin not succumb to the flaccid grip of settled habits, refusing to play at Grandeur (the poet) and Servitude (the politician), he also still finds enough energy—alongside his president and behind him—to keep alive the dream of a Europe still on its feet, at a time when everything indicates that this white elephant was up to now the clear expression, for eight Europeans out of ten, of a very firm *will to powerlessness.*

Here is a conjecture, an attempt to understand: what if the key to this anomaly—and these days anyone who takes risks is an anomaly—is to be sought in the direction of poetic activity, and of what, even for the conservatives themselves, is invincibly revolutionary in it? Of course, every foreign minister has his own personal planisphere, and in Villepin's geography, black Africa, Latin America, the Antilles are nei-ther peripheries nor gray zones (although Asia remains in the background, a curious fact for someone who knows India well): this opening of horizons helps to make the transat-lantic squabbles less obsessional. Of course, every minister has his inclinations and his convictions (some of Hubert Védrine had some excellent ones, just as he had his own geogra-phy)—and precisely from this he shapes his own world amid the daily flood of telegrams falling from every direction onto his green felt writing pad. But we may wonder whether there is some secret attunement between the entry into interiority and the entry into dissidence, between the frequenting of inner spaces and the rejection of false appearances on the outside. Politics, it is said, is an anti-poetry. But what if, quite to the contrary, poetry provided an apprenticeship in the strange ferocity of the real? The thieves of fire have a bad reputation among our Turelures and our Prudhommes. It is not well known that they are on the side of things.[7] It is thought that they prefer incantation to analysis, and the intoxication of hyperbole to exactitude. This is a mistake. The poet is a man who resists—both words and the halo of words. The poet is the non-dupe who rejects the chaff of routines and lays bare the grain, in its insolent, unsettling and living freshness. It is the rhetoricians who embellish and equivocate in the reassuring and flowery language of a sub-prefect. Those who clear the way into the extraordinary do not suffer from the myopia induced by the administrative formulas that gently lull us into our everyday blindness, and make us turn our backs on the world as it is, in order to seek refuge in cardboard comforts. The poet, having escaped from sleep-inducing prose, demands, from himself and from others, to be paid in good and durable coin. Scalpel in hand, he cuts the shortest possible path to the future. You want to save some time? Drop the newspapers and read the poets.

In this way, the two mysteries—the internal and the public—would then be only one, and would cancel each other out. Nothing forbids us from enlarging life with magical shortcuts (to put it plainly), and simultaneously enlarging one's country—Europe too, let us hope—with words that are true.

---

[7] *Le parti pris des choses*: this is the title of a well known book by the poet Francis Ponge.—Trans.

TO THE GLORY OF FRANCE

BY CARLOS FUENTES

"The ridiculous francophobia displayed by the more jingoistic 'patriots' of North America is further proof that, at times, the superpower deserves the name 'United States of Amnesia.'"

Carlos FUENTES (Mexico)

Mexican novelist and essayist, Fuentes also works in theater and cinema, while at the same time being involved in a large number of cultural activities in both of the Americas. He received the Cervantes Prize for the totality of his work in 1987 and the Prince of the Asturias Prize in 1994. He has just published En esto creo *(2002), in the form of a personal primer that offers the synthesis of his work as novelist and essayist, as well as two novels,* Inez *and* La silla del Aguila *(2003). The latter is an ironic meditation on the machinery of the leading power in Mexico.*

The ridiculous francophobia displayed by the more jingoistic "patriots" of North America is further proof that, at times, the superpower deserves the name "United States of Amnesia."

Indeed, it can be said that without France, the United States would not exist. Without the support of the French monarchy, no doubt Washington and his men would not have won the War of Independence. What is certain is that they won with the powerful help of the French. In 1776, Benjamin Franklin appeared at the French court as an ambassador of the Revolution, attracting attention for the simplicity of his dress and for his lively and brilliant intelligence. That same year, Louis XVI agreed to give George Washington's armies a supply of munitions worth one million French pounds. In 1778, France signed the Treaty of Amity and Commerce with the rebel colonies of North America. This treaty included a most favored nation clause and obliged France to maintain the independence of the United States of America. The treaty was signed in February and, naturally, the war between France and England broke out in June. Many high level officers in the French army intervened directly in favor of Washington and the rebels. Charles Hector d'Estaing commanded the first fleet sent to blockade the British in New York Harbor in 1778.

The Marquis de Lafayette joined the revolutionary forces and in 1777 was named a revolutionary commander (as was the Argentine Ernesto "Che" Guevara many years later in Cuba). In 1776, it was Lafayette who convinced Louis XVI to send an expeditionary force of 6000 men to fight alongside Washington. The end of the War of Independence would be inconceivable without the decisive intervention of French arms. In 1780, the French fleet of Admiral de Grasse surrounded the English army in Virginia, preventing any escape by sea. The siege launched by the French fleet and the support provided to Washington's revolutionary army sealed the fate of the English in the thirteen colonies. In Virginia, General Cornwallis was summoned by the Comte de Rochambeau in October 1780, thus consummating the independence of the United States of America.

General John Pershing, commander of the American Expeditionary Force in World War I, hastened to pay his respects at the tomb of the French hero of the American revolution, with these words: "Lafayette, we are here."

But General Pershing had a sense of military honor and of national recognition completely lacking to the irascible and bloodthirsty secretary of defense under President Bush, Donald Rumsfeld. The fact that it was Rumsfeld who first sealed the alliance between the United States and Saddam Hussein in 1983—providing him with the weapons of mass destruction now disturbing the sleep of the Dracula in the Pentagon—further proves the existence of a twofold truth. The United States is the Dr. Frankenstein of the modern world, and its specialty is the creation of monsters who, in the end, turn against their creators. Saddam in Iraq and Bin Laden in Afghanistan—these are the offspring of the obtuse, mercenary, and contradictory foreign policy of a nation that, when it wants, can be both enlightened and pragmatic. Imagine what the world would look like today if Bill Clinton were still in the White House or if Al Gore had won the last presidential election (which he did, in fact, in terms of the popular vote). Bill Clinton fulfilled his inevitable obligations as the leader of a superpower with a wisdom and a capacity for negotiation and reconciliation totally foreign to the Manichaean bluster ("For us or against us," "The Axis of Evil") of the gun-toting evangelist who succeeded him in the White House. I am certain that, after September 11, Clinton and Gore would have concentrated the effort of their country on fighting terrorism—an unconventional enemy that must be combated with unconventional means—rather than diverting their forces and sacrificing global solidarity in the war against Iraq.

Bush and company, through their atrabilious acts aimed at destroying international order, are going to transform the world into a breeding ground for terrorists. Today, thanks to the blindness of the current U.S. government, Bin Laden has an army of potential terrorists who—irony of ironies—will no doubt be spared Saddam Hussein's anti-fundamentalist repression.

But what is even more serious, of course, is the White House's enshrining of the doctrine of preemptive strike. If the Cold War did not become hot, it was because the parties involved had recourse to dissuasion and restraint. Once these principles have been supplanted by a discretionary use of force, every nation that is opposed to another can consider itself authorized to deal the first blow. The best example of a preemptive strike was given by Japan at Pearl Harbor, on December 7, 1941—"a day that will live in infamy," as the greatest U.S. president of the twentieth century, Franklin D. Roosevelt, said. Will the attack on Iraq become another "day of infamy"? I don't know. But even without being infamous, it was, is and will be a day of the greatest dangers. Unless the international community unites in its efforts to create a solid juridical and political order for the twenty-first century, we will tumble from crisis to crisis all the way to a precipice that does have a name: nuclear apocalypse.

It is for this reason that the wise firmness of France, its president, Jacques Chirac, and its foreign minister, Dominique de Villepin, is rendering a service not only to the world, but also to the United States of America, by keeping open the damaged prospects of a world order founded on law. Forgetful, frivolous and ignorant, the current U.S. government simply cannot understand this reasoning. The extremists on the Right think they're insulting France—in the most ridiculous way—by baptizing their French Fries as "Freedom Fries." Perhaps for a while they'll stop drinking Evian and—for an even shorter time—champagne.

But as soon as one enters New York Harbor, the Statue of Liberty—a gift from the French to the United States—reminds the North Americans that if they believe they saved France in two world wars, France, for its part, contributed decisively to the very creation of the United States of America.

Today, after September 11, 2001, and in the absence of a countervailing power, the power of the United States dominates the entire globe, as demonstrated by the document issued to Congress by George Bush on September 21, 2002. The cenacle in power in Washington is infinitely more skillful than the dictators who preceded them in other countries. It hides behind the nation and confers on the latter a total and exclusive ecumenical value. "The United States is the single surviving model of human progress," declared Bush Jr., and his national security advisor, Condoleezza Rice, provided the corollary to this arrogant remark: the United States must "proceed from the firm ground of its national interest" and forget about "the interests of an illusory international community." This is as clear as can be. The United States believes that it is the only model for the world, and its plan is to impose this model, without any regard for the rest of humanity—all of us, Latin Americans, Europeans, Asians, and Africans—who constitute nothing more than "an illusory international community."

But there is more: the plot thickens. Bush claims to be acting in the name of the people of the United States, "the single surviving model of human progress." And what is the "big lie" of Bush's regime? In historical and cultural terms, it is the claim that Brazil or France, India or Japan, Morocco or Nigeria offer no valuable model of human progress, despite their distinct traditions, modalities and objectives, all as worthy of respect as those that make up the North American model. What is terrifying about Bush's declaration is that it announces, subliminally and eventually in practice, the extinction of every model of progress different from the North American one.

And there is still more. The current government of the United States is merely a political façade for certain very obvious economic interests. Since the period leading up to the muddled election of November 2000, I have been saying that the Bush-Cheney clique quite obviously represents economic interests tied to the oil industry. I have documented this assertion elsewhere. Now I find the situation quite alarming. Saudi Arabia, the world's largest oil producer, has oil reserves equal to 262 billion barrels. Iraq is second, with a reserve of 130 billion barrels, and Iran is fifth, with 90 billion barrels. Add these figures together and you will see that by taking control of Iraq's energy resources, the United States will become the largest oil power in the world, reducing Russia, all of Europe, and Japan to client states or petro-colonies. This is the reality behind the disturbing mixture of arrogance, paternalism, and exaltation of human values that one finds in Bush's message to Congress. That message, along with U.S. public opinion, could be transformed by patriotic or electoral factors into the props of this new form of collective autocracy—impersonal and insidious—now developing in the superpower.

"There are no endless wars," Susan Sontag bravely writes, "but there are declarations of the extension of power by a state that believes it cannot be challenged." The words of this great liberal writer bring us back to the subject of civil liberties in the United States, dangerously violated by the program announced by the Bush administration—a program involving denunciation, imprisonment without defense or trial, the secret deprivation of personal freedoms, and so on. I believe that it is on this point that the North American people—who, as Lincoln said, can be fooled some of the time but not all the time, and only some of them but not all—can and must react, in order to return true meanings to names and words. Will they do so?

We have entered a new era in which an imperial government and its leaders no longer deserve historic or mythic epithets. Il Duce Bush, Zorro Cheney, Bluebeard Ashcroft, Lady Condoleezza of the Potomac, Lone Ranger Rumsfeld and Tonto Powell. No need. It's too much. These characters exercise power whose faces are interchangeable, shifting and even disposable. They can be replaced without major surgery. Hitler or Stalin were permanent fixtures. Not so with Bush or Cheney. There is thus some hope that the coterie that took over the White House will be expelled in November 2004. For the moment, however, they are wreaking all the havoc that can be inflicted by a power with no external limits, although—and this is the great difference from the imperial powers of the past—with some serious internal democratic safeguards. Externally, there is no one who can stand up to the United States government. Internally, the electorate (even if the elections have all been taken over by power and money), the media (however intimidated they are by the patriotic argument), Congress and the courts (to the extent that they insist on their rights), together make the United States the first superpower of the globalized world, but also the first global empire subject to potential internal controls. What can we call a power that is so extensive, so intense, and so contradictory? What name can we give to its quasi-anonymous leaders? What fate can we foresee for the American nation? Expansion or explosion?

Mysticism or criticism? What's in a name?

Indeed—what's in a name? In a word? "My name was useful," said Franco's sister Pilar, in a frank explanation of her privileges. But a rose would smell as sweet by any other name, said Shakespeare. And a rose is a rose is a rose, confirmed Gertrude Stein. And the finest of all: "Roses are the most important things that happen here," wrote Carlos Pellicer. In light of what I have written so far, one thing becomes perfectly clear: we are not living in the best of all possible worlds. But if we must live in the world that exists, we must maintain the verbal creativity that never encloses a name or a word within a prison, but that gives to language that quality of freedom, "unfinished and infinite," to which Emilio Lledo refers when he considers Don Quixote. Members of the

Spanish-speaking community, faced with the dangers of the present world, let us turn to our greatest book—written in the midst of the Counter Reformation—for this breath of nominative freedom that puts all dogmas and absolute certainties in check. The name of the town in La Mancha is uncertain. The names of the protagonist and his lady are uncertain as well. So is the authorship of the book itself. But there is the certainty of our freedom to challenge peremptory claims, and to build, instead, a world whose contours are not fixed but can be changed by the freedom speak and name. Yes, there is a clash of civilizations, but it is not the one that pits Islam against the West, the North against the South, the United States ("the single surviving model of human progress") against all the rest—against ourselves.

Rather, it is the clash between the authoritarian, ignorant and exclusive power of brute force, and the democratic, wise and inclusive power of human creativity. Will we be able to resist? Will we know how to choose? War is not peace. Freedom is not slavery. Ignorance is not strength.

As for Mexico and France, the bilateral relations between our two countries have only grown and prospered. In every area—culture, trade, finance, politics—the bilateral Franco-Mexican friendship has grown deeper and stronger since World War II. Today we are entering the fourth circle, in which Mexico and France find themselves united once again in the defense of the fundamental principles necessary for creating a new international order. The twenty-first century has had a stormy beginning, and many doubts are gathering on the horizon. But France and Mexico are united by the same faith in multilateralism, without which there can be no international order. Unilateralism wins wars, but it gropes in vain for peace. Multilateralism is the response to a very present fact, which is not about to disappear, and which is called globalization. Just as the industrial revolution of the eighteenth and nineteenth centuries did not disappear, despite the protestations, the agitations... Now it is a matter of giving globalization its legality, of rendering reality legal, of granting the facts their proper rights. These rights, for which France and Mexico are working together, imply first of all a cooperation in the domain of education. Everyone knows that without education there is no information, and that without information there is no production. We are united on questions of health, for example, which have become an international preoccupation because of the epidemics spreading throughout the world— AIDS among others. We are united on the attention that must be paid to the elderly and to children. We are united in the struggle to give women the rights that are due to them. And, in the domain of international relations, I would like to stress the solidarity of Mexico and France in dealing with two fundamental problems of our world. The first is the protection of the environment, which means adhering to the Kyoto Protocol. And the second is the struggle against crimes against humanity, and for the defense of universal human rights, which in turn means adhering without reserve to the International Criminal Court.

Finally, we have a diplomatic activity in common with which we both strongly identify and which presents us with some very clear objectives. Defending diplomacy means defending negotiation, dialogue, law, patience, pauses and compulsion, if necessary, or war—but solely as a last resort and on a fully juridical basis. Preemptive war cannot be tolerated. It is a barbaric principle leading directly to the arms race, to war-mongering based on mere suspicion, to rivalries between neighbors, and possibly to nuclear war. We must be united for the sake of assuring a better life in the century that is just beginning. The brilliant foreign minister, Dominique de Villepin, asks a very important question: "What kind of world do we want, in what kind of world do we want to live?" I see that the response of Mexico and France is clear.

We want to live in a world where law prevails over force, not in a world where force vanquishes law.

BRITAIN, FRANCE, AND THE FUTURE OF EUROPE'S FOREIGN POLICY

BY CHARLES GRANT

"The biggest problem of all, however, is that European governments have sharply contrasting views on how to deal with America. This is despite the fact that the Europeans—Britain and France included—agree on most of the world's major foreign policy challenges."

Charles GRANT (Great Britain)

In 1998, Grant stopped working with The Economist *in order to take the directorship of the Centre for European Reform, in London. He is also a member of the Committee for Russia in the European Union. He holds a chair at the Council of experts at the School for Political Science in Moscow. He is the author of several books, including* EU 2010: An Optimistic Vision of the Future, *and has just published a pamphlet entitled* Transatlantic Rift: how to bring the two together.

The European Union has many achievements to its credit, such as the single market, the euro and progressive rounds of enlargement. But the EU's oft-proclaimed goal of establishing an effective "Common Foreign and Security Policy" (CFSP) remains elusive. In the early 1990s the EU had no common line on the Gulf war or the breakup of Yugoslavia. In recent years there seemed to be some signs for hope: the EU launched plans for a common defence policy, and then its diplomacy helped to keep the peace in Macedonia and Montenegro. But in 2003 the EU split down the middle over the war in Iraq.

There are many reasons why the European Union has failed to impress as a player in its own right in foreign policy. The various member-state governments do not share a common strategic culture. They have different perceptions of the security threats they face, and different ideas on how to deal with any given threat. Hopefully, the EU security strategy that is emerging under the guidance of Javier Solana, the High Representative for foreign policy, will overcome some of these differences.

Another problem is that the EU institutions which attempt to co-ordinate the member-states' foreign policies are badly designed. For example, it is hard to imagine a less efficient system for external representation than the rotating presidency, under which a different member-state takes over the chairmanship if the EU every six months. The new constitution that is currently under discussion promises to make some sensible improvements, such as the establishment of a new president and a new foreign minister, who would both speak for the Union to the outside world.

The biggest problem of all, however, is that European governments have sharply contrasting views on how to deal with America. This is despite the fact that the Europeans—Britain and France included—agree on most of the world's major foreign policy challenges. Iraq is the exception, not the rule. On the Middle East Peace Process, on Iran and on the Balkans, the Europeans usually have a common position. They agree about the Kyoto protocol, the International Criminal Court and all the arms control treaties. They do not have any fundamentally different interests in their relations with Russia.

The problem is that the Europeans—and in particular Britain and France—do not agree on what to do if America strongly opposes a common European position. The British tend to shift their stance towards that of the U.S., in the hope of gaining influence in Washington, while the French tend to criticise the U.S. in public. For example in the spring of 2003, both Britain and France wanted a strong role for the UN in the reconstruction of post-war Iraq. But the U.S. decided to allow only a minimal UN role, and the UK—with some reluctance—shifted towards the U.S. position, while France criticised that American policy.

More fundamentally, Britain and France disagree over the rationale for a stronger European foreign and defence policy. The British want a strong EU so that it can be a useful partner in helping the U.S. to sort out the world's problems. If Europe's stance is generally co-operative, thinks Tony Blair, the U.S. is more likely to listen—and understand the benefits of multilateralism. But the French want a strong EU that is capable of standing up to the U.S., and—perhaps with Russia, China and others—preventing the emergence of a 'unipolar,' meaning U.S.-dominated, world.

Extra meetings of the 'big three' (Britain, France and Germany) or the 'big six' (the big three plus Italy, Poland and Spain), or of all the members, plus a lot of good will, can help to overcome this difference of approach. But the *sine qua non* of a common European line on America is a *rapprochement* between London and Paris.

If prime minister Tony Blair and president Jacques Chirac could achieve some reconciliation of their views on how to deal with the U.S., Germany and other European countries would be happy to follow their lead. Then a real and effective Common Foreign and Security Policy would become feasible.

When Britain and France fall out over fundamental strategic issues, as they did over Iraq, they damage much more than each other. The animosity between London and Paris over Iraq has undermined the United Nations, NATO and the EU's embryonic foreign and defence policies. Conversely, both Blair and Chirac would be stronger if they could learn to work with each other. And more importantly, Europe would be stronger.

A Franco-British reconciliation should be feasible. On counter-proliferation, for example, both countries favour a tough, UN-based multilateralism that binds in the U.S., Russia and China. They have similar views on the European constitution: both favour the 'inter-governmentalist' emphasis of the constitution drawn up by Convention President Valéry Giscard d'Estaing. They have a similar interest in development issues and—much more than most other EU countries—pay serious attention to Africa's problems. However, a serious *rapprochement* requires both countries to shift their attitudes to the U.S. In a nutshell, France needs to become less instinctively anti-American, and Britain less unconditionally pro-American. This short essay offers four suggestions to the French government, and four to the British government, which, if adopted, would minimise their divisions over the U.S., and enhance their authority within the EU.

A NEW LINE IN PARIS

France needs to soften the Gaullist character of its foreign policy. Plenty of senior figures in France's foreign policy establishment understand that France's active opposition to the U.S. on Iraq weakened three foundations of French power—the UN, NATO and the EU. The French government's policies and pronouncements on Iraq did much to divide those three institutions (and of course those in the opposing camp also did much to open up the divisions). What damaged France's interests was not its opposition to the war *per se*, but rather the manner in which it opposed military action in Iraq. President Vladimir Putin opposed the war without making flamboyant public pronouncements, or leading a vigorous diplomatic campaign against the U.S., in the manner of French leaders. Putin therefore antagonised the pro-war camp much less than French leaders.

France's first objective should be to oppose the U.S. on big issues rather than small ones. For example if the Americans want to start a war of which France disapproves, it should certainly oppose the war. But France has tended to oppose the U.S. on relatively minor security issues, often to cede in the end. France's decision to block NATO military aid for Turkey in January and February 2003 fuelled Francophobia in the U.S.—on an issue which even to many opponents of the Iraq war appeared to be theological. France's prickly behaviour over many years has annoyed its allies and deepened the well of anti-French sentiment in the U.S. France should conserve its powder for the big battles.

Second, France's leaders could achieve a lot by changing some of their language. If they talked more about partnership and working together to solve common problems, they would disarm many of their critics in Washington. In particular, they should avoid talking about the need for a 'multipolar' world. That word goes down well in Moscow and Beijing. But it causes concern in many European capitals, particularly in the eastern half of the continent, where people remember how much Yevgeny Primakov, the former Russian prime minister, promoted the idea of multipolarity.

To many Europeans, multipolarity is word which conjures up Bismarkian 19th-century power politics: the concept implies that the rise of any pre-eminent power provokes the emergence of an opposing coalition whose purpose is to contain that power. The underlying philosophy of the European Union is integration and the sharing of interests and responsibilities, rather than balance of power politics. That is why, as François Heisbourg has observed, multipolar is a word which divides Europeans, while multilateral is a word which brings them together. If French leaders could talk more about the need for a multilateral world, they would keep everyone in Europe with them—including the British.

The problem may be that language represents substance. In May this author heard an Elysee official say that France, Germany and Russia had learned to trust one another, that when dealing with the U.S. they had developed a common vision, and that their alliance was "capital" for the future. He said that this alliance was helping to integrate Russia with the West, and that it was also "a base" for France's future foreign policy.

Such ideas worry not only other European countries, but also some French diplomats. For if France became serious about this triple alliance, it would ensure that Europe remained divided and that the EU never became a power. Many other Europeans would disapprove of a long-term French alliance with a Russia which, despite its evident progress under Putin, still has an uncertain trajectory and a far from perfect human rights record.

Third, France should avoid divisive initiatives, such as ideas that would lead to the establishment of a "core Europe." Senior French officials sometimes drop hints that, if the British are not prepared to clarify that their commitment is to Europe rather than the alliance with the U.S., France and Germany will have to proceed on their own to establish an inner core that would include defence cooperation.

The April 29th summit that France held with Germany, Belgium and Luxembourg, with the purpose of creating an inner grouping for European defence, appeared to confirm that France was ready to embrace some kind of *noyau dur*. Whatever the intrinsic merits of promoting defence integration through an *avant-garde* group, this initiative was hugely divisive. The countries left out—including Britain, Spain, Italy and the East Europeans—resented a venture that seemed to be implicitly anti-American and anti-NATO. The timing, shortly after the war which had split Europe into two camps, could not have been worse. The April 29th summit helped to keep open the wound between "New Europe" and "Old Europe," thus delighting Donald Rumsfeld and the Pentagon hawks.

An enlarged EU will require an element of 'variable geometry': the Euro Group will dominate much economic policy-making; progress on defence may require smaller groups to move ahead; and not every member will participate fully in the Schengen agreements. But such inner circles must operate within an EU framework. There should be no 'inner core' that embraces a whole range of policy areas, for the result—a clear division into two classes of membership—would be very damaging. If the French president tried to lead a mini-Europe, built around the six founding members, he would by definition be unable to lead Europe as a whole. And so long as core Europe had an anti-American flavour, most EU countries would oppose it. France has to make a strategic choice: to aspire to lead the new, wider Europe, or to build an inner core centred on France and Germany.

Fourth, if France wants to be truly influential in the new Europe, its government will need to make new friends. It will have to make a special effort with the Central and East Europeans, for two reasons. One is that the leaders of these countries believe that comments by the French president and others in the early months of 2003 insulted them, and as far as they are concerned they have not received an apology. The other is that many French leaders have appeared to be in a state of denial about EU enlargement. Viewing enlargement as an unpalatable prospect, some French politicians have simply refused to think through the consequences. As a result France has made very little effort to build alliances with the accession countries. This attitude will have to change, simply for *raison d'état*: the eight new members from Central and Eastern Europe have many votes in the Council of Ministers, and they will not want to be allies of a France that is systematically opposed to the U.S.

If France could modify its approach towards the U.S., it would win friends in Washington and many European capitals. It would also reduce the chances of Europe splitting apart in the future as it did over Iraq. If France altered its stance, Germany—always more reluctant than France to oppose the U.S.—would almost certainly follow.

A NEW LINE IN LONDON

The other side of this equation is that British foreign policy will also have to shift. As with France, there are compelling reasons for the UK to re-examine its position in international affairs. Since the summer of 2002, the perception across many parts of Europe that Britain is unconditionally supportive of the U.S.—combined with the UK's decision not to join the euro any time soon—has damaged British influence.

Not everyone in the British government understands that there is a problem. Some senior figures in the government have at times appeared to believe that Britain can be George Bush's best friend and also the pre-eminent leader of Europe. But despite the fact that several European governments supported Tony Blair's stance on Iraq, he will have to work at restoring his authority in Europe. If Blair could shift his line on the U.S., he would strengthen his position on the continent and make it easier for the big three—Britain, France and Germany—to take a common approach. The UK, like France, need not change a great deal of the substance of its foreign policy.

First, Britain should be less uncritical and unconditional in its support of the U.S. Blair has been reluctant to criticise the U.S. in public, on the grounds that he has more influence if he is publicly supportive. That is surely correct; but one of Blair's problems on the continent is that nobody knows if he is critical in private, and very few people believe that he has much influence in the White House. He should be prepared to make more explicit criticisms of the U.S. in public, for example on issues such as the International Criminal Court, Kyoto, Iran and—if Bush fails to fulfil his promises to Blair—the Middle East peace process. If Blair is serious about leading in Europe he will have to take some risks in his relationship with George Bush. Those risks should be manageable: before making a criticism, Blair could warn Bush, explaining that it was all in the cause of enhancing British influence in Europe, and that that was good for the U.S. Some of the top officials in the Foreign Office believe that British influence in Washington would survive the occasional public criticism of the president, and they are probably right.

Second, the British government needs to tell a different story about British foreign policy. As already stated, on most of the key foreign policy issues, Britain agrees with its European partners. But Blair and his ministers seldom make speeches that highlight this truth. They need to spell out that the UK is with the other Europeans on the Balkans, Israel-Palestine, the International Criminal Court and so on. On some of these issues they will need to stress that the UK-European line is different from that of the U.S. British ministers should speak out on Javier Solana's EU security strategy, praising this attempt to bring about a convergence of European viewpoints on security threats. Until now the security strategy has gone unmentioned in their speeches.

Third, Blair and his ministers should avoid actions which prolong the division between New and Old Europe. The "letter of eight," signed by Blair and seven other European leaders in the run-up to the Iraq war, widened an already deep rift that had opened up between two hostile European camps. The British government also needs to handle the relationship with France more sensitively: British words and actions affect the internal debates of the French government. At the time of the Iraq war some ministers' attacks on the French, almost blaming them for the war, were over-the-top and unhelpful.

Fourth, Blair needs to show the rest of Europe that Britain is enthusiastically committed to the European Security and Defence Policy (ESDP). Nothing did more to convince other EU governments that he was genuinely pro-European than the St Malo initiative. But in the subsequent five years, Britain's support for the concept of an EU role in defence has appeared hesitant. For example, after the UK's tabloid press viciously attacked the 'European army' at the time of the Nice summit in December 2000, Blair and his ministers said very little in public about the ESDP for over a year. And sometimes the UK has appeared over-sensitive to the concerns of the Pentagon: in spring 2003 British officials talked of postponing plans for the EU to take over the peacekeeping in Bosnia, because the Pentagon had got cold feet. Of course, a key task for the British in building the ESDP has been to persuade the Americans that the purpose is not to weaken NATO. That may justify some British caution. Nevertheless, Blair also needs to convince his European partners that he is faithful to the objectives of the St Malo initiative, including the idea that the EU should be able to run its own military missions.

Sometimes the UK government seems to understand this point. The British-French declaration at Le Touquet in February 2003 sketched out a way forward for the ESDP, even mentioning the possibility of pooling some military capabilities. And Britain gave strong support the EU's first autonomous military mission, to Bunia in the Congo, in June 2003—despite American misgivings about the operation. But British support for the ESDP needs to be more unequivocal, constant and public. That is the best way of dissuading other governments from divisive initiatives such as the four-country summit in April.

SOME ENCOURAGING SIGNS

By the autumn of 2003, there were some tentative signs that the British and French governments had taken on board at least some of these points. France seemed to have stopped opposing the U.S. on some of the smaller issues. Thus in May 2003, during the negotiation over UNSC resolution 1483 on Iraq, it showed some flexibility. It also supported the plan for NATO to take over the peacekeeping in Kabul, as well as the scheme for NATO to help the Poles run their sector of Iraq. And in September France said that it would not use its UNSC veto to block America's plans for further a resolution on Iraq.

French leaders also seemed to be talking much less about the need for a multipolar world. They seemed to have become less enthusiastic about a triple alliance with Germany and Russia, perhaps because the Russians did not seem to be interested in forming a permanent front whose rationale would be, in part, to oppose the Americans. The French government also seemed to be playing down the idea of a core Europe that would exlude Britain. In September, when Chirac met Blair and Germany's Gerhard Schroder in Berlin, France and Germany made it clear that they wanted Britain to be part of any leadership group in European defence. For his part, Blair said that he would not oppose such a leadership group, so long as it did not damage or appear to damage NATO. All three countries appeared ready to seek compromises on the sensitive issues surrounding European defence.

British ministers have curbed their inclination to bad-mouth the French. In May defence secretary Geoff Hoon even worked hard to persuade the Pentagon to scale back its exclusion of the French from some kinds of military cooperation. And when Tony Blair addressed Congress in July, he came very close to offering constructive criticisms of U.S. foreign policy. He said he agreed that the mission should determine the coalition, rather than the reverse. He then added, in a veiled rebuke to the administration's unilateralists: "But let us start preferring the coalition and acting alone if we have to; not the other way round." And he concluded that America must listen as well as lead.

On Iran, Europe's big three have shown that they can act together, and in some respects in opposition to U.S. policy. In the summer of 2003, Britain, France and Germany persuaded the other EU governments to adopt a tougher stance on Iraq: EU foreign ministers decided that if Iran failed to sign the International Atomic Energy Authority's additional protocol, which would allow more intrusive inspections of its nuclear facilities, they would cut off contacts, including talks on a trade and cooperation agreement.

However, while the U.S. was pleased to see this tougher European line on Iran, there remained a gap between U.S. and European policies. The EU believes in offering carrots as well as sticks: if Iran does the right things, the EU says, it should be rewarded with trade, aid and technology transfers. The U.S. disapproves of such offers, believing that President's Khatami's regime is incapable of transforming Iran for the better. When the British, French and German foreign ministers wrote a letter to their Iranian counterpart, offering incentives for good behaviour, the White House expressed its annoyance to 10 Downing Street.

While there are signs that Britain and France are making efforts to overcome their divisions, they remain a very long way from a common attitude to the U.S. There is still the danger that, when the U.S. strongly opposes a European policy, the British will try to shift closer to the U.S., thereby opening up a gap between themselves and other Europeans, notably France. This could happen on Iran, if the Khatami government does just enough to satisfy the Europeans but not enough to impress the Americans.

And it could certainly happen on the Middle East peace process. This author listened to British and French diplomats discussing the peace process at a dinner in October 2003. They agreed absolutely on the requirements for a peace settlement. But they did not agree on what to do if the situation on the ground deteriorated and if the U.S. disengaged: the British argued that the Europeans should continue to apply discreet pressure to the U.S. administration to re-engage, and that criticising the U.S. in public would achieve nothing. The French argued that the Europeans would have no choice but to criticise the U.S. and to come up with their own peace plan.

So, the key to a more effective CFSP remains an evolution in both French and British positions on how to deal with the U.S. They should lead their European partners to support a common EU stance: in favour of a stronger Europe that is usually supportive of U.S. policies; but a Europe which can act autonomously, and which, on matters of vital importance, is capable of opposing the U.S.

October 2003

FRANCE AND AMERICA, 2003 AND BEYOND
REFLECTIONS ON A DISCOURSE OF FRENCH FOREIGN MINISTER DOMINIQUE DE VILLEPIN[8]

BY AMBASSADOR ROBERT E. HUNTER

"Iraq . . . has been the 'fire bell in the night' for all the allies, not least for the United States and France, as both need to recognize the essential quality of their relationship, whether in Europe or beyond."

Robert E. HUNTER (United States)

*Principal advisor at the Rand Corporation in Washington, D.C.,
NATO ambassador from 1993 to 1998, he was representative
of the United States in the European Union. He was the major
architect of NATO and negotiated the transformation of the
Alliance and its engagements in Bosnia. He has more than seven
hundred and fifty publications to his name.*

---

8 (PREVIOUS PAGE) All the quotations from Dominique de Villepin are from his
Dimbleby Lecture, October 20, 2003, as broadcast by the BBC.
See http://news.bbc.co.uk/1/hi/world/europe/3207948.stm.

" At a time when the world seems to be out of control, when it is split over the painful ordeals of Iraq and the Middle East, we need not more lectures but clarity, determination and boldness to find our way back to the path of unity and action."

—Dominique de Villepin,
Dimbleby Lecture, October 19, 2003.

This advice was offered at the six-month mark following the end of the critical phase of major combat operations in the Iraq War—itself reflecting the deepest divide among allies in the history of NATO and the most serious strains between France and the United States since at least President Charles deGaulle's decision in 1966 to withdraw French forces from the allied integrated command. What Dominique de Villepin had to say on this occasion was sensible—indeed remarkable—advice, particularly coming from the foreign minister of the nation most at odds with the United States, who had himself been believed in Washington to have played a major role in causing, or at least nurturing, the Franco-American rift. This advice was not offered in an effort to mollify or—even less—to apologize; but at the same time, it did not represent a radical departure from years of French engagement with the United States and the North Atlantic Alliance. Sensible advice: Reflecting awareness in France as well as in every other nation of the Alliance that all of its states are fated to live together, and—put positively—are indeed now offered the chance to work together in shaping international society as the same allies, with stunning success, had done in prosecuting and then winning both the Cold War and a sustainable peace in Europe.

At this relatively short distance, looking back at the Iraq crisis of 2002–3, perspective is still likely to be lacking. Indeed, in the United States, being "anti-French" is still highly popular, a renewal of a saga with deep roots and a long history. Some commentators have said, a bit whimsically, that this reflects in part the failure of either great nation to forgive the other: the United States to forgive France for Yorktown, which secured American independence from Britain; and France to forgive the United States for Normandy, releasing the French from Nazi bondage. Neither can accept that it needed the other for its salvation.

But what happened in 2002–3 should properly be seen not as the continuation of some sort of on-again, off-again troubled relationship, often marked by deep differences of vision, action, and interpretation—intensified by a long history of close interaction, of mutual expectation and sometimes disappointment—but rather as an aberration from steadily strengthening bonds and common action, including in the post–Cold War years.

The fact is, to begin with, that France has become as deeply intertwined with the United States economically as any other European nation. To be sure, there are continuing differences of interests and policy, for example over the EU's Common Agricultural Policy and U.S. genetically modified organisms (GMOs), but these so pale beside transatlantic interconnections—in trade, finance, investment, cross-owner-ship, job-creation, and the like—as to make the economic ties indissoluble. The United States does not single out France for attention when there are economic difficulties; and France does not go out of its way to be painful to America.

More apposite to the problems of 2002–3, there are precious few—if any—major strategic disagreements between France and the United States, certainly in what matters most to these two countries, what threats and challenges they face, and where each of them could have to be engaged to protect their individual and common national interests. Thus, with its EU partners, France shares the U.S. concerns with combating international terror; with stopping the spread of weapons of mass destruction (WMD); and with tackling a congeries of problems in the Middle East. U.S. President George W. Bush could as easily have pronounced foreign Minister de Villepin's Dimbleby Lecture words on these subjects:

> Let's also beware of the possible connections between terrorism and the proliferation of weapons of mass destruction. Such a combination can be a destabilizing factor for whole regions. More serious still, it could result in blackmail or even a direct threat to our security interests. Here we are facing a major global risk: from North Korea to the Middle East, an arc of proliferation has taken shape with its trafficking in technology and materials, and the underground activities of scientists.

Nor is this anything new—French attitudes paralleling those of the United States in the wake of "9/11." Throughout the 1990s, France and the United States found that they were able to accommodate one another's interests and preferred methods in the transformation of European security as effectively—if not even more so—than they had found practical means of working together to prosecute the Cold War. Neither sought to abandon the transatlantic connection or to have American power withdraw from the Continent; neither ignored the need to deal decisively with the final elements of the 20th century security and political agenda— most critically to pursue President George H. W. Bush's vision of a "Europe whole and free"; and both saw NATO as the cornerstone of transatlantic security.

Indeed, from about 1993 onwards, the U.S. and France tried to create the conditions whereby France could return to full membership in NATO's integrated command structure leading up to President Jacques Chirac's decision in December 1995. The arrangements that followed, including France's return to the NATO Military Committee and the recreation of the North Atlantic Council in Defense Ministers Session, came within an ace of full integration, foundering on the issue of NATO's Southern Command. But this was a "95% solution" for both NATO and France; and there were no inhibitions on France's full participation in all of NATO's military and peacekeeping actions in the Balkans—indeed, France gave more support than did Britain to U.S. efforts to have NATO use its airpower in Bosnia during 1993–95.

Franco-American differences over security and foreign policy issues in the post–Cold War period—and there were several—had less to do with strategic perspective than with views on the future organization of European security. Throughout this period, France has sought to enhance its role within the European Union—an unremarkable approach and an ambition pursued by some other key EU states—and also to promote the possibilities for both a European "foreign policy" and European "defense policy"—the latter in some measure in competition with transatlantic defense connections represented in NATO. France has had ambitions to enlarge its range of action and maneuver; to create a greater role for Europe in the world, necessitating (by French lights) some lessening of American influence on the Continent—*provided, however, that the United States does not lessen its commitment to Europe's freedom, independence, security, and shared interests beyond Europe*; and to have some alternatives, for itself and its European partners, to dependence on the United States in a number of areas. For example, to quote de Villepin:

> Only a Europe capable of speaking with one voice will be a credible partner for the U.S. and respected as such. This is in the interest of the U.S., our common closest ally. How can we, for example, cooperate with the U.S. in the area of intelligence, if Europe hasn't got its own strategic analysis? How can we fight proliferation together, if Europe hasn't got its own assessment of the relevant programmes and a determined policy to put an end to them?

Some details of this assessment and its larger framework have proved objectionable to the United States (and to some of the European allies), but the underlying principle has enjoyed more then a decade of U.S. support. During the Cold War, the U.S. wanted a strong "European pillar" to the alliance, but it also wanted this pillar to be clearly subservient to U.S. direction and leadership, and for a valid purpose: to ensure the central management of the critical strategic and nuclear relationship with the Soviet Union. By the early

1990s, however, it was clear that objective circumstances had changed, and thus U.S. policy changed, as well. The Clinton Administration embraced the concept of a European Security and Defense Identity (ESDI)—called "Policy" (ESDP) in the EU to denote broader ambitions—provided it were developed within NATO and be "separable but not separate from it." Washington took this approach for several reasons, including historic American support for European integration; the stimulus that pursuit of an ESDI/ESDP might give to European countries in terms of modernizing their armed forces and keeping up defense spending beyond what might otherwise have been done; and the political value of having a European "capability of last resort" in case, for some unknown reason, the United States would be unprepared to use its military forces to secure some European interest—reasoning, incidentally, that is shared by France.

As the European defense structure developed—first in the Western European Union and latter in the EU itself—the United States and its European allies, notably France, debated the terms and conditions of the relationship between NATO and the EU's defense "identity" or "policy." The upshot of long and complex debate was a dual decision at a European Union summit in Helsinki in December 1999, which created a Headline Goal Task Force ("rapid reaction force") capable of deploying limited amounts of military power, and agreed that this force would only be used "where NATO as a whole is not engaged." In less diplomatic terms, this meant that NATO had the right of first refusal; in effect, if the United States were prepared to engage in a military operation desired by the EU states, it would be undertaken and commanded by NATO. In the process of negotiating practical arrangements between the two bodies, other ties were created, including for planning, commanding the EU force, the loaning of NATO military "assets" to the EU, and ensuring that, should it be called for, military actions undertaken by the Europeans on their own, but which escalated in intensity, could smoothly be transferred to NATO's integrated command.

Discussion and debate across the Atlantic on these complicated issues has continued, most often pitting France and the United States against one another, leading in 2003 to another major disagreement over the EU's potential creation of a planning headquarters at Tervuren, Belgium, for use in circumstances where the United States chose not be engaged militarily and, in addition, some NATO country would block the transfer of military assets to the EU force. The tempest that followed in this particular teapot could hardly have been mostly about the merits—the planning staff could hardly rival that of NATO; the principle of "where NATO as a whole is not engaged" went essentially unchallenged in Europe, and was accepted (even if grudgingly) by France; and the United States indeed welcomed EU independent action in the Congo, in Macedonia peacekeeping, and prospectively in assuming responsibility for the Bosnia Implementation Force in 2004. The issues at stake were more political, including about the relative influence of the United States and France in Europe's security future—issues of moment and of intensity, but with legitimate views on both sides and hardly the stuff of crisis; and they also were, as much as anything else, a surrogate for the great debates over Iraq and the rest of the Middle East that erupted with full force from late 2002 onward. They were also about contending views of the role of the use of force—where and when it should be employed, who should make the decisions, and how military force should be related to other elements of power and policy.

Much of the debate and disagreement was triggered by the attacks on the United States on September 11, 2001, which radically transformed American perceptions about the nature, locus, and intensity of threats—for the first time in nearly two centuries palpably against the continental homeland. Notably, however, there was no opposition in Europe to America's prompt and vigorous military response—and certainly not in France, where *Le Monde* proclaimed: *Nous sommes tous Americains*. Indeed, there was strong European political and military support for reduction of the Taliban regime in Afghanistan, including the direct engagement of forces from several European states—to the limits that fit within the military needs and tactics of U.S. forces—including France. It is also remarkable, in the time since then, NATO itself has expanded its own role, by unanimous agreement: beyond the Balkans to assuming command of the International Security Assistance Force (ITAF) in Afghanistan and to providing needed support to a Polish-led division in post-war Iraq. A debate that had long bedeviled the Alliance, as it adapted itself both to complete the 20th century security agenda in Europe and to open a fresh agenda beyond for the 21st century—whether to act "out of area"—has been decisively concluded, including ally France as much as any other member of NATO.

Division across the Atlantic over the proper uses of military force developed over what, if anything, to do about Iraq—and, more broadly, over the 2002 U.S. proclamation of the right of preemptive attack, especially in circumstances involving the potential spread of weapons of mass destruction. What transpired in 2002-3 in terms of the cacophony of disagreement need not be rehearsed here, although several points need to be recognized: that during much of this period neither American or French political leaders covered themselves with glory—or even civility—in their dealings with one another; that the critical issues in dispute were often buried beneath mutual acrimony; and that some opportunities for compromise and accommodation were accordingly lost. At the same time, however, there was no dispute on the need to prevent Iraq from acquiring WMD— as de Villepin has recalled, "Last winter, France advocated Iraq's complete, immediate and verifiable disarmament on the basis of Security Council Resolution 1441"; nor was there dispute that the Middle East would be a better place with the departure of Saddam Hussein.

There were, in fact, legitimate differences of view that were substantially obscured by the intensity of disagreement; and U.S. opposition to positions taken by the French and German governments also obscured that both were in good company in Europe and that they spoke more for European public opinion than did countries like Britain which sided with the United States on the Iraq War. Ironically, one key concern, widely expressed in Europe, was that circumstances in post-conflict Iraq would develop in precisely the way that they did. Another was that a precedent would be set for similar American pre-emptive or preventing action elsewhere. It was also believed widely in Europe that it is essential to create a generally respected post–Cold War code of conduct and source of legitimacy regarding the use of force; that other efforts would need to be made in parallel with a war on Iraq and its aftermath, notably vigorous prosecution of Israeli-Palestinian peacemaking to the point of success; and that terrorism might actually be abetted rather than of countered by a strike against Iraq that did not garner sufficient international support and legitimacy, such as attended President

George H.W. Bush's leadership in expelling Iraq from Kuwait a decade earlier. On this point, de Villepin has spoken in terms that are actually mainstream American:

> Not backed by force, law is powerless. But force alone is futile. A strategy focusing solely on the use of force cannot destroy the roots of terrorism. It would risk giving political legitimacy to individuals acting in the shadows.

But all of this, as they say, is now history. For good or ill, the old security system in the Middle East has been shattered. The West will be perforce engaged for a generation or more in building a new political and security system, founded in part on the transformation of regional societies. Nor is this just an American task, with some European allies perhaps quietly reveling in American discomfort. No one can afford to have the United States fail; and no European country can afford to have the process of Middle East transformation fail. "Have no doubt about it," de Villepin says, "despite the difficulties, despite our differences, France will spare no effort to achieve stability and security." The logic is impeccable and compelling. European interests and concerns—French interests and concerns—include Muslim migration to Europe, Middle East oil and gas, WMD, terrorism, the Israeli and Palestinian futures, economic and political development, and the elusive quality "stability"—whether or not democracy building is an essential part of this process, where many Europeans are more skeptical than leaders of the U.S. government. On this last point, de Villepin again speaks instructively:

In Iraq just like in the whole of the Middle East, we must embark on the road to democracy. In a world where peoples must be able to assert their identities, reform is indispensable. It has to come from within, it mustn't be dictated from outside. We would be seriously mistaken if we were to think that democracy can be exported as if it were a mere set of formal rules. Democracy has to be nurtured. It requires a whole apprenticeship. It is our duty to foster dialogue, freedom and respect in these countries.

Lessons from the Iraq war and its aftermath will no doubt be learned for a long time to come. But a few are already evident and they embrace both Europe and North America, France and the United States. The U.S. is learning that even great power is not the same as great influence, that translating the one into the other requires the same kind of stewardship, cooperation with friends and allies, and institution-building, such as marked the Cold War era. It is not that the United States could not on its own undertake most if not all of the inescapable tasks that now face the world in the Greater Middle East; it is that the American people will not accept that the U.S. should do so alone—whether paying in blood or in treasure—or that the United States should assume the burdens of a modern empire. Nor should the United States have to assume all these burdens, when it has so many similar-minded allied who are prepared to share responsibility, in their own self-interest and in the interest of preserving, protecting, and extending the community of values built up so painstakingly over half a century. In working together in dealing with the mass of problems in post-war Iraq, the West has a ready instrument in NATO; with a proper UN mandate and blessing, it can be the framework for sorting out Iraq's long-term military-related problems, while a consortium of the U.S., EU, and others can take responsibility for nonmilitary nation building.

Meanwhile, the European allies are learning that military power remains relevant in the 21st century; that there are threats and challenges beyond Europe that they must help to meet; that the United States needs and deserves European partners, not just in Europe but beyond; and that the stakes overall are too great for Europe to be inward looking to the point of self-damage. For their part, the Americans must learn, once again, the importance, wherever possible, of dealing in timely fashion with causes of future conflict rather than just conflict itself and the aftermath.

Together, the transatlantic allies must understand the requirements of shaping a world than can be less likely to see major terrorism, less likely to see the spread of WMD, and less likely to be subjected to forms of conflict we have not yet even thought of—in a globalizing world, with its intensifying disparity between haves and have-nots. In an increasingly global "nation," we must collectively respond to the words of President Franklin D. Roosevelt: "We cannot be content, no matter how high [the] general standard of living may be, if some fraction of our people—whether it be one-third or one-fifth or one-tenth—is ill-fed, ill-clothed, ill housed, and insecure." Or in the words of Dominique de Villepin: "Power is no longer a mere matter of military and technological might. Power also means an ability to listen to others and understand their concerns.... Let us be careful not to recreate the conditions for a new clash between North and South, East and West, Christianity and Islam."

Minister de Villepin could easily have added that there needs to be a new strategic partnership between North America and Europe, and especially a partnership between the United States and the European Union—with France's leadership a key element—to tackle the tasks beyond Europe that will largely determine both challenge and opportunity in the period ahead.

"Iraq," in this sense, has been the "fire bell in the night" for all the allies, not least for the United States and France, as both need to recognize the essential quality of their relationship, whether in Europe or beyond. De Villepin instructs the United States:

> To go the unilateral route is utopia. It is also, more importantly, obsolete. We all know that no one State is in a position to respond on its own to the challenge of security, economic growth and social development.

Finally, tying together four isolated but complementary and reinforcing comments from Foreign Minister Dominique de Villepin's Dimbleby Lecture, are points to be pondered and ingested by France, Britain, America, and all the rest of the transatlantic world:

> The links between Europe and the U.S. are paramount. . . . There is no contradiction between our determination to see Europe play a world role and strengthening the transatlantic link. . . . [We need to lay] the foundations for fruitful and constructive cooperation. . . . What unites us is stronger than what separates us.

PROPOSALS

BY BERNARD-HENRI LÉVY

"France is one of the few nations that, since De Gaulle in any event, feels authorized to dream of an ambitious, offensive diplomacy that is not always or necessarily guided by realpolitik alone.... this constantly repeated desire to speak in the name of Truth, Justice, and Goodness, this strange and beautiful ambition... imposes a certain number of duties on our country."

Bernard-Henri LÉVY (France)

Writer, philosopher, journalist, and the founder of the esteemed literary journal La Règle du jeu, *Bernard-Henri Lévy also has an editorial column in the newspaper* Le Point. *He has published numerous books, including, most recently,* Who Killed Daniel Pearl? *and* War, Evil, and the End of History, *for which he received the 2003 Aujourd'hui Prize, France's equivalent of a Pulitzer Prize.*

In the modern age and since the end of the Cold War more than ever, France, together with the United States, is the only great nation that, without too much deception or ridicule, can still lay claim to a universalist view of the world.

France is one of the few nations that, since De Gaulle in any event, feels authorized to dream of an ambitious, offensive diplomacy that is not always or necessarily guided by *realpolitik* alone—it is one of the very last countries capable of propelling itself into the world without this prominence becoming the mere extension of its own narrowest state interests.

This exceptional position, this constantly repeated desire to speak in the name of Truth, Justice, and Goodness, this strange and beautiful ambition that, incidentally, is recognized as being legitimate by many of our partners, and this acquired right—which Dominique de Villepin here asserts as well— to speak loud and clear on the international stage, imposes a certain number of duties on our country.

THE QUESTION OF EUROPE

It is everywhere repeated that Europe is in crisis.

It is also true that there is optimism, a European euphoria, a form of believing that Europe is going in the direction of

History and that it will be constructed no matter what happens, whatever the good or ill will of its builders may be, by virtue of a kind of providential necessity, determined in the secret course of things. It is true there is a European *progressivism* that seems seriously damaged by a few of the communal machinery's recent developments or events. It is to be understood, furthermore, that everyone contributed to this—including, unfortunately, the government of which Dominique de Villepin is a part, who in this area did not want to be outdone. Ah! the little game that consists of giving verbal support to the European rules and breaking them as soon as it concerns preparing a budget or getting out of a social crisis.

All the more reason, then, to react.

All the more reason not to resign oneself to what could pass for a serious penchant of the day, helped along by dejection and pessimism.

All the more reason to see a great European country—and why, in that case, not France?—sound the alarm in the communal house and take the initiative of restarting the process.

Today, Europe's grand accomplishment, its only true and successful cultural revolution is the Euro.

One idea: transpose the same approach, in the same spirit, and with the same determination, to an area that is just as vital since it is the one where the first truly European generation will or will not be trained: education.

The project: to launch, starting with France, the idea of unifying instruction and degree courses, of substituting European diplomas for the various national diplomas—of initiating the idea of a European ENA [a college that trains senior civil servants], a European Academy, a European Political Science Department.

Another project: picking up on Franz Werfel's old academic dream and putting Europe on the rails by which it should perhaps have begun, as the apocryphal but correct phrase of Jean Monnet states—those of knowledge, memory, intelligence, and culture.

A task for France.

A mission for that France that sees itself as truly loyal to the few principles set forth in the "European" chapters of this book.

THE QUESTION OF ISLAM

I am more and more convinced that it is no longer enough to struggle with words—although that is essential, of course—against the criminal assimilation of Islam with fundamentalism and of the latter with terrorism.

I am more and more convinced that, in the face of that other LePen-ification of the mind, which is what Islamophobia is here, and in the face of the rampant Islamization of the civil societies there, France has the duty to support—concretely and through actions with real and important meaning—moderate Muslims, lay people, the tenets of enlightened Islam that, with its back to the wall, struggles against its dark double.

The minister who expresses himself herein seems conscious of what is at stake. He seems to have understood the urgency that lies in making Islam not the adversary but the support of democracy, especially among youth. He has understood, and he says so, that the great task of Arab-Muslim intellectuals in the coming decade, the fervent obligation of the forces of progress, of enlightened circles, and of the women of these countries will be to bring on a theoretical and political *aggiornamento* capable of thwarting the present incompatibility of the Koranic message and of the ideal of the Enlightenment. And therein we must help them. Therein we must contribute by giving them courage as we provide them with some of our strength and our memory. Precise and concrete gestures are needed in which our politics are in agreement with our professions of faith.

On the Chechnyan question, let us revive the point of view that, albeit very late, was ours in Bosnia and Kosovo.

In the face of the suffering of the civilian population of Grozny, let us be careful not to repeat the error—if not the insult—of which the late Commander Massoud was a victim before and during his visit to France in June 2001, while Lionel Jospin and Jacques Chirac were in cohabitation at the pinnacle of the state.

Let us invite Maskadov to Paris.

Let us support the democrats in that potentially terrorist state of Pakistan, instead of Musharraf alone, prisoner of the military—although he pretends otherwise—of the ISI[9], and of the MMA[10] fundamentalists.

Let us help Indonesia that, should it topple...

And, finally, why not take a highly symbolic, grand political-cultural initiative, such as the creation of a Euro-Arab university, spanning France and one or several moderate Arab nations, in which Islam and Democracy, Islam and a spirit of tolerance, would be combined and where the liberal elites of Muslim countries, those who dream of joining the West with the East, would come to build up their inventory of methods, knowledge, and hope?

The urgency lies, and I repeat, in systematically and openly giving support to the moderates who struggle for democracy in the very heart of the Islamic world. And that, too, is France's task—France is the great democratic country that, if it follows through on its intuitions and its agenda as formulated here, can most effectively contribute to this.

---

9 The ISI is the Pakistani Secret Service.
10 MMA stands for the Muthida Majlas-e-Aamal.

THE NEAR EAST AND THE
ISRAELI-PALESTINIAN CONFLICT

I do not agree with Dominique de Villepin's analysis when he makes this war into the mother of all the wars that are presently devastating the planet.

I am particularly convinced that the settlement of the above-mentioned war would in essence not change very much in the state of affairs of terrorism. With the terrorist epicenter being in a region of the world (broadly speaking in Islamic Asia, more specifically Pakistan and Afghanistan) where they have no concrete experience with either Israel or Palestine and where the question of Kashmir, for example, is seen as a far more burning issue than that of the Palestinian Intifada, I am convinced that peace in Jerusalem would there, by definition, have a far less palpable effect than one might think.

All the same.

This peace must be made.

It must be made for itself, if I may say so, independent of the impact that it would or would not have on the planetary terrorist context and because the two peoples there have an equal interest in and right to it.

And for all those who, like myself, have for thirty-five years been striving for a fair and equitable peace, for all those who tirelessly plead for the division of the land and the reciprocal compromise about dreams and forms of messianism, for all those who campaign against every form of fanaticism, for the very principle of a political and metapolitical transaction, there is today something like an imperceptible quiver indicating that we are perhaps not condemned to the perpetual return of the worst, after all. Obviously, I am thinking of the so-called Geneva protocol made public early in November by distinguished

Palestinian and Israeli figures; I am thinking of the extraordinary lesson given there by civilian societies to the politicians on both sides who are bogged down in their prejudices; I am thinking of the manner these men had, to use Villepin's words, of causing the lines to budge that for thirty-five years condemned every peace plan to failure and deadlock. Well then! I say that France is again the country in the world that, faced with the failure that is as much the Quartet's as the promoters' of the travel warrant, is perhaps best placed to accept the challenge and convert it into a political plan.

Not, of course, that France has a more vigorous affinity than the others do with the Kantian ideals of perpetual peace.

And I'm careful not to forget it is here in France that we are witnessing the most disconcerting political blunders, among certain fringes of the sphere of influence of Alter-Globalization, for example. I am not forgetting the indulgence with which words of such Franco-Islamist tenor that assimilate French Jews with Israel, Israel with Sharon, and Sharon with Hitler are heard even beyond the extreme left, as I write these lines.

But then I read the texts and speeches collected in this volume.

I see the care that was taken to hold together and tie the double thread.

I perceive the double modulation, almost in my ears, that runs through them and that to me is like an echo of the cry sent forth a few months ago by a group of French intellectuals, Jews and Muslims both, asserting they were both "Zionist and pro-Palestinian."

I hear how this strange diplomacy, both inclined to dreaming and fearsomely pragmatic, never wastes an opportunity to restate the absolute legitimacy of the Palestinians' right to a state in the West Bank and Gaza, nor to proclaim France's attachment to the beautiful idea of a Jewish State, which it once carried to the baptismal fonts of the United Nations, and which fifty years later certainly has not kept all its promises but continues to be the principle of an open and dynamic society, a democratic oasis in a region that is threatened by collective regression.

Why, in the face of the present deadlock, not take this double petition to the end?

Why not support holding a great conference of the Israeli-Palestinian peace forces in Paris?

Why not try, in Paris, to make the voices heard of those who do not always know each other but who make peace their common hope, as opposed to those of the politicians who make war their trade?

Why not, under the aegis of France, have a States General of Peace, an intellectual and moral referendum bearing on the main clauses of the compromise?

In a word, why not adopt the Geneva plan, pass it on, appropriate it—why not make it, as it amply deserves to be, into the founding text, the referendum common to all the partisans of what I, for one, have called the "dry peace"?

FINALLY, BAGHDAD:

The interminable nightmare where we see Gulliver entangled, in the process of losing the peace after having won the war.

And the no less interminable quarrel with a country—France—whose true wrong seems to be having been right too soon and then, in turn, making the mistake sometimes of putting too much emphasis on this.

My personal position on this point was extremely clear from the start: the military operation in Iraq was morally correct but politically disastrous. Certainly, the unilateral intervention had the moral merit of causing the fall of a dictator but it had the triple flaw of first of all being based on a lie (the presence in Baghdad of weapons of mass destruction that everyone knew did not exist); secondly, of giving a sort of anticipated blank check to all possible candidates for unilateralism (what will we say, what will the United States say, to those in Africa, for instance, who would argue from a higher "law" in order to make their power respected?); thirdly, for getting the address and the enemy wrong (Saddam was a tyrant in the autumn of his life, the map of rogue nations had changed since George Bush, Sr., and the bases of al-Qaeda were to be found far more in Ryad and Karachi than in Baghdad and Basra). In other words, France was right to do everything to convince its American ally, until the last moment, not to become involved in that improbable and absurd adventure.

All the same.

Apart from the fact that this correct position went hand in hand with a few blunders, it seems to me even so that it is our duty today to do everything to move beyond the quarrel.

An American failure—and this should be stated over and over again—would be a shared failure.

Whether the Americans prepared their post-war situation badly, whether they are getting stuck in a trap they themselves set, whether they have become incapable—contrary to what they were able to do in post-war Germany and Japan—of playing the double role of "nurse" and "policeman," none of that changes the fact that their defeat, if there were to be a defeat, would be a defeat for all with clearly cataclysmic regional and international consequences.

Finally, American francophobia is abhorrent; it is expressed in a rhetoric that is reminiscent of the worst moments of that great country's history. In Washington and New York, I have met editorial writers, intellectuals, and neoconservative leaders, who seem to think quite sincerely that France, a feminine nation if such exists, Venus, is the worst of contemporary rogue states. But French anti-Americanism, that political passion which, as we never sufficiently remember, appeared in France in the political spectrum of the French Fascists in 1930, that ideological frenzy that ill masks feelings as questionable as the hatred of Tocquevillian democracy, the unavowed disdain for an artificial country founded on the fiction of a quasi-Rousseauist social contract, the yearning for true communities rooted in a soil, a race, a common memory, and finally the fantasy of a cosmopolitan country living under a Jewish lobby, French anti-Americanism, then, attracts the worst, and its seductions will be all the more dangerous if a symbolic stop, coming from up high, is not put to it very quickly.

Thus, the urgency for reconciliation.

An obligation, political and moral this time, to fly to the rescue of Mars ensnared.

In these past fifty years, France and America have known and overcome other disputes: the Suez crisis, leaving NATO, views on Phnom Penh, Bizerte, and Algeria, and I am surely skipping some. This crisis is neither the most profound nor the most seriously motivated of the ones our countries have gone through and there is no reason whatsoever why we should have greater trouble getting through this one.

Besides, it has already been accomplished in a way.

We are allies of the Americans in their struggle against the al-Qaeda terrorists.

With my own eyes I have seen French commandos side by side with the British and the Americans patrol the border of Afghanistan and Pakistan in pursuit of Bin Laden.

But we have to go farther.

Instead of continuing to the tune of that famous "giving Iraqi power back to the Iraqis themselves," which for the time being is only the other name of a subterfuge and which, if one were to reach that point, would serve no purpose other than to give the power to the Shiites, indeed, to hasten the return of Saddam's supporters, we should find a way to reinforce the Americans.

In the face of the requirements of the common fight against the new army of terrorist crime, we must, without delay, give a concrete meaning to those articles, speeches or interviews in this book, in which our communal destiny with America is confirmed—and, if they do not do so, we must suggest the terms and details of a new great Alliance to our partners.

Do we invite the hundred or thousand American opinion makers to come to France, a fraction of whom blindly believes that France is a country where synagogues are burned?

Do we set up a great Franco-American Commission modeled on the one that exists with Russia and the others?

Do we send the masterpieces from the Louvre to the Metropolitan Museum?

Do we rely on those who on the other side of the Atlantic have kept a cool head and will come back to do business tomorrow?

Do we dare to create a Euro-Arab army corps and send it into the field, a body that would have the triple merit of soothing the Americans, of internationalizing the Iraqi question, and of reminding the moderate Arab countries that the making of a democracy in the region is their business, too?

The future lasts a long time and it is worth persevering in a policy of world equilibrium in which the concern with the world's multi-polarity would not distance us from our essential alliances.

A FINAL WORD:

I know very well that no diplomacy, no matter how ambitious, can feel accountable for all the world's afflictions.

And I appreciate that Villepin, like any great Minister of Foreign Affairs, was obliged for the past two years to focus his strengths and efforts on those issues of the moment where he felt, rightly or wrongly, that he could be of influence.

Nonetheless, I do regret the absence of certain themes and places in this volume.

I regret having found but a scarce echo of the other, terrible, senseless, sometimes incomprehensible wars that are ravaging Africa, for example, and which I know are present in the mind of the President of the Republic and his Minister, the author.

In a word, I regret that the country that in the very end was able to bring the international community to support the Bosnian cause and then, more recently, successfully lead an operation of political and diplomatic mediation in Côte d'Ivoire as it was laid to waste, cannot find the same drive to carry its weight to end the war in Burundi or southern Sudan. I am dreaming of a true and "great policy" that would also connect with the fate of those faceless and helpless dead, whose primary mistake was to have lived in absolutely forsaken lands and who have departed from universal History, so to speak.

Who would be better justified than a country such as France, which remembers its historic responsibility in the Rwandan genocide, to announce, indeed to attempt to impede, the new genocide that threatens Bujumbura?

If our country, which is one of those where the memory of the Shoah is most vividly maintained, does not worry about the fate of the animist and Christian Nuba Mountain populations that have been exterminated by the Khartoum Islamists, who will?

And what about Angola? And what about Congo? And the horrifying war in Sri Lanka that causes as many deaths each week as the entire second Intifada did in two years?

Well then, Mr. Minister, let us make another effort to be truly universalist.

Long live that France that would be faithful to the best of its vocation by resolutely and, if I may say so, generously siding with those the world has forgotten.

France, homeland of the stateless. France, land of the echo of martyrdom of the nameless, the uncounted, the dead without record or grave, utterly scorned by the community of nations. That is my wish. I would like it to be the wish of this book's author as well.

DREAMS THAT NO MONEY CAN BUY

BY NORMAN MAILER

"The U.S. now feels like two nations, and Iraq is there to remind us daily of our surrealistic hubris."

Norman MAILER (United States)

Norman Mailer, whose novel The Naked and the Dead *made him internationally famous in 1948, has written numerous books about American politics, such as* Armies of the Night *(1968). He was president of the American PEN Center from 1986 to 1989. His most recent book is* The Spooky Art *(2003), a collection of articles on writing.*

Half of the nation is outraged over the lies that embedded us in Iraq.

For those whose pride in America runs deep, this sense of alienation from our country is full of woe, sharp as a divorce. The U.S. now feels like two nations, and Iraq is there to remind us daily of our surrealistic hubris. Confident we could bring American-style democracy to the Middle East, we proceeded to ignore an entrenched horde of Islamic mullahs who see American democracy as the literal embodiment of Satan.

So, why did Bush & Co. go to war? The probable answer is that an escape was needed from our problems at home. Joblessness gave no sign of diminishing, and corporate greed had been caught mooning its corrupt buttocks onto every front page. The Catholic Church was looking to overcome a paucity of young seminarians even as it staggered under a horde of ghastly lawsuits. The FBI was badly spattered by connections to a Mafia killer, Whitey Bulger, and to a KGB mole, high in the Bureau, the extreme right-winger Robert Hanssen. The CIA had become much too recognizable as an immense intelligence agency whose case officers did not speak Arabic. The stock market was offering intermittent signs that it might gurgle down to the bottom of the bowl. An easy war looked then to be George W. Bush's best solution. What he needed and what he got was a media jamboree that provided our sweet dose of patriotic ecstasy. At the time, we did not know that we had just entered a perceptual system designed to serve as a stand-in for reality. Bush would give us *The Twin Towers, Part 2—America's Revenge*. We had all seen Part 1—the audacity of the terrorists, the monumental viciousness of the attempt, and its exceptional filmic success—who will ever forget the collapse of those monoliths? The TV viewer had been overpowered by the kind of horror that belongs to dreams. One was witnessing what seemed a video game on a cosmic scale. The exploitation film had finally come alive! Two gleaming corporate castles disintegrated before our eyes. Two airplanes did it. David had struck Goliath, and David was on the wrong side. The event had gone right into the nervous system of America but Bush now had his mighty mission, and he knew the game that would handle it—Virtual Reality.

Virtual Reality is built on whatever parameters have been laid into it. You are, for instance, steering a car on a video screen. Roads and road obstacles loom up as you take the vehicle down a winding mountain road. Suddenly, a truck comes around a narrow turn. Video-wise, there is no choice. You have to run off the road. Whereupon you plunge down a hill, avoid a large tree, and manage to twist to a stop before a stone wall. It all happened on video, but to a degree, you were able to choose your moves. You had to exercise enough manual skill to keep from being wiped out on any of these traps. Your prowess in the game could be measured by your ability to skid to a stop before you slammed into the stone wall. The pre-designed situations, plus the responses permitted within the limits of the game, measured your success or failure. Virtual Reality is a closed system.

In life, we encounter not only parameters but chaos. Closed systems look to forbid unexpected patterns, confusion, and all that seems meaningless. They declare what the nature of reality can be, and allow for no other. In that sense, Communism was Virtual Reality and religious fundamentalism is still another foray into a totally structured system. You are free to make no choices other than the ones allowed you in advance. Obviously, it helps to live in such a matrix if you believe the parameters are established by a higher authority.

Ergo, Bush's decision to invade Iraq came from the Lord. Virtual Reality decided which conclusions we would obtain before we went in. We had all the scenarios in hand. We were prepared for everything but chaos.

Given our human distaste for chaos, Virtual Reality is the choice of every ethical system that is not interested in lively and difficult questions, especially if they lead to even livelier and more difficult questions. The emphasis is always to go back to the answer you had before you started.

So, Bush laid out the parameters. There was a hideous country out there led by an evil madman. This monster possessed huge weapons of mass destruction. But we Americans, a brave and militant band of angels, were ready to battle our way up to the heavens. We would forestall him. That was our duty. Safeguard our land and all other deserving lands from such evil.

Stocked with new heroes and new dragons, he was quick to sense that his presentation would be lapped up by half the nation—all those good Americans who were longing for the pleasure of being able to cheer for America again. He turned church-going into high drama. One could offer prayers up to George W's adventure. 9/11 had transmogrified him from a yahoo out of Yale to an awesome angel. We were in the war against evil. A spiritual adventure, full of slam-bang.

Truth, it may have been Bush's political genius to recognize that the U.S. public would rather live with Virtual Reality than reality. For the latter, out there on the sweaty hoof, bristled with questions, and there were no quick answers. Whereas Virtual Reality gave you American Good versus Satanic Evil—boss entertainment! Evil was now easy to recognize! Everything from Islamic terrorists to hincty Frenchmen. Freedom Fries! Be it said that TV advertising with its investiture into the nerves and sinews of our American senses had long been serving as the midwife to bring Virtual Reality into our lives—all those decades of sensuous promises in the commercials.

We are at one of the major turns in our history. It is possible that the Republican and Democratic parties are at the edge of major transitions, an upheaval of ideologies, a schism in each of our two major political configurations that will bend every one of our notions to Left or to Right.

For close to three-quarters of a century, ever since FDR, the Democratic party has been internationalist. So were most of the Republicans. The power of their corporate center enabled them to withstand intense isolationist sentiments in their own ranks.

All that has altered. Since the Second World War, the success of the Corporate Economy has encouraged a vanity that the Corporation is a virtuous body. One manifestation of this moral superiority is its physical presence. The world is now teeming with its aesthetically neutered monuments—precisely those high-rise hotels and offices that surround every major airport and capitol in the world, those monotonous, glassy behemoths coming forth as the virtuous architecture of the new corporate religion, an El Dorado of technology.

One fundamental error has begun to rock the globe. It was assumed by us that the most powerful of these corporate entities, that is to say, America, knew what was best for the rest of the world. The U.S. was ready to solve every nation's problem, all of them, all the way from Old Europe to the flea- and fly-bitten turpitudes of the Third World.

It could be remarked that the men who set sail with Columbus in 1492 had more idea of where they were going. The best to be said for the gung-ho *capitalistas* of the Bush administration is that they taught us all over again how extreme vanity is all you need to sail right off the edge of the world.

You cannot bring democracy to tyranny by conquering it. Democracy can be neither injected nor imposed. It comes into existence through a rite of passage. It has achieved its liberty by the actions of its own martyrs, rebels, and long-enduring believers. It is not a system, it is an ennoblement. Democracy must come from within. Brought into oppressed nations by way of external force, it collides with all the habits that tormented population was obliged to develop, those humiliating compromises that came from submitting to ugly and superior force. Now, all of that has been jammed into an abruptly ground-up gruel of chopped psychic reflexes, even as a strange people arrived from outside in mighty machines with guns attached, new people whose motives one could not trust. How could one? The prevailing law within a tyranny is to trust nobody. There have been too many shameful adaptations within oneself, as well as decades of long-swallowed rage. The recollection of humiliations early and late have been incorporated into the psychic core. Existence has been imprisoned too long in the Virtual Reality imposed by the tyrant.

We did not have an administration who could comprehend that. We came in with our guns, our smiles, and our assumption that democracy was there to hand over to these Iraqis. Our gift! Our form of Virtual Reality, superior to yours!

The truth is we don't belong in any foreign country. We are not wise enough, honest enough, nor a good enough nation to tell the rest of the world how to live—indeed, such a nation has never existed. But even if we were just so fabulous, so unique, other humans would still not be ready to savage their national pride for the dubious joy of receiving *our* crusade against evil. We would do well to become a little more aware of Christian militancy that marches into war against any evil but its own.

The time has come to solve our problems, our ongoing American problems. We have a direct need to focus on ourselves over the coming span of years and thereby become less displaced from reality For we are the most mighty of all the nations, and we are secure. Despite all, we are relatively secure. We can absorb new terrorist attacks if they come. We do not need military invasions into foreign lands to protect us. From 1968 through the year 2000, the world suffered an average of 424 terrorist incidents a year, and each year, that resulted in an average of 300 deaths. In 2001, however, came 9/11. Three thousand lives were lost. A huge number. Yet in that same period from 1968 to 2001, Americans suffered more than 40,000 deaths each twelve-month from auto accidents. If one takes the ratio for the prime year 2001, the proportion of 40,000 to 3,000 is still 13 to 1. If it be asked why such focus is now being put on automobile mortalities, it is because such tragedies are not without analogy to losing one's life to a terrorist. You leave your home, you kiss your wife goodbye, and you are dead ten minutes or ten hours later. To those who are left to grieve, there seems not enough reason to such death. Not enough logic! More than any other event in our lives, our own demise excites just such a need for logic in those who remain. Lung cancer, we know, kills 154,000 people a year. That is near to four times more than automobiles, but we can comprehend that. We are ready to decide that cigarettes have something to do with it. But death without any grip upon the explanation bothers people more. It does no good to tell ourselves that 2,400,000 people die each year in America. We are fixed on the 3,000 lost humans of 9/11. They seem more important. In truth, they have been so important to America that we have come to what may be a point of no return. Will we continue to protect our freedoms, or will we conclude that all effort must go to saving ourselves from every conceivable form of terrorist attack? The second course pursued to conclusion will lead to nothing less than a unique variety of fascism. Brown-shirts or black-shirts will not be needed. Our only certainty is that whatever it will be called, "fascism" will not be the word. Should Bush still remain in office, we can count on Virtual Reality to suggest the face of the new regime. Of course, this is the essence of fascism—one must give the populace a version of cause and effect that has very little to do with how things are.

The question, then, is whether we will be brave enough to dispense with foreign adventures. We do know, or we should know, that any nation which would look to attack us would face the might of our armed forces. Any nuclear attack that originated in North Korea or Iran would be an absolute disaster for either. Our power to retaliate is awesome. When it comes to terrorist attacks, however. we are also at the mercy of building good and decent relations with the rest of the developed world. Military forays are not the answer—you do not wipe out terrorists with airplanes and tanks. Rather, we will be obliged to use—that dread word!—collective efforts to build an international police force ready to guard against major attacks comparable to 9/11. Even the best of such collaborative organizations will not prevent small terrorist acts, any more than a local police force can root out all local crime. But, to be able to inhibit a terrorist effort that could be equal to the demolition of the Twin Towers, a global police system with a world-wide network of informants can be developed. It is one thing for terrorists to succeed in suicide bombings; it is another for them to find the necessary cadres, skills, and materials to bring off an immense coup against the sophisticated forces of proscription that can be put in place. We will never be able to prevent all minor attacks. It is illogical to be ready to sacrifice our remaining liberties in search of a total security that will never come to pass. Terrorism, in parallel to cancer, is in total rebellion to established human endeavor. If democracy ever did begin to work in Iraq, the incidence of terrorist acts would, doubtless, increase. Suicide bombers are stimulated by the presence of the enemy, whether that presence is foreign soldiers or a political system that is anathema to one's beliefs. If Islam ever took over America, our fundamentalists would be the first to become terrorists.

It comes to one thing: our freedom now depends on what we learned in elementary school. We must live with arithmetic! Over the last three years, 850 Israelis have been killed by suicide bombers. That, by rough calculation, comes to one Israeli in 20,000 for each year of those three years. If we in America were to suffer at the same rate, we would, given our population which is fifty times as great as Israel, suffer approximately 14, 000 deaths a year. That comes to one-third of our American loss of life from driving automobiles. Short of a major disaster, we are not likely to face 14,000 such deaths a year. We do not have the daily problems that Israelis have with Palestinians and Palestinians with Israelis. We have more freedom to explore into what we can become as a nation.

The time has come for us to understand that not everyone to the right is on the hunt for more money, more power, more conquest, and more worship of the flag, Not every conservative is for suburbs scourged by the blank-faced orgies of suburban malls, nor is every conservative ready to cheer every corporation that puts its name on a new stadium for professional athletes. Not every conservative believes that our mission as a nation was to needle the serum of democracy into nations who have no vein for democracy. No, there are conservatives who believe that the U.S. has been boiling up an unholy brew under the lid of the corporate pot. There are conservatives who believe that educating our children is degenerating into a near to autistic mess, and there are conservatives who do not think that all the answers to crime can be solved by building more prisons, no, there are conservatives who would argue, just like Democrats, that no matter how much we spend on our schools, it doesn't seem to be working all that well, there are even conservatives who have sensitive feelings on these matters—as sensitive as the Democrats', by God. Yet, neither side knows how to speak to the other. Still, this variety of conservative, decent not bigoted, open to discussion rather than given over, body and soul, to talk-radio, is also aghast at the uneasy but real possibility that George W. Bush might be the worst and most unqualified President America has ever had, yes, such conservatives, whatever their number, are in the same state of inanition and ideological impotence as all those Democrats who cannot believe where the country is going. Let us as Democrats consider the possibility that such conservatives can also be part of a future where Democrats draw their political sustenance from the best ideas of Left and Right. At present, that is not easy to believe, but there are new political conceptions in the air, ideas that have not been calcified into the iron masks of ideology that sit upon the elephant's head and the donkey's back. This country was created, after all, by the amazing notion (for the time) that there was more good than evil in the mass of human beings, and so, those human beings, once given the liberty not only to vote, but the power to learn to think, might be able to show that more good than evil could emerge from such freedom. It was an incredible concept. All society until then had assumed that the masses were incapable of exercising a wise voice and so must be controlled from the top down.

That question has remained alive through the two centuries and twenty-odd years of our national existence, and often it has seemed that the answer was affirmative. Now, doubt is with us again. In 2004, we will face what could become the most important election in our history. Since our candidate will never have funds to equal the bursting coffers of an opposition inflamed by power, bad conscience, and all the Virtual Reality of religious fundamentalism itself, the contest will have to be an electoral war between money, moral righteousness, mental restriction and paranoia washing down on us from their side, versus our hope that moral revulsion still exists in more than half of our voting public, enough to let us set forth, despite all our own impurity, to overthrow the Colossus on the other bank. May our wit be clean, our indignation genuine, and our ideas new enough and fine enough to pierce the caterwaul of political advertising that will look to flood our campaign down the river and over the falls.

APPOINTMENT IN SAMARA

BY FERNANDO SAVATER

"...the worst is not that the explicit motives for the war were false, but rather that the authentic ones, which we could discern behind them, are more disturbing."

Fernando SAVATER (Spain)

Professor of philosophy at Complutense University in Madrid, he works with the daily newspaper El Pais *and is general editor of the review* Claves de Razon Practica *together with Javier Pradera. He is the author of a novel,* Caronte aguarda, *and of many essays, among them* Ethics for Amador, *which was translated into thirty languages. He has just published* El valor de elegir (The Value of Education), Mira por donde, *an autobiography, and an essay on Borges,* La ironia metafisica.

Those in the know (but Allah still knows more) tell the story of a servant in Baghdad who one day went to the Caliph of the faithful:

"Lord, I have just met Death in the marketplace and he made a threatening gesture to me. I think he is coming for me. Please allow me to flee to Samara where my parents live, so that I can hide there and he won't find me."

The Caliph granted his servant permission to leave immediately for Samara. A little later, as we was walking in his garden, the Caliph met Death and asked him:

"Why did you threaten my servant?"

Death answered: "It was not a threatening gesture I made but one of surprise. Surprise to find your servant in Baghdad this morning when I have an appointment with him in Samara tonight."

It is precisely there in Samara that the marines freed several North American soldiers who were prisoners of the Iraqis. It is one of the last episodes in this lightning war (but lightning, which is beautiful, is the visible part of the thunderbolt, which is deadly and cruel), whose aftermath is even more problematic and can undoubtedly become still more harmful than the actual military operation. At the time, I carefully read the arguments that justified or excused the invasion of Iraq by the Anglo-American coalition such as they were explained by the intellectuals whose analyses I often share and whose integrity I do not doubt: Emilio Lamo de Espinosa, Michael Ignatieff, Adam Michnick, Michael Waltzer, and Pascal Bruckner. In all honesty, they did not manage to convince me that this armed conflict was inevitable or even commendable. In contrast to the first Gulf War, this one seemed unnecessary to me and I certainly do not think that it responded properly to the formal requirements of international law. Contrary to the one in Kosovo, legally not any less dubious, I do not believe that it obeyed an ethnic necessity either.

The reasons given for its being acceptable were feeble or unbelievable: for example, the existence of weapons of mass destruction. From the start, everything seemed to indicate that Iraq would be invaded not for having possessed any weapons but precisely for not having had any, which facilitated the invasion. Today, only the faithful endowed with an invulnerable *Sancta simplicitas,* or selfishly pretending to be thus endowed, still hope that some stockpile of diabolical arms will be discovered in Iraq. It is beyond any doubt that Saddam Hussein and his peers constituted a danger, but a danger for the Iraqis themselves above all and not exactly for the bordering countries and of course not for the United States or Europe. It is difficult to accept that the best solution for liberating the Iraqis from the dictator was to bomb them, destroy their towns, at the same time crippling all their political and social institutions, and thereby creating the present state of chaos in that defenseless country. Not to mention that having challenged the credibility of the United Nations and supported the dissension in Europe are greater risks for the Western powers than the one that the tyrannical Saddam represented in his time.

However, the worst is not that the explicit motives for the war were false, but rather that the authentic ones, which we could discern behind them, are more disturbing. The attacks of 11 September convinced the present American administration that it should reorganize the world in its own image and to its own liking, without letting itself be drawn in by multilateral considerations that take the plurality of legitimate interests into account, which must be enacted today so that the planet's society can attain security through a fair equilibrium. We once believed that the great political project of the twenty-first century—once the tension of the Cold War was eliminated—would be the consolidation of the supranational institutions invented in the twentieth century, as deficient in results as they were promising in intention, and their being made operative in all areas. But apparently the government of those who hold sway over Bush prefer accelerating the liquidation of all these institutions by reducing them to a humanitarian, wishful, and begging role, while he replaces the international political spaces with the boards of directors of great corporations and with the categorical directives of the Pentagon. The greatest military force in history seems to be less disposed to backing up the universal expansion of democracy and its rights than to grandly asserting its own interests, which we will all be obliged to identify with humanity's progress. The outlook could not be more disconcerting.

After having witnessed the enormous demonstrations against the war in almost every European country, it is obvious that in their time many people across the entire globe felt this same alarm. It is without a doubt a good civic sign that these demonstrations were held (the same thing can be said, for instance, about the movements critical of globalization), since a democratic system that automatically *acquiesces* is deprived of its best political substance. But the intention that must be assumed in these protests—it is always preferable to see masses take to the streets to demand peace rather than to support a war—was more promising than the displayed slogans and texts. Declaring disapproval of wars and weapons satisfies courting the soul but it does not force the intelligence to any arduous exertion. In fact, it does not even require us to reflect upon the relationship between our way of living or our values and the massacres of the past, anymore than it asks us to question ourselves about the appropriate struggle against those who threaten, while they claim to be the followers not of the divine but of still worse forms of despotism, which we appreciate. If we want to have a clear image of the international state of the world, today's occupied Baghdad offers us an adequate metaphor with its unscrupulous plunderers, its pro-Saddam terrorists lying in ambush, its apathetic marines concerned only with self-defense (becoming increasingly difficult each time), its boycotted humanitarian aid, its assassinated UN members, its attacks against moderate religious leaders, and so on. We are living in a global and planetary Baghdad, even though in the best of cases our countries inside the European Union enjoy the benefits of the State of rights and of judicial and police forces that guarantee these. As we see the embezzling Mafiosi or the suicide killers operate on television in the lawless global city, while the civil population and especially the weakest ones suffer the consequences of this turmoil daily, we demand (not really knowing of whom) that "somebody do something." Baghdad needs a police force that will allow for the reconstruction of its vital peaceful rhythm and its flouted liberties: laws that protect and guarantee civilization's rights, just as "someone" who, by righteous coercion, protects and guarantees the execution of these norms. On the global scale our need is the same. That is exactly what the supranational institutions promised without achieving it, not in Iraq, not in Palestine, and not in so many other places. Taking advantage of the empty power of these institutions (beginning with the UN, which in order to be effective, requires a fundamental democratic reform, sufficient financial resources equitably collected from all its members, as well as an army that is truly a deterrent), the imperial coalition, led by the present American administration, acts today merely on its own behalf. It is not enough to grumble or stamp one's feet against it, it is also absolutely necessary to expect the international bodies to be entirely relevant, otherwise we will always depend on the ideological whims and the economic interests of the strongest. In this endeavor, a politically united European community, with a respected and firm voice where global questions are concerned, is today as necessary as it is difficult to achieve.

In Spain, public opinion is to a large extent appalled by the arrogant and short-sighted attitude of its government that flew to assist the Anglo-American intervention. Perhaps it is my irascible character, but I am still not convinced of the pertinence of a "democracy without anger." Indignation, it seems to me, can sometimes be as profoundly democratic and even represent a form of civic health. By supporting Bush's policy and without any real national necessity, Aznar's executive compromised the civilian harmony of a state that has a serious internal problem of totalitarian terrorism with the threat of the ETA. I don't see what we gained by this, but what we are already losing seems obvious to me. Undoubtedly, comparing support from the nationalist groups for ETA crimes to the support for the Iraq war from the government (as some of the left wing parties did) is excessive, in view of the unquestionable character of the national laws contrasted with the debatable evanescence of international norms. But the political and moral distress of those who clutch on to these parallelisms does not excuse the rulers who incited them thereto by their carelessness. Spanish democracy found itself demolished by those who do not wish (nor know how) to improve it but who take advantage of its rifts. For instance: Euskaltelebista (the autonomous Basque television) refuses to back the campaign of Alava's institutions provided for by the constitution, seeing it as "political propaganda," but it shows the web site of the Basque government that offers the possibility of protesting against the war in Iraq. As in Baghdad, invaded and bombed, one sees the Mafia make a secret appearance and with a moral certificate of good behavior!

Just as in the tale of *A Thousand and One Nights*, Death has given a sign to our unjust and self-satisfied civilization, unsparing with fine words that nobody seeks to make prosper, even though many are ready to protest when they are not kept. But let us remember that it is useless to flee from Samara to escape death, because it is there in truth that it awaits us at night. Better yet, let us remember that the only tragedies that cannot be avoided are those we do not know how to or do not resolve to avoid.

FALSE START AND NEW ORDER

BY SIMON SERFATY

"The quagmire is no longer just in Iraq or the Middle East, it is also at the core of the Atlantic Alliance, affected by the imperial temptation of its most powerful partner, as well as at the core of the European Union . . . . "

Simon SERFATY (United States)

Director of European Studies at the Center for Strategic & International Studies (CSIS) where he holds the Zbigniew Brzezinski Chair for Geopolitical Studies, he is also Professor of American Foreign Policy at Old Dominion University (ODU) in Norfolk.

"It is important," Dominique de Villepin declared a few weeks after his arrival at the Quai d'Orsay, "that we have a relationship of confidence, of frankness—abruptly so if necessary—with the United States."[11] By engaging in a "diplomacy of change and action" based on the ability of the French government to "act as one," he satisfied two of the three criteria he had set himself. A frank and abrupt relationship—but, unfortunately, developed in the climate of mistrust that surrounded the false start regarding Iraq in 2002 and that opened a period of conflict in 2003 threatening the anticipated new order, both on the level of bilateral relations and of transatlantic relations.

FALSE START

On May 10, 1967, at the end of a ministers' meeting dealing with the entry of Great Britain into the Common Market, Charles de Gaulle exclaimed in his usual manner:

"Eventually they will defer to what France wants. That is not an unpleasant situation.[12]"

In Iraq, France seems to have found itself in a comparable position. In essence, the French government was not wrong.

[11] "France wants a relationship of candor with the United States," statement by Dominique de Villepin recorded by François Bonnet and Claifre Tréan. Le Monde, 30 July 2002.
[12] Cited by Alain Peyrefitte. C'était de Gaulle, p. 272. Paris: Fayard, 2000.

In January 2003, the threat from Iraq was not imminent and the deployment of UN inspectors, reinforced by the presence of American forces in the region, confined the Baghdad regime to a cage that rendered it harmless on the whole. The need to "take time" was confirmed by the necessity of focusing our— American and allied—resources on other priorities, tests of our ability to get rid of terrorism both in confrontation and in reconciliation in Afghanistan and, on the other hand, in the Middle East where the conflict between Palestinians and Israelis, the main source of the cultural unrest between the West and a component of Islam, was on the verge of a tragic explosion. In short, from the very start France understood the need to prepare for the post-war period better than its American ally did. Liberation is one thing—the first step in a four-step dance, followed by pacification, reconstruction, and possibly reconciliation. Changing regimes without knowing beforehand what will follow is risking a quagmire in which it is easy to disappear but from which it is difficult to extricate oneself. This was Villepin's message when, early in another debate in the UN, he spoke of "the temptation [...] to reiforce the security measures without reclaiming the political field."[13]

With the certain knowledge of present events, it is a pity that the logic of this was not heard. Since the end of combat on May 1, 2003, the American power, which is unparalleled, is today in tow of events that it neither knew how to anticipate or how to control. Consequently, George W. Bush was reduced to solicit international assistance in the fall of 2003 to extricate himself and the rest of the world from the Iraqi quagmire. Listening to both him and his Vice President Richard Cheney, one would have preferred rebuking them. And yet, the situation is far more "unpleasant" than it was when De Gaulle pursued a nonrisk strategy since, in the face

---

[13] "Irreversible Gestures Needed," interview with Dominique de Villepin. Statement recorded by Alain Franchon and Bruno Philip, reported in *Le Monde*, 23 August 2003.
[14] Quoted in the *Washington Post*, 20 September 2003.

of the Cold War Soviet danger, the protection of the Alliance, to which France remained loyal, could be seen as an asset. This time the danger is by no means insignificant. It lies in the prospect of a serious failure that, even if it is to be attributed to American errors of judgment in the future, will still be a failure whose responsibility goes beyond the mere members of the coalition. For in Iraq, to use the phrase of Albert Camus, we are all "penitent-judges": the sentences we pronounce are also those we will have to suffer.

Thus, Senator Ted Kennedy maintained that the war was a "fraud"—okay, its only a liberal Kennedy who can easily be ignored, he's almost deserving of being sent off to France.... But the criticism becomes more serious when it is expressed by General Wesley Clark, the victor in Kosovo, a supporter of Nixon and Reagan in his younger years, who today is a candidate for the presidency of the United States, seeking the nomination of the Democratic party.

"I would never have voted in favor of the war," he confirmed on September 19, 2003, the day after he declared his candidacy.

"There was no imminent threat. There was no need for a preventive war. I would have voted for the kind of lever needed to come to a diplomatic solution, an international solution challenging Saddam Hussein."[14] At the UN, Wesley Clark would have sided with France and its Minister of Foreign Affairs.

On both sides of the Atlantic, in a dangerous era of conflicts and rifts, our respective attitudes reflect an atmosphere of mistrust, indeed, of hostility.[15] Beyond our differences in analysis, it is the tone that contributed to the false start on 8 November 2002, when the Security Council unanimously adopted a resolution of "change and action" developed by Dominique de Villepin and his American counterpart,

---

[15] See, by the author, *La France vue par les États-Unis*: Réflections sur la francophobie à Washington. Paris: IFRI, 2002; "Les bourbiers," Le Monde, 4–5 October 2003; *La Tentation impériale*. Paris: Odile Jacob, 2004.

Colin Powell. Was this the price of "frankness" or the result of an approach that in the spring of 2003 was frequently too "abrupt"? What wonderful things could have happened for Europe thanks to French diplomacy that finally enjoyed the trust of the United States! It is understandable that it is not a priority of France to be acknowledged in Europe as the privileged ally of the United States, which was confirmed on 8 November 2002 after Resolution 1441 passed in the UN Security Council. But it may also be pointed out that for the twelve weeks after the resolution was adopted American diplomacy took a rather bad, quite inexplicable course before the brutal rupture early in 2003.

In the end, however, who is blackmailing whom? In the drama that is unfolding in Iraq, not just at this moment but for the past twenty years—and in the even worse tragedy that threatens to shatter the Middle East—an influential France in a united Europe would need to operate within credible bilateral and transatlantic partnerships in order to assert itself in common actions. This way a better management of differences could be introduced, differences that seem to separate us more on the level of action than on the level of objectives. The new breach between France and the United States, then, was not compensated for by any political rapprochement in Europe while, although more divided than ever in its decisions and choices than at any other moment in its communal history, the latter is presently directing itself at its "aim." In January 2003, even if it was inconceivable to follow the United States into Iraq, it should have been possible to avoid hindering them by not organizing the "coalition of the unwilling," an approach that, after the fighting ended, stood in the way of the unity required to stabilize Iraq and launch the peace process for the Middle East again.

NEW ORDER?

It is completely understandable that the imperial temptation that has been driving the United States since the end of the Cold War and even more since the events of September 11, 2001 should provoke anxiety in France and all over Europe. By definition, America is an imperial power because of its means, its interests, its influence, and henceforth by its zeal. This is neither the fruit of an ambition nor the result of a plan. Some people are already mentioning the American imperial venture as a stillborn empire, briefly noticed in Afghanistan, but hereafter challenged in Iraq, crippled in the Middle East, and threatened by financial ruin in its obsessive hunt for terrorists: four wars, all bogged down, without counting the real risks of half a dozen other conflicts: in Iran, North Korea, Colombia, Taiwan, Pakistan, and of course in Palestinian territories, and all of them likely to explode depending on the harm done by terrorists or the bad calculations by the governments in place.

But we shouldn't have any illusions. American power is too great not to impose itself—whether by its presence or its absence. If it is the ambition of "Europe-as-power" to exercise its influence by counterbalancing America, this is an ambition not ready to be realized. If it is the vocation of "Europe-as-influence" to teach institutional classes established to discipline the imperial power, the lessons will not be heard.

In and of themselves, the terrorist attacks of September 11 did not really change the world. But to the extent that they changed the world view of the Americans—the vision they have of their allies and friends, of their power and the intentions of their enemies—this may actually be enough to change the world. The changes in perception of the Americans concerning their own security, but also those of the rest of the world concerning America, make the definition "of a framework of methods and dialogue" necessary, as the French minister asked in August 2003. It would be a framework that comes forth from a transatlantic charter—and why not?—whose elaboration cannot be imagined without an agreement on Iraq beforehand.[16] In other words, it is precisely the future of the Alliance that, once again, is part of the ongoing debate for another UN resolution on Iraq.

Some like to imagine that these conditions are limited only to the American president of the moment—George W., not well liked, uneducated in matters of importance, and too sensitive to the irresponsible convictions of the neoconservatives around him. That, too, is an illusion. This analysis, which is common in Europe, corroborates the strategic difference that separates Americans and Europeans whom History has placed in different time zones. In France and other European states, 9-11 seems to refer to the events of November 9, 1991—the collapse of the Berlin Wall: the "landscape after the battles" is that of the end of a century of total wars, the end of slaughter, and the integration of national sovereignties in the disciplinary context of institutions that presumably forced Europe to rethink and reconstruct itself. Will the Kantian dream henceforth define the law-and-order landscape of which France would be the herald and Jacques Chirac the hero? In the United States and for a large section of the Americans who express themselves politically against Bush Junior, "9-11" refers to the events of September 11, 2001—to a territorial assault that expressed a Hobbesian nightmare for a country that thanks to a protective geography had thus far escaped it. When it is a question of killing in order not to be killed, one may wish to be multilateralist, but anyone who can is unilateralist.

---

[16] 11th Conference of Ambassadors, Opening Address. Paris, 28 August 2003.

But let us stop analyzing the past. Dominique de Villepin insists that to pursue "the roads of reconstruction," as he writes on September 13, 2003, we need "to forget the quarrels of the past" and accept Iraq as a "task to be shared." At the crossroads—one Americanized West or two, one Europe or two?—the prevailing strategy that has been tempting the United States since the end of the Cold War is badly adapted to the multipolar plans mentioned by Jacques Chirac. In fact, Condoleeza Rice finds the "admiration" with which multipolarity is evoked "troubling," as if it were a "good thing" that deserved to be "sought after as an end in itself."[17]

Rice's reaction to the idea of a multipolar world, probably inevitable in some more or less distant future, is surprising unless it is set in a context in which the predominance of the United States itself is judged as "a good thing," and an "end in itself." At the present time, succumbing to the imperial temptation of the United States requires that those who comply with it grant it credibility as a proof of lasting commitment, whatever the price and the consequences. That is not the strong point of American public opinion, known for its impatience and its mood swings. That is precisely the reason why "the dialogue balanced between regional poles," mentioned by Chirac in December 1999, would be worthwhile, particularly if it included a strong European union, as he emphasized at his meeting with Tony Blair in Saint-Malo. For it is only in the strengthening of the American pole by the European pole that the United States will be able to build its credibility in view of its tenacity in actions that start off as easy but are more difficult to pursue. Was that what Dominique de Villepin meant when, on August 28, 2003, he stressed that "in no case does the French vision of multipolarity aim at generating competition, but rather responsibility, stability, and initiative"?

---

[17] Remarks by C. Rice at the Institute for International and Strategic Studies (IISS) in London, 26 June 2003. Speech by President Jacques Chirac for the 20th Anniversary of the Institut Français des Relations Internationales (IFRI) in Paris, 4 November 1999.

As we await the confirmation of this view of things—and, above all, let Europe affirm itself as enough of a "counterbalance" to present an "equivalent" rather than an "opposite direction"—it would be preferable to follow one another so as to have an influence rather than to impede each other and not gain the influence sought. The call for a transatlantic easing of tension responds to a sense of urgency: it is impossible to play down the importance of what is at stake. The quagmire is no longer just in Iraq or the Middle East, it is also at the core of the Atlantic Alliance, affected by the imperial temptation of its most powerful partner, as well as at the core of the European Union, upset by the pressures of the calendar to which its members must submit. To work our way out of these predicaments, we need to go back to a very simple idea: in the absence of common policies, there could be complementary policies with a view to common although partial interests.

In order to accomplish this, both sides should play three cards: unity, solidarity, and complementarity. Without its unity, Europe cannot have a dialogue on equal footing with its mentor, which is much too big and much too powerful for any single European state, whichever that may be. Being in a *ménage à trois* with Russia so as to assert its power goes counter to European history. It would be a grave mistake that would risk blowing up the large family of the European Union. It would be better to play the card of transatlantic solidarity, which could be rethought more effectively in a relative equilibrium of forces between a Europe able to be influential and an America available for dialogue. And both should be more aware of their respective weaknesses in order to stimulate a partnership that would express itself in complementary actions when the latter cannot be pursued in complete agreement. For, in the end, the lesson taught by the events of 11 September 2001 and their impact on the bilateral and transatlantic relationships during the two years that followed, seem to signify—taking our respective strengths and weaknesses into account—that we should all try to do everything even if it continues to be impossible to do everything together.

THE GREAT ATLANTIC DIVIDE

BY SUSAN SONTAG

*"There has always been a latent antago-
nism between Europe and America, one
at least as complex and ambivalent as
that between parent and child."*

Susan SONTAG (United States)

Author of four novels, short stories, and several plays, her book
On Photography *received The National Book Award. She has just
published an essay,* Regarding the Pain of Others. *In 2003, she
was awarded the Peace Prize of the German Book Trade. "The
Great Atlantic Divide" is an excerpt from her acceptance speech.*

Irate, dismissive statements about Europe, certain European countries, are now the common coin of American political rhetoric; and here, at least in the rich countries on the western side of the continent, anti-American sentiments are more common, more audible, more intemperate than ever. What is this conflict? Does it have deep roots? I think it does.

There has always been a latent antagonism between Europe and America, one at least as complex and ambivalent as that between parent and child. America is a neo-European country and, until the last few decades, was largely populated by European peoples. And yet it is always the differences between Europe and America that have struck the most perceptive foreign observers: Alexis de Tocqueville, who visited the young nation in 1831 and returned to France to write *Democracy in America*, still, some hundred and seventy years later, the best book about my country, and D. H. Lawrence, who, eighty years ago, published the most interesting book ever written about American culture, his influential, exasperating *Studies in Classic American Literature*, both understood that America, the child of Europe, was becoming, or had become, the antithesis of Europe.

Rome and Athens. Mars and Venus. The authors of recent popular tracts promoting the idea of an inevitable clash of interests and values between Europe and America did not invent these antitheses. Foreigners brooded over them—and they provide the palette, the recurrent melody, in much of American literature throughout the 19th century, from James Fenimore Cooper and Ralph Waldo Emerson to Walt Whitman, Henry James, William Dean Howells, and Mark Twain. American innocence and European sophistication; American pragmatism and European intellectualizing; American energy and European world-weariness; American naïveté and European cynicism; American goodheartedness and European malice; American moralism and the European arts of compromise—you know the tunes.

You can choreograph them differently; indeed, they have been danced with every kind of evaluation or tilt for two tumultuous centuries. Europhiles can use the venerable antitheses to identify America with commerce-driven barbarism and Europe with high culture, while the Europhobes draw on a readymade view in which America stands for idealism and openness and democracy and Europe a debilitating, snobbish refinement. Tocqueville and Lawrence observed something fiercer: not just a declaration of independence from Europe, and European values, but a steady undermining, an assassination of European values and European power. "You can never have a new thing without breaking an old," Lawrence wrote. "Europe happened to be the old thing. America should be the new thing. The new thing is the death of the old." America, Lawrence divined, was on a Europe-destroying mission, using democracy—particularly cultural democracy, democracy of manners—as an instrument. And when that task is accomplished, America might well turn from democracy to something else. (What that might be is, perhaps, emerging now.)

The past is (or was) Europe, and America was founded on the idea of breaking with the past, which is viewed as encumbering, stultifying, and—in its forms of deference and precedence, its standards of what is superior and what is best—fundamentally undemocratic; or "elitist," the reigning current synonym. Those who speak for a triumphal America continue to intimate that American democracy implies repudiating Europe, and, yes, embracing a certain liberating, salutary barbarism. If, today, Europe is regarded by most Americans as more socialist than elitist, that still makes Europe, by American standards, a retrograde continent, obstinately attached to old standards: the welfare state. "Make it new" is not only a slogan for culture; it describes an ever-advancing, world-encompassing economic machine.

However, if necessary, even the "old" can be rebaptized as the "new."

It is not a coincidence that the strong-minded American Secretary of Defense tried to drive a wedge within Europe—distinguishing unforgettably between an "old" Europe (bad) and a "new" Europe (good). How did Germany, France, and Belgium come to be consigned to "old" Europe, while Spain, Italy, Poland, Ukraine, The Netherlands, Hungary, the Czech Republic, and Bulgaria find themselves part of "new" Europe? Answer: to support the United States in its present extensions of political and military power is to pass, by definition, into the more desirable category of the "new." Whoever is with us is "new."

All modern wars, even when their motives are the traditional ones, such as territorial aggrandizement or the acquisition of scarce resources, are cast as clashes of civilizations—culture wars—with each side claiming the high ground, and characterizing the other as barbaric. The enemy is invariably a threat to "our way of life," an infidel, a desecrator, a polluter, a defiler of higher or better values. The current war against the very real threat posed by militant Islamic fundamentalism is a particularly clear example. What is worth remarking is that a milder version of the same terms of disparagement underlie the antagonism between Europe and America. It should also be remembered that, historically, the most virulent anti-American rhetoric ever heard in Europe—consisting essentially in the charge that Americans are barbarians—came not from the so-called left but from the extreme right. Both Hitler and Franco repeatedly inveighed against an America (and a world Jewry) engaged in polluting European civilization with its base, business values.

Of course, much of European public opinion continues to admire American energy, the American version of "the modern." And, to be sure, there have always been American fellow-travelers of the European cultural ideals (one stands here before you), who find in the old arts of Europe a liberation and correction to the strenuous mercantilist biases of American culture. And there have always been the counterparts of such Americans on the European side: Europeans who are fascinated, enthralled, profoundly attracted to the United States, precisely because of its difference from Europe.

What the Americans see is almost the reverse of the Europhile cliché: they see themselves defending civilization. The barbarian hordes are no longer outside the gates. They are within, in every prosperous city, plotting havoc. The "chocolate-producing" countries (France, Germany, Belgium) will have to stand aside, while a country with "will"—and God on its side—pursues the battle against terrorism (now conflated with barbarism). According to Secretary of State Powell, it is ridiculous for old Europe (sometimes it seems only France is meant) to aspire to play a role in governing or administering the territories won by the coalition of the conqueror. It has neither the military resources nor the taste for violence nor the support of its cosseted, all-too-pacific populations. And the Americans have it right. Europeans are not in an evangelical—or a bellicose—mood.

So America now sees itself as the defender of civilization and Europe's savior, and wonders why Europeans don't get the point; and Europeans see Americans as a reckless warrior state—a description that the Americans return by seeing Europe as the enemy of America: only pretending, so runs rhetoric heard increasingly in the United States, to be pacifist, in order to contribute to the weakening of American power. France in particular is thought to be scheming to become America's equal, even its superior, in shaping world affairs— "Operation America Must Fail" is the name invented by a columnist in the *New York Times* to describe the French drive toward dominance—instead of realizing that an American defeat in Iraq will encourage "radical Muslim groups—from Baghdad to the Muslim slums of Paris" to pursue their jihad against tolerance and democracy.

It is hard for people not to see the world in polarizing terms (*them* and *us*) and these terms have in the past strengthened the isolationist theme in American foreign policy as much as they now strengthen the imperialist theme. Americans have got used to thinking of the world in terms of enemies. Enemies are somewhere else, as the fighting is almost always "over there," Islamic fundamentalism having replaced Russian and Chinese communism as the threat to "our way of life." And terrorist is a more flexible word than communist. It can unify a larger number of quite different struggles and interests. What this may mean is that the war will be endless—since there will always be some terrorism (as there will always be poverty and cancer); that is, there will always be asymmetrical conflicts in which the weaker side uses that form of violence, which usually targets civilians. American rhetoric, if not the popular mood, would support this unhappy prospect, for the struggle for righteousness never ends.

THE WAR AND EUROPE

BY TZVETAN TODOROV

"...a search for the truth is doomed if we convince ourselves in advance that everything must turn out well. Is the reign of law over force viable, or does it consist of an illusion, momentarily tempting but potentially misleading?"

Tzvetan TODOROV (France)

Director of Research at the CNRS (Centre National de la Recherche Scientifique), historian and philosopher, he has published many books, among them Mémoire du Mal, tentation du bien [Hope and Memory?], Devoirs et délices [Duties and Delights], Une vie de passeur [A Smuggler's Life], *an intellectual autobiography, and most recently* Le Nouveau Désordre mondial: Réflexions d'un Européen [The New World Disorder: Reflections of a European].

My goal here is not merely to comment on Dominique de Villepin's writings, but rather to reflect on certain aspects of French foreign policy as seen through the 2003 Iraq conflict.

The American strategy during this conflict has been criticized by a number of countries, including several of its allies—most notably France. The most common argument held that the United States was employing a politics of force, whereas international relations should obey the rule of law, represented in this case by the United Nations, the Security Council and its resolutions. On March 7, 2003, several days before the attacks began, the Minister of Foreign Affairs Dominique de Villepin addressed the Security Council: "Some believe that we can solve these problems by way of force and thus create a new order. This is not the conviction of France." On March 18, 2003, the night of the invasion, President Chirac, justifying his position in the Security Council, told the press that, in contrast to the United States, which wanted to "privilege force over the law," France "acted with the primacy of the law in mind, and by virtue of its conception of the relationships among people and among nations." He therefore asked that "international law be respected."

Once the war began, the French leaders did not change their minds. Speaking before the International Institute of

Strategic Studies in London on March 27, 2003, Villepin reiterated his faith in the "collective norms seeking to contain the use of force," adding that "only a consensus and a respect for the law gives the use of force its necessary legitimacy." He concluded that "force should be put at the service of the law." After the war was over, he revisited this theme in an interview in *Le Monde* (May 13, 2003): "Now more than ever, the United Nations is irreplaceable," he declared. "The United Nations embodies a universal conscience above those of the States" and constitutes a step towards a "constitution for a global democracy." Other European leaders expressed the similar opinion that today the reign of force is coming to an end and is progressively being replaced by the rule of law; once this happens, war could be definitively banished.

Such a vision of the world certainly sounds seductive. But before we embrace it, we must ask ourselves: does it take into account the existing real world? Or are we confusing fantasy with reality? To judge correctly, we must know the answers to these questions, since a search for the truth is doomed if we convince ourselves in advance that everything must turn out well. Is the reign of law over force viable, or does it consist of an illusion, momentarily tempting but potentially misleading? Are "International law" and "global democracy" nothing more than juridical fantasies?

During the Enlightenment, encyclopedists and philosophers cherished the hope that progress, occurring separately within each country, would spread to affect the relations among all nations; the entire world could be thought of as a "collective society" consisting of individual societies, which could be thought of as citizens. It was Jean-Jacques Rousseau who sought to move away from these fragile constructions: "From man to man," he wrote, "we live in a civil state and are subject to laws;

from peoples to peoples, each enjoys natural liberty" (Complete Works, III, 610). To extend his logic further, the relationships between countries operate in a natural state; on the contrary, a societal state governs each individual country. Why is it like this? Because each nation's citizens have relinquished the use of violence, entrusting it instead to their governing state; meanwhile, the states, not belonging to one universal State, cannot find a body to which they can delegate their force; therefore they keep it for themselves. Short of a threat from a common enemy—coming, for example, from another planet—the States privilege their own particular interest over the general interest (illustrated by the difficulty of reaching an agreement on issues like global warming, among others).

Every State is aware of this double regime: the same principles do not govern domestic and foreign politics. Inside the state, force submits to law, the army is controlled by the government, and the police guarantees that justice is served. Outside, it is force that governs the relationships between countries, tempered only by voluntary contracts which can be broken at any time. International law does not have the same authority as national law because it does not possess a corresponding arm of enforcement—unless the states all consent and agree to act. Rather than being submissive to the law, interstate relations fall under an international order made up of treaties, conventions and participation in international organizations; however, this order is not enforced by global police, which is no more real than a Universal State. Thus it is quite futile, as many did during the Iraq conflict, to speak of an "illegal war." War—all war—is by its very definition a rupture of the preexisting international order; but this order has never achieved the power of law.

In this context it is therefore useless to invoke the "primacy of law," "the respect for law," or "collective norms":

existing contracts between States, which can always be broken unilaterally, are not laws; what we call international law is simply not in the same category as military power. It is true that this reasoning does not apply to the member countries of the European Union and their mutual relations; they have renounced the use of force against each other. But this renunciation does not extend beyond the frontiers of the European Union: wars with nonmember countries are conceivable, and no law could prohibit them.

What, then, is the role of the UN, an organization encompassing every country in the world? Is it not a symbol of international law prevailing over force? In order to dispel this myth, we must first remind ourselves that at the heart of the UN lies the choice, based on no law whatsoever, to grant a "right-of-veto" to the five permanent members of the Security Council. In other words, these five members—the great powers—are exempt from the obligations shared by all other countries since they can exercise their veto on any resolution concerning them. A great power couldn't possibly make an error in judgment! Thus, in the recent past, the USSR escaped any condemnation of its military interventions because it blocked any resolution addressing them. This protection can be extended from the "veto members" to their allies: in this manner Israel, protected by the United States, no longer faces an UN-backed intervention. Far from restraining the hegemony of the great powers, the global organization therefore enshrines it.

I must add that even when the UN is not paralyzed by one of its powerful members, it has never proven to be the embodiment of justice in action. The UN has not known how, or even wished, to prevent numerous massacres: genocides in Cambodia and Rwanda, massive killings in Sudan and Ethiopia, civil wars in Angola and Sierra Leone.

The specific reasons vary, but their origin is the same: the powerlessness of an organization that does not have its own force and must borrow the forces of its individual members. Add to that the inevitable sluggishness of a remote bureaucratic machine and the diverging interests of its members, each of whom is always ready to derail any action.

It's asking a lot that the behavior of every state be dictated only by consideration for the law. You will remember how in March 2003, American and French diplomats raced around the world trying to secure favorable votes on the Iraq issue from such and such a country. Do we really see here a manifestation of this "universal conscience" Villepin mentions? Do we see a triumph of justice in the workings of the UN's Commission on Human Rights (currently presided over by Libya!), which never sought to condemn countries like China, Vietnam, Algeria, Syria, the Sudan, or Zimbabwe for their human rights abuses?

Since the Iraq crisis, the UN has been faced with a difficult task. The Security Council has had to choose between two unfavorable solutions: either submit to the United States in a show of servility, or oppose them and demonstrate its own impotence. For the most part it opted for the latter, and one can argue that, in doing so, the UN saved its honor; its weakness would have eventually come to light anyway. The Lilliputians who tried to restrain Gulliver with ropes scattered once the giant decided to rise. France prided itself in winning the battle at the UN, but she ultimately lost the one taking place outside of the meeting rooms because the war happened. A policy is judged on its results, not its intentions; this was therefore a questionable one.

Meanwhile, France, extremely vocal on questions of law when it applies to stronger nations, does not always submit to the UN when its own affairs are concerned. General de Gaulle didn't hesitate to declare his unwillingness to obey an organization to which so many dictators belonged. Even in 2003, France had not completely abandoned "solving its problems by way of force," to use Villepin's terms. It did not request the UN's authorization to intervene in the Ivory Coast, and this was undoubtedly a good thing: a new round of massacres would probably have taken place before the UN had reached a necessary consensus. One cannot help but believe that France insisted so heavily on the necessity of passing through the UN and its Security Council during the Iraq crisis because it was the sole place where it could assume a position of world power.

All of these instances detailing the shortcomings of international institutions should not incite us to sabotage them further (a contract is always preferable to chaos or blackmail); rather, they should temper our enthusiasm. The UN can be useful in all sorts of situations; simply put, during war, it will always be subjected to the will of hegemonic states. International justice can reinforce the rule of law, especially if it effectively governs the relations among nations rather than merely deluding itself with illusions of global cooperation. However, humanity being what it is, the international order will not replace the will of the State, and thus the will of military power. The UN will never be able to stop aggressors, ensure peace, impose justice; for that, force is necessary, and force belongs to the State. It is therefore useless to oppose the right of force: without force, as Pascal ruefully stated, law is powerless.

How can we ensure peace in the world? Some, like France, respond thusly: entrust it to international law and to organizations like the UN. Unfortunately, this solution is mistaken: we know very well that international relations do not obey international laws unless the countries choose to do so voluntarily. Others, like the United States, respond like this: entrust it to our force, the most powerful in the world. Every country need only submit and follow this policy, even when it disapproves: such is the price that must be paid for peace. Are we condemned to accept this alternative? No, "peace through law" and "peace through empire" do not exhaust all the possible options. These two solutions both seek safety in unity: the real unity of the American empire for the one; the illusory unity of a global governing body for the other. To these two options, we must add that of the plurality, in which peace is maintained by an equilibrium among several powers. The European leaders who opposed military escalation during the Iraq conflict also raised this possibility, expressing their wish for a constitution for a multi-polar world; but they did so as if international law and pluralism were synonymous. While they are not contradictory, these two strategies do not overlap. Although several forces, instead of only one, assure peace and global equilibrium, we are still talking about the use of force.

On a global scale, one lone European country, even if it is the most militarily powerful like Great Britain or France, would not be sufficient to establish a plurality of force. Only the European Union, an entity that compares favorably with the other great powers, can play this role (even if it doesn't rival the United States on a military level, which it does not need to). A newly powerful Europe would be capable of contributing to the very equilibrium which its leaders call for. In this manner, Europe would ensure its own defense rather than relying on the shield of the American military, which would in turn eventually allow it to disassociate itself from the United States if the latter persisted in pursuing its imperialistic policies. We can even think of this strategy as a favor to the United States, helping it to resist the "do-gooder temptation" to which it occasionally succumbs.

Can we say that during the Iraqi conflict France seized an opportunity to promote a united European policy? The French government seemed to have coordinated its position with its closest ally, Germany, but not with the others. We know the result: the public position taken by the French and German governments provoked a reply ("the letter of eight") from other European countries, some of whom were already members of the EU, like Great Britain, Spain and Italy, and the rest destined to join in 2004, like Poland, Hungary, and the Czech Republic.

Let's first take the case of the Eastern European countries. We know that ten days after the letter appeared, French president Jacques Chirac publicly admonished them, saying that they "had missed a good opportunity to be quiet" and had behaved like "children who were not well raised," even compromising their future acceptance into the European Union. Is this the only lesson to be learned from this attempt to prevent the war against Iraq?

The leaders of the ten countries in question have confided nothing to me. It seems, however, that their actions cannot be explained by the lack of a good education, by an excessive sense of gratitude towards the Americans for their role in the Cold War, or, finally, by the overt pressure applied by Washington.

If the countries of Eastern Europe decided to declare their unconditional support for the United States' policy, it is because another immense country, Russia, lies farther to the east. Even if the Russian government is not pursuing a politics of expansion, the difference in size between Russia and the Eastern European countries is such that they will always feel threatened by their gigantic neighbor. These countries know what Russian domination entails—they experienced it briefly as part of the Soviet Union, and some, like Poland, lived under it even longer. The question they must ask themselves is this: In case of a direct threat, are we better protected by the United States or by the combined forces of France and Germany? The answer is obvious. The American military shield is credible; France's is not. Faced with the impossibility of standing firm all alone against the great powers, Poland prefers to be an American satellite rather than a Russian one; the United States is a more liberal and distant protector. We can glean the following from this "letter of eight" episode: Europe must establish itself as a power before it is able to break free from the American guardianship. In so far as it has not yet accomplished this, a purely moral condemnation of this guardianship does not hold any water.

Concerning the other five countries, who are already members of the European Union but disagree with the Franco-German position, there is a different lesson to be learned. We must understand that no country in the EU, even if it is thoroughly convinced that it is right, cannot claim to speak for the others, and that a common voice would be much more powerful than several scattered ones. If the union does not draw together now, it has a slim chance of future success. Furthermore, if France is convinced that the Union is necessary, it must accept the eventuality of being put in the minority and having to submit to the opinions of other nations. Therefore, in order to constitute a European power, each of the member states must cede some of its national sovereignty, thereby gaining increased security and a superior collective sovereignty.

The world of tomorrow will not be a place where force is forever banished. France should continue to prepare to defend itself. And the future of that self-defense lies in Europe.

THE LESSER EVIL

BY MARIO VARGAS LLOSA

"...my opposition to U.S. and British military intervention in Iraq, presented in unequivocal terms on February 16, 2003, was nuanced, not to say corrected, after my trip to Iraq. "

Mario VARGAS LLOSA (Peru)

Mario Vargas Llosa is a prolific writer (novels, essays, theater) and a journalist (he contributes to El Pais on a regular basis), whose work has been translated into thirty-two languages. In 2003, he received the Roger Caillois Prize in Paris and the Budapest Prize in Hungary. A Mario Vargas Llosa Library was inaugurated at the Cervantes Institute in Berlin.

If one takes the trouble to read this text in its entirety, it will be clear that my opposition to U.S. and British military intervention in Iraq, presented in unequivocal terms on February 16, 2003, was nuanced, not to say corrected, after my trip to Iraq.[18] That was precisely one of the two reasons I had for going there: to verify on the ground—and from the Iraqi point of view—whether the arguments put forth by the French foreign minister for condemning military intervention were still as convincing as when I was considering the matter in the abstract, in Europe, far from the theater of events.

I continue to believe that it was a very grave error for the coalition governments to brandish, as a justification for military action, the existence of weapons of mass destruction in the hands of Saddam Hussein and the link with al-Qaeda and the perpetrators of the massacre of September 11, 2001, since there was no definitive proof for these claims, and now, at this late stage, they seem rather like pretexts than conclusive reasons.

Because the destruction of Saddam Hussein's dictatorship, one of the cruelest, most corrupt and demented in modern history, was in itself sufficient to justify the intervention—just as it would have justified preemptive action on the part of the democratic governments against Hitler and his regime before Nazism plunged the world into the apocalypse of World War II.

---

18 Vargas Llosa traveled to Iraq from June 25 to July 6, 2003, and wrote this account upon his return.

"Saddam Hussein had to fall, but by the internal action of the Iraqis themselves," said the French president Chirac, in a statement that reveals a profound misunderstanding of the regime ruled by Saddam Hussein. Like his models, Hitler and Stalin, the Iraqi dictator had dispossessed his entire people of their sovereignty, and by means of a vertiginous terror, he had colonized the spirits of the Iraqis to the point of annihilating, in the more or less long term, every realistic possibility of an effective revolt against the regime that would open the door to a process of democratization. A palace revolution would no doubt have been possible, but that would have merely replaced one despot with another; or, perhaps, a fundamentalist insurrection could have installed a regime in Baghdad identical to that of the Iranian ayatollahs. Was that the road to freedom for the decimated people of Iraq?

The coalition's military intervention can no doubt be criticized for its unilateralism, and for not having the support of the United Nations; nevertheless, it has created the possibility, for the first time in the history of Iraq, for this country to break out of the vicious circle of authoritarianism and totalitarianism in which it has lived since Britain granted its independence. The readers of this report will see that, even with all the suffering and hardship that the military intervention has brought the Iraqis, it is still less than what they had to endure under the Ba'ath regime, with its policies of genocide, abjection and systematic repression. But don't take my word for it: a recent Gallup poll, published in the *New York Times* on September 24 [2003], reported that 67 percent of the Baghdadis consulted said just that. Almost two thirds of the Iraqi population, then, acknowledge that despite the lack of water and electricity, the insecurity of the cities, and the grave economic crisis, they are better off than they were under the iron rule of Saddam Hussein. Now, at least, despite the terrorists' bombs, they have hope, and they are seeing the beginnings of a genuine liberation.

It would no doubt be dangerous to establish a norm by which democratic nations can assert the right to take military action against dictatorships in order to facilitate democratic processes, since in certain cases such a principle might be used as a smokescreen for colonial ventures. This type of action can be legitimate only in exceptional cases, when the extremity, the criminal excesses, and the genocidal practices of a dictatorship have blocked every opening to freedom that would allow its people an opportunity to engage in peaceful resistance, or when, through its belligerent initiatives against its neighbors and its attacks on human rights, it becomes a serious threat to global peace. All the testimonies from Iraqis that I was able to gather during my short stay there convinced me that the regime of Saddam Hussein was precisely such an exceptional case.

Certainly, an intervention of this type should have been legitimated by the international legality represented by the United Nations. But the opposition of France, which threatened to use its veto in the Security Council, closed every door to this possibility.

The war in Iraq goes far beyond the borders of ancient Mesopotamia. It has served to highlight and to aggravate the differences between the United States and its longtime allies, like France and Germany, and it has stirred up hatred against the United States, by legitimizing with an aura of pacifism and anti-colonialism a new anti-Americanism, in which those who are nostalgic for fascism and communism rub shoulders with nationalists, social-democrats, socialists and the anti-globalization movements. By a strange turn of the screw, the war in Iraq has made it possible, in Europe and America, to cast Saddam Hussein as the Third World David resisting the petro-colonial ventures of Bush-Goliath, and to demonize the United States as the prime source of the international crisis affecting the world since September 11, 2001. It is deplorable to see that the frivolity displayed by the French government in this affair, together with its increasing nationalism, has contributed to a denaturalization of historical reality, one of the most serious effects of which has been the division within the European Union, which threatens to delay or even to paralyze indefinitely the process of European integration.

Finally, the war in Iraq—or rather the post-war period—has begun to define what wars will be like in the twenty-first century. These confrontations will be fought less and less by two opposing conventional armies, as in the past, and increasingly by open societies and governments against terrorist organizations which, with the resources available to them, are able to acquire military technology with enormous destructive power and cause immeasurable damage to unarmed populations—as al-Qaeda demonstrated on September 11, 2001. During the weeks since my trip to Iraq, the situation has grown worse, and at least three of the people whom I interviewed and who helped me in my investigations—the Imam al-Hakim, Sergio Vieira de Mello and navy captain Manuel Martín-Oar—have perished, victims of terrorist attacks. This is naturally very painful and grave, especially for the Iraqi people, since they are the ones undergoing the worst ravages of this new type of armed confrontation. But we must not draw pessimistic conclusions from this, or suggest, as some have done, that we should abandon the Iraqis to their fate and give free rein to what remains of Saddam Hussein's supporters and to all the international terrorist organizations who have migrated to Iraq to prevent it from being a free country. This battle can still be won if the community of democratic nations acknowledges its role and acts accordingly. For the result of the confrontation taking place today in Iraq will determine, in large part, whether in the future democratic culture will be victorious over terror and authoritarian fanaticism—as it ultimately triumphed over the totalitarian ideologies of fascism and communism—or whether the entire world will return to the barbarity of the old despotisms and satrapies which constitute the most stubborn political legacy of human history.

It is my hope that this report on the daily experience of the Iraqi people who survived the dictatorship of the Ba'ath party will be of some help to those who are trying to exercise proper judgment and who do not judge according to conditioned reflexes and the stereotypes of the "politically correct"—I hope that it will help such people have a more precise idea of what the now vanquished tyranny of Saddam Hussein meant for the Iraqi people (a tyranny that is nonetheless experiencing some ferocious death throes before completely disappearing) and to ask themselves in that light whether this war—which like all wars is cruel—was not the lesser evil.

FOR A COUNCIL OF SAGES

BY ABRAHAM B. YEHOSHUA

"... *an action that lacks a clear and forceful moral validity is condemned to fail in the end, however much force is used to carry it out.*"

Abraham B. YEHOSHUA (Israel)

Presently Professor of Literature at the University of Haifa, he is one of Israel's finest contemporary writers. He was recognized in the New York Times *as "a kind of Israeli Faulkner." A novelist and a playwright, A. B. Yehoshua has received several literary prizes, including the Prize of Israel and Bialik. He has just published* La Mariée libérée [The Liberated Bride] *and* A Journey to the End of the Millennium.

Even today many people still believe that the demands of moral behavior stop at the national and social border. At the international level, where confrontations take place between the powerful interests of societies, states, or peoples who have different cultural, religious or moral norms and codes, it might seem excessive to demand a moral evaluation of their behavior, since a hesitant approach might very well be harmful.

I do not think that this is the case, although I recognize how difficult it would be to apply completely rigorous moral rules in dealing with a state or a society that violates all the rules of international law and every moral code. I continue to think that whenever an international, economic, diplomatic, and especially a military action is undertaken on a clear moral basis, corresponding to the Kantian principle of its generality—a principle that does not necessarily contradict the existence of egoistic national interests, as it does in relations between individuals—this action will ultimately succeed in reality. On the other hand, an action that lacks a clear and forceful moral validity is condemned to fail in the end, however much force is used to carry it out.

In Vietnam, no moral justification invested the United States with the power to intervene in the civil war between the Communists in the North and the regime of the South, which in any case was not democratic. That is why, despite the immense force used by the United States in this war, they were met with total defeat. On the other hand, the liberation of a Kuwait conquered by Saddam Hussein was clearly a moral act—despite the simultaneous existence of other interests—and that is why it was easily and successfully carried out. The Six-Day War in June 1967, whose goal was to push back the forces of destruction launched by the Arab countries against Israel, was morally justified, as the world recognized in Security Council resolution 242, a resolution stipulating that the territories occupied in the course of this war would be restored only in exchange for peace. Indeed, this war, which lasted only six days and was fought against three Arab states, ended in an overwhelming victory, and without great losses for Israel.

But the same Israeli army, with all its power and sophistication, suffered a resounding defeat in its invasion of Lebanon in 1982—an invasion that had no moral justification—even though it was facing forces much weaker than those it had fought against in 1967. After eighteen years, this same army was forced to retreat from Lebanon unilaterally and without a peace agreement.

The same is true of the unjust and immoral idea of a "French Algeria," the source of a bloody and painful struggle that, despite the superior force of the French, ended in a clear defeat for the latter, and in the precipitous evacuation of the colonists when Algeria won its independence. Another example: the failure of Soviet intervention in the civil war in Afghanistan. I am deliberately choosing extreme examples, in which states with great military, economic, and diplomatic power have failed in a war against forces that were quite inferior to them. I am doing this because I want to emphasize that in the absence of very solid moral grounds and justifications, no international action can bear any lasting fruit.

Obviously, one can find examples in history that contradict this notion, examples of unjustified international actions that succeeded. But if we look very closely, we will see that the majority of such "immoral" successes lasted only a short time, and were highly vulnerable.

But here some difficult questions arise: What is moral, and what is not? What is justified, and what is not? Who decides, and on what grounds? For example, the invasion of Iraq by the United States, whose goal is to overturn a regime of cruel tyranny and to prevent the production of weapons of mass destruction—is this a moral action or not? And if it is, what is permitted or forbidden at the outset or *a posteriori*?

Whenever there is a debate within any of the international authorities concerning the moral aspects of an action, suspicions immediately arise that the various moral arguments serve only to disguise narrow national interests. The basis for any mutual moral confidence between states is lacking, to the point that whenever a particular state undertakes a very forceful international action, like a war or economic sanctions—or, conversely, when a state opposes such decisions— it is immediately accused of acting not from "idealistic motives" and in the name of Good and Justice, but rather from a desire to serve its apparent or hidden interests. Even when one uses international law as a criterion, there are always differences in the interpretation of this law, and one can always find precedents that contradict a given position. Indeed, international law refers to theoretical and abstract cases, and one can always claim that in a particular case the circumstances are so complex and specific that the formal and theoretical rules of the UN Charter or of international law do not provide a sound and adequate justification for one decision or the other.

Once again, we can take the last war in Iraq as an example of such complexity, and of the international community's inability to provide an unequivocal moral judgment for or against the war.

Public opinion within countries that are not directly involved in the conflicts, despite the vitality and the spontaneity of its judgments, is too fluid as well, subject as it is to shifting moods and to an "emotional calculus." Given that public opinion has no particular quality that would authorize it to lead organized and systematic moral debates concerning international problems—which is not the case for internal social and national questions—the moral judgments expressed by public opinion, most often in sporadically and haphazardly conducted surveys and polls, have no moral value.

That is why I will limit myself to presenting only the broad outlines of a proposal that would perhaps help to consolidate the moral aspect of international politics—something we all greatly hope for—a politics that would have a more solid basis in moral considerations and that would thus have more pertinence. I am speaking of the creation of a forum—whether under the aegis of the UN or another organization—made up of individuals who, because of their formation and training, are particularly suited to debate moral questions related to radical actions like war, intervention in civil wars, or economic sanctions.

These individuals would be philosophers, specialists in political science, historians, religious leaders, as well as a few artists and journalists who have earned a reputation for outstanding moral authority. There would be people from many different countries—it is very important that there be as many representatives from the second and third worlds as from the first world—people who in the course of their lives have earned a well established moral authority. They would debate national or international actions of the order of the day: the invasion of Iraq based on suspicions that it has weapons of mass destruction; the ousting of the Milosevic regime in Serbia; the imposition of economic sanctions against Israel for the Jewish settlements. These men and women would engage in a moral debate on Good and Evil, on the Just and the Unjust—and not on international law and the existing conventions.

This forum should not have more than a few dozen members, named by winners of the Nobel Peace Prize—with the exception of politicians—who themselves would be natural partners. They would make every effort to show a maximum of objectivity, and its members would abstain from participation in debates concerning their countries of origin.

Their decisions or their recommendations and the arguments behind them would deal with the moral—and not the juridical—dimensions of the problem under examination. This would accustom public opinion to concentrate exclusively on the moral kernel of the problem at hand, by attempting to set aside, for a sufficient amount of time, the constant temptation to search for egotistical motives hidden behind everything, the sordid calculations of economic profit, or the personal political manipulations of a particular leader—motives often presented as central and essential.

There are many people who have felt an urgent need for there to be such a debate concerning the war waged by the United States against Saddam Hussein.

It is precisely because this question was complex and ambiguous, and because as an Israeli I had a very clear national interest in relation to this war, that I would have liked very much to hear the reasoned moral opinion of objective observers—observers who would be neither commentators nor researchers, but rather who have been guided in their life by moral questions on Good and Evil, on what is wise and what is not, on the Just and the Unjust. An opinion that would have explained whether or not it was justified, all things considered, to undertake this war. And if so, how to undertake it, and at what point it would be necessary to change course or turn back.

I imagine that this forum would also occasionally take the initiative to open debates on questions that are not immediately urgent—for example, the imposition of economic sanctions against Israel because of the Jewish settlements; or the suspension of aid to the Palestinians, until they have put an end to terrorism.

Of course, I am not so naïve as to think that this forum would be able to weigh concretely on the international policies of states. If the United States was so conspicuous in foregoing the Security Council's authorization to begin a war in Iraq, why would the learned document of this moral forum, which will be immediately accused of using a double standard—to the point that some will insist on rummaging in the biographies of its members—why would such a document make any impression on Washington?

But in the long term, the very existence of this forum, the prestige that it would acquire thanks to the people of great value whose purity of intentions it would be difficult to question, as well as the possibility of accustoming the larger public to this kind of debate and to its high level—all this would have a very deep and lasting pedagogical function. Perhaps in the future we will be able to gather its beneficial fruit, for the good of a more human world.

APPENDIX

UNITED NATIONS S/RES/1441 (2002)
Security Council
Distr.: General
8 November 2002
02-68226 (E)
0268226
RESOLUTION 1441 (2002)

Adopted by the Security Council at its 4644th meeting, on 8 November 2002

The Security Council,

Recalling all its previous relevant resolutions, in particular its resolutions 661 (1990) of 6 August 1990, 678 (1990) of 29 November 1990, 686 (1991) of 2 March 1991, 687 (1991) of 3 April 1991, 688 (1991) of 5 April 1991, 707 (1991) of 15 August 1991, 715 (1991) of 11 October 1991, 986 (1995) of 14 April 1995, and 1284 (1999) of 17 December 1999, and all the relevant statements of its President,

Recalling also its resolution 1382 (2001) of 29 November 2001 and its intention to implement it fully,

Recognizing the threat Iraq's non-compliance with Council resolutions and proliferation of weapons of mass destruction and long-range missiles poses to international peace and security, *Recalling* that its resolution 678 (1990) authorized Member States to use all necessary means to uphold and implement its resolution 660 (1990) of 2 August 1990 and all relevant resolutions subsequent to resolution 660 (1990) and to restore international peace and security in the area,

Further recalling that its resolution 687 (1991) imposed obligations on Iraq as a necessary step for achievement of its stated objective of restoring international peace and security in the area,

Deploring the fact that Iraq has not provided an accurate, full, final, and complete disclosure, as required by resolution 687 (1991), of all aspects of its programmes to develop weapons of mass destruction and ballistic missiles with a range greater than one hundred and fifty kilometres, and of all holdings of such weapons, their components and production facilities and locations, as well as all other nuclear programmes, including any which it claims are for purposes not related to nuclear-weapons-usable material,

Deploring further that Iraq repeatedly obstructed immediate, unconditional, and unrestricted access to sites designated by the United Nations Special Commission (UNSCOM) and the International Atomic Energy Agency (IAEA), failed to cooperate fully and unconditionally with UNSCOM and IAEA weapons inspectors, as required by resolution 687 (1991), and ultimately ceased all cooperation with UNSCOM and the IAEA in 1998,

Deploring the absence, since December 1998, in Iraq of international monitoring, inspection, and verification, as required by relevant resolutions, of weapons of mass destruction and ballistic missiles, in spite of the Council's repeated demands that Iraq provide immediate, unconditional, and unrestricted access to the United Nations Monitoring, Verification and Inspection Commission (UNMOVIC), established in resolution 1284 (1999) as the successor organization to UNSCOM, and the IAEA, and regretting the consequent prolonging of the crisis in the region and the suffering of the Iraqi people,

Deploring also that the Government of Iraq has failed to comply with its commitments pursuant to resolution 687 (1991) with regard to terrorism, pursuant to resolution 688 (1991) to end repression of its civilian population and to provide access by international humanitarian organizations to all those in need of assistance in Iraq, and pursuant to resolutions 686 (1991), 687 (1991), and 1284 (1999) to return or cooperate in accounting for Kuwaiti and third country nationals wrongfully detained by Iraq, or to return Kuwaiti property wrongfully seized by Iraq,

Recalling that in its resolution 687 (1991) the Council declared that a ceasefire would be based on acceptance by Iraq of the provisions of that resolution, including the obligations on Iraq contained therein,

Determined to ensure full and immediate compliance by Iraq without conditions or restrictions with its obligations under resolution 687 (1991) and other relevant resolutions and recalling that the resolutions of the Council constitute the governing standard of Iraqi compliance,

Recalling that the effective operation of UNMOVIC, as the successor organization to the Special Commission, and the IAEA is essential for the implementation of resolution 687 (1991) and other relevant resolutions,

Noting that the letter dated 16 September 2002 from the Minister for Foreign Affairs of Iraq addressed to the Secretary-General is a necessary first step toward rectifying Iraq's continued failure to comply with relevant Council resolutions,

Noting further the letter dated 8 October 2002 from the Executive Chairman of UNMOVIC and the Director-General of the IAEA to General Al-Saadi of the Government of Iraq laying out the practical arrangements, as a follow-up to their meeting in Vienna, that are prerequisites for the resumption of inspections in Iraq by UNMOVIC and the IAEA, and expressing the gravest concern at the continued failure by the Government of Iraq to provide confirmation of the arrangements as laid out in that letter,

Reaffirming the commitment of all Member States to the sovereignty and territorial integrity of Iraq, Kuwait, and the neighbouring States,

Commending the Secretary-General and members of the League of Arab States and its Secretary-General for their efforts in this regard,

Determined to secure full compliance with its decisions,

Acting under Chapter VII of the Charter of the United Nations,

1. *Decides* that Iraq has been and remains in material breach of its obligations under relevant resolutions, including resolution 687 (1991), in particular through Iraq's failure to cooperate with United Nations inspectors and the IAEA, and to complete the actions required under paragraphs 8 to 13 of resolution 687 (1991);

2. *Decides*, while acknowledging paragraph 1 above, to afford Iraq, by this resolution, a final opportunity to comply with its disarmament obligations under relevant resolutions of the Council; and accordingly decides to set up an enhanced inspection regime with the aim of bringing to full and verified completion the disarmament process established by resolution 687 (1991) and subsequent resolutions of the Council;

3. *Decides* that, in order to begin to comply with its disarmament obligations, in addition to submitting the required biannual declarations, the Government of Iraq shall provide to UNMOVIC, the IAEA, and the Council, not later than 30 days from the date of this resolution, a currently accurate, full, and complete declaration of all aspects of its programmes to develop chemical, biological, and nuclear weapons, ballistic missiles, and other delivery systems such as unmanned aerial vehicles and dispersal systems designed for use on aircraft, including any holdings and precise locations of such weapons, components, subcomponents, stocks of agents,

and related material and equipment, the locations and work of its research, development and production facilities, as well as all other chemical, biological, and nuclear programmes, including any which it claims are for purposes not related to weapon production or material;

4. *Decides* that false statements or omissions in the declarations submitted by Iraq pursuant to this resolution and failure by Iraq at any time to comply with, and cooperate fully in the implementation of, this resolution shall constitute a further material breach of Iraq's obligations and will be reported to the Council for assessment in accordance with paragraphs 11 and 12 below;

5. *Decides* that Iraq shall provide UNMOVIC and the IAEA immediate, unimpeded, unconditional, and unrestricted access to any and all, including underground, areas, facilities, buildings, equipment, records, and means of transport which they wish to inspect, as well as immediate, unimpeded, unrestricted, and private access to all officials and other persons whom UNMOVIC or the IAEA wish to interview in the mode or location of UNMOVIC's or the IAEA's choice pursuant to any aspect of their mandates; further decides that UNMOVIC and the IAEA may at their discretion conduct interviews inside or outside of Iraq, may facilitate the travel of those interviewed and family members outside of Iraq, and that, at the sole discretion of UNMOVIC and the IAEA, such interviews may occur without the presence of observers from the Iraqi Government; and instructs UNMOVIC and requests the IAEA to resume inspections no later than 45 days following adoption of this resolution and to update the Council 60 days thereafter;

6. *Endorses* the 8 October 2002 letter from the Executive Chairman of UNMOVIC and the Director-General of the IAEA to General Al-Saadi of the Government of Iraq, which is annexed hereto, and decides that the contents of the letter

shall be binding upon Iraq;

7. *Decides* further that, in view of the prolonged interruption by Iraq of the presence of UNMOVIC and the IAEA and in order for them to accomplish the tasks set forth in this resolution and all previous relevant resolutions and notwithstanding prior understandings, the Council hereby establishes the following revised or additional authorities, which shall be binding upon Iraq, to facilitate their work in Iraq:

—UNMOVIC and the IAEA shall determine the composition of their inspection teams and ensure that these teams are composed of the most qualified and experienced experts available;

—All UNMOVIC and IAEA personnel shall enjoy the privileges and immunities, corresponding to those of experts on mission, provided in the Convention on Privileges and Immunities of the United Nations and the Agreement on the Privileges and Immunities of the IAEA;

—UNMOVIC and the IAEA shall have unrestricted rights of entry into and out of Iraq, the right to free, unrestricted, and immediate movement to and from inspection sites, and the right to inspect any sites and buildings, including immediate, unimpeded, unconditional, and unrestricted access to Presidential Sites equal to that at other sites, notwithstanding the provisions of resolution 1154 (1998) of 2 March 1998;

—UNMOVIC and the IAEA shall have the right to be provided by Iraq the names of all personnel currently and formerly associated with Iraq's chemical, biological, nuclear, and ballistic missile programmes and the associated research, development, and production facilities;

—Security of UNMOVIC and IAEA facilities shall be ensured by sufficient United Nations security guards;

—UNMOVIC and the IAEA shall have the right to declare, for the purposes of freezing a site to be inspected, exclusion zones, including surrounding areas and transit corridors, in which Iraq will suspend ground and aerial movement so that nothing is changed in or taken out of a site being inspected;

—UNMOVIC and the IAEA shall have the free and unrestricted use and landing of fixed- and rotary-winged aircraft, including manned and unmanned reconnaissance vehicles;

—UNMOVIC and the IAEA shall have the right at their sole discretion verifiably to remove, destroy, or render harmless all prohibited weapons, subsystems, components, records, materials, and other related items, and the right to impound or close any facilities or equipment for the production thereof; and

—UNMOVIC and the IAEA shall have the right to free import and use of equipment or materials for inspections and to seize and export any equipment, materials, or documents taken during inspections, without search of UNMOVIC or IAEA personnel or official or personal baggage;

8. *Decides* further that Iraq shall not take or threaten hostile acts directed against any representative or personnel of the United Nations or the IAEA or of any Member State taking action to uphold any Council resolution;

9. *Requests* the Secretary-General immediately to notify Iraq of this resolution, which is binding on Iraq; demands that Iraq confirm within seven days of that notification its intention to comply fully with this resolution; and demands further that Iraq cooperate immediately, unconditionally, and actively with UNMOVIC and the IAEA;

10. *Requests* all Member States to give full support to UNMOVIC and the IAEA in the discharge of their mandates, including by providing any information related to prohibited programmes or other aspects of their mandates, including on Iraqi attempts since 1998 to acquire prohibited items, and by recommending sites to be inspected, persons to be interviewed, conditions of such interviews, and data to be collected, the results of which shall be reported to the Council by UNMOVIC and the IAEA;

11. *Directs* the Executive Chairman of UNMOVIC and the Director-General of the IAEA to report immediately to the Council any interference by Iraq with inspection activities, as well as any failure by Iraq to comply with its disarmament obligations, including its obligations regarding inspections under this resolution;

12. *Decides* to convene immediately upon receipt of a report in accordance with paragraphs 4 or 11 above, in order to consider the situation and the need for full compliance with all of the relevant Council resolutions in order to secure international peace and security;

13. *Recalls*, in that context, that the Council has repeatedly warned Iraq that it will face serious consequences as a result of its continued violations of its obligations;

14. *Decides* to remain seized of the matter.

S/RES/1441 (2002) ANNEX

Text of Blix/El-Baradei letter United Nations Monitoring, Verification International Atomic Energy Agency and Inspection Commission The Executive Chairman The Director General

8 October 2002

Dear General Al-Saadi,

During our recent meeting in Vienna, we discussed practical arrangements that are prerequisites for the resumption of inspections in Iraq by UNMOVIC and the IAEA. As you recall, at the end of our meeting in Vienna we agreed on a statement which listed some of the principal results achieved, particularly Iraq's acceptance of all the rights of inspection provided for in all of the relevant Security Council resolutions. This acceptance was stated to be without any conditions attached.

During our 3 October 2002 briefing to the Security Council, members of the Council suggested that we prepare a written document on all of the conclusions we reached in Vienna. This letter lists those conclusions and seeks your confirmation thereof. We shall report accordingly to the Security Council.

In the statement at the end of the meeting, it was clarified that UNMOVIC and the IAEA will be granted immediate, unconditional and unrestricted access to sites, including what was termed "sensitive sites" in the past. As we noted, however, eight presidential sites have been the subject of special procedures under a Memorandum of Understanding of 1998. Should these sites be subject, as all other sites, to immediate, unconditional and unrestricted access, UNMOVIC and the IAEA would conduct inspections there with the same professionalism.

H.E. General Amir H. Al-Saadi
Adviser
Presidential Office
Baghdad
Iraq

S/RES/1441 (2002)

We confirm our understanding that UNMOVIC and the IAEA have the right to determine the number of inspectors required for access to any particular site. This determination will be made on the basis of the size and complexity of the site being inspected. We also confirm that Iraq will be informed of the designation of additional sites, i.e., sites not declared by Iraq or previously inspected by either UNSCOM or the IAEA, through a Notification of Inspection (NIS) provided upon arrival of the inspectors at such sites.

Iraq will ensure that no proscribed material, equipment, records or other relevant items will be destroyed except in the presence of UNMOVIC and/or IAEA inspectors, as appropriate, and at their request.

UNMOVIC and the IAEA may conduct interviews with any person in Iraq whom they believe may have information relevant to their mandate. Iraq will facilitate such interviews. It is for UNMOVIC and the IAEA to choose the mode and location for interviews.

The National Monitoring Directorate (NMD) will, as in the past, serve as the Iraqi counterpart for the inspectors. The Baghdad Ongoing Monitoring and Verification Centre (BOMVIC) will be maintained on the same premises and under the same conditions as was the former Baghdad Monitoring and Verification Centre. The NMD will make available services as before, cost free, for the refurbishment of the premises.

The NMD will provide free of cost: (a) escorts to facilitate access to sites to be inspected and communication with personnel to be interviewed; (b) a hotline for BOMVIC which will be staffed by an English speaking person on a 24 hour a day/seven days a week basis; (c) support in terms of personnel and ground transportation within the country, as requested; and (d) assistance in the movement of materials and equipment at inspectors' request (construction, excavation equipment, etc.). NMD will also ensure that escorts are available in the event of inspections outside normal working hours, including at night and on holidays.

Regional UNMOVIC/IAEA offices may be established, for example, in Basra and Mosul, for the use of their inspectors. For this purpose, Iraq will provide, without cost, adequate office buildings, staff accommodation, and appropriate escort personnel.

UNMOVIC and the IAEA may use any type of voice or data transmission, including satellite and/or inland networks, with or without encryption capability. UNMOVIC and the IAEA may also install equipment in the field with the capability for transmission of data directly to the BOMVIC, New York and Vienna (e.g. sensors, surveillance cameras). This will be facilitated by Iraq and there will be no interference by Iraq with UNMOVIC or IAEA communications.

Iraq will provide, without cost, physical protection of all surveillance equipment, and construct antennae for remote transmission of data, at the request of UNMOVIC and the IAEA. Upon request by UNMOVIC through the NMD, Iraq will allocate frequencies for communications equipment.

Iraq will provide security for all UNMOVIC and IAEA personnel. Secure and suitable accommodations will be designated at normal rates by Iraq for these personnel. For their part, UNMOVIC and the IAEA will require that their staff not stay at any accommodation other than those identified in consultation with Iraq.

On the use of fixed-wing aircraft for transport of personnel and equipment and for inspection purposes, it was clarified that aircraft used by UNMOVIC and IAEA staff arriving in Baghdad may land at Saddam International Airport. The points of departure of incoming aircraft will be decided by UNMOVIC. The Rasheed airbase will continue to be used for UNMOVIC and IAEA helicopter operations. UNMOVIC and Iraq will establish air liaison offices at the airbase. At both Saddam International Airport and Rasheed airbase, Iraq will provide the necessary support premises and facilities. Aircraft fuel will be provided by Iraq, as before, free of charge.

On the wider issue of air operations in Iraq, both fixed-wing and rotary, Iraq will guarantee the safety of air operations in its air space outside the no-fly zones. With regard to air operations in the no-fly zones, Iraq will take all steps within its control to ensure the safety of such operations.

Helicopter flights may be used, as needed, during inspections and for technical activities, such as gamma detection, without limitation in all parts of Iraq and without any area excluded. Helicopters may also be used for medical evacuation.

On the question of aerial imagery, UNMOVIC may wish to resume the use of U-2 or Mirage overflights. The relevant practical arrangements would be similar to those implemented in the past. As before, visas for all arriving staff will be issued at the point of entry on the basis of the UN Laissez-Passer or UN Certificate; no other entry or exit formalities will be required. The aircraft passenger manifest will be provided one hour in advance of the arrival of the aircraft in Baghdad. There will be no searching of

UNMOVIC or IAEA personnel or of official or personal baggage. UNMOVIC and the IAEA will ensure that their personnel respect the laws of Iraq restricting the export of certain items, for example, those related to Iraq's national cultural heritage. UNMOVIC and the IAEA may bring into, and remove from, Iraq all of the items and materials they require, including satellite phones and other equipment. With respect to samples, UNMOVIC and IAEA will, where feasible, split samples so that Iraq may receive a portion while another portion is kept for reference purposes. Where appropriate, the organizations will send the samples to more than one laboratory for analysis.

We would appreciate your confirmation of the above as a correct reflection of our talks in Vienna.

Naturally, we may need other practical arrangements when proceeding with inspections. We would expect in such matters, as with the above, Iraq's cooperation in all respect.

Yours sincerely,
(*Signed*)
Hans Blix
Executive Chairman
United Nations Monitoring,
Verification and Inspection Commission

(*Signed*)
Mohamed El Baradei
Director General
International Atomic Energy Agency

UNITED NATIONS S/RES/1483 (2003)
Security Council
Distr.: General
22 May 2003
Resolution 1483 (2003)

Adopted by the Security Council at its 4761st meeting, on 22 May 2003

The Security Council,

Recalling all its previous relevant resolutions,

Reaffirming the sovereignty and territorial integrity of Iraq,

Reaffirming also the importance of the disarmament of Iraqi weapons of mass destruction and of eventual confirmation of the disarmament of Iraq,

Stressing the right of the Iraqi people freely to determine their own political future and control their own natural resources, *welcoming* the commitment of all parties concerned to support the creation of an environment in which they may do so as soon as possible, and *expressing* resolve that the day when Iraqis govern themselves must come quickly,

Encouraging efforts by the people of Iraq to form a representative government based on the rule of law that affords equal rights and justice to all Iraqi citizens without regard to ethnicity, religion, or gender, and, in this connection, *recalls* resolution 1325 (2000) of 31 October 2000,

Welcoming the first steps of the Iraqi people in this regard, and *noting* in this connection the 15 April 2003 Nasiriyah statement and the 28 April 2003 Baghdad statement,

Resolved that the United Nations should play a vital role in humanitarian relief, the reconstruction of Iraq, and the restoration and establishment of national and local institutions for representative governance,

Noting the statement of 12 April 2003 by the Ministers of Finance and Central Bank Governors of the Group of Seven Industrialized Nations in which the members recognized the need for a multilateral effort to help rebuild and develop Iraq and for the need for assistance from the International Monetary Fund and the World Bank in these efforts,

Welcoming also the resumption of humanitarian assistance and the continuing efforts of the Secretary-General and the specialized agencies to provide food and medicine to the people of Iraq,

Welcoming the appointment by the Secretary-General of his Special Adviser on Iraq,

Affirming the need for accountability for crimes and atrocities committed by the previous Iraqi regime,

Stressing the need for respect for the archaeological, historical, cultural, and religious heritage of Iraq, and for the continued protection of archaeological, historical, cultural, and religious sites, museums, libraries, and monuments,

Noting the letter of 8 May 2003 from the Permanent Representatives of the United States of America and the United Kingdom of Great Britain and Northern Ireland to the President of the Security Council (S/2003/538) and recognizing the specific authorities, responsibilities, and obligations under applicable international law of these states as occupying powers under unified command (the "Authority"),

Noting further that other States that are not occupying powers are working now or in the future may work under the Authority,

Welcoming further the willingness of Member States to contribute to stability and security in Iraq by contributing personnel, equipment, and other resources under the Authority,

Concerned that many Kuwaitis and Third-State Nationals still are not accounted for since 2 August 1990,

Determining that the situation in Iraq, although improved, continues to constitute a threat to international peace and security,

Acting under Chapter VII of the Charter of the United Nations,

1. *Appeals* to Member States and concerned organizations to assist the people of Iraq in their efforts to reform their institutions and rebuild their country, and to contribute to conditions of stability and security in Iraq in accordance with this resolution;

2. *Calls upon* all Member States in a position to do so to respond immediately to the humanitarian appeals of the United Nations and other international organizations for Iraq and to help meet the humanitarian and other needs of the Iraqi people by providing food, medical supplies, and resources necessary for reconstruction and rehabilitation of Iraq's economic infrastructure;

3. *Appeals* to Member States to deny safe haven to those members of the previous Iraqi regime who are alleged to be responsible for crimes and atrocities and to support actions to bring them to justice;

4. *Calls upon* the Authority, consistent with the Charter of the United Nations and other relevant international law, to promote the welfare of the Iraqi people through the effective administration of the territory, including in particular working towards the restoration of conditions of security and stability and the creation of conditions in which the Iraqi people can freely determine their own political future;

5. *Calls upon* all concerned to comply fully with their obligations under international law including in particular the Geneva Conventions of 1949 and the Hague Regulations of 1907;

6. *Calls upon* the Authority and relevant organizations and individuals to continue efforts to locate, identify, and repatriate all Kuwaiti and Third-State Nationals or the remains of those present in Iraq on or after 2 August 1990, as well as the Kuwaiti archives, that the previous Iraqi regime failed to undertake, and, in this regard, *directs* the High-Level Coordinator, in consultation with the International Committee of the Red Cross and the Tripartite Commission and with the appropriate support of the people of Iraq and in coordination with the Authority, to take steps to fulfil his mandate with respect to the fate of Kuwaiti and Third-State National missing persons and property;

7. *Decides* that all Member States shall take appropriate steps to facilitate the safe return to Iraqi institutions of Iraqi cultural property and other items of archaeological, historical, cultural, rare scientific, and religious importance illegally removed from the Iraq National Museum, the National Library, and other locations in Iraq since the adoption of resolution 661 (1990) of 6 August 1990, including by establishing a prohibition on trade in or transfer of such items and items with respect to which reasonable suspicion exists that they have been illegally removed, and *calls upon* the United Nations Educational, Scientific, and Cultural Organization, Interpol, and other international organizations, as appropriate, to assist in the implementation of this paragraph;

8. *Requests* the Secretary-General to appoint a Special Representative for Iraq whose independent responsibilities shall involve reporting regularly to the Council on his activities under this resolution, coordinating activities of the United Nations in post-conflict processes in Iraq, coordinating among United Nations and international agencies engaged in humanitarian assistance and reconstruction activities in Iraq, and, in coordination with the Authority, assisting the people of Iraq through:

(a) coordinating humanitarian and reconstruction assistance by United Nations agencies and between United Nations agencies and non-governmental organizations;

(b) promoting the safe, orderly, and voluntary return of refugees and displaced persons;

(c) working intensively with the Authority, the people of Iraq, and others concerned to advance efforts to restore and establish national and local institutions for representative governance, including by working together to facilitate a process leading to an internationally recognized, representative government of Iraq;

(d) facilitating the reconstruction of key infrastructure, in cooperation with other international organizations;

(e) promoting economic reconstruction and the conditions for sustainable development, including through coordination with national and regional organizations, as appropriate, civil society, donors, and the international financial institutions;

(f) encouraging international efforts to contribute to basic civilian administration functions;

(g) promoting the protection of human rights;

(h) encouraging international efforts to rebuild the capacity of the Iraqi civilian police force; and

(i) encouraging international efforts to promote legal and judicial reform;

9. *Supports* the formation, by the people of Iraq with the help of the Authority and working with the Special Representative, of an Iraqi interim administration as a transitional administration run by Iraqis, until an internationally recognized, representative government is established by the people of Iraq and assumes the responsibilities of the Authority;

10. *Decides* that, with the exception of prohibitions related to the sale or supply to Iraq of arms and related materiel other

than those arms and related materiel required by the Authority to serve the purposes of this and other related resolutions, all prohibitions related to trade with Iraq and the provision of financial or economic resources to Iraq established by resolution 661 (1990) and subsequent relevant resolutions, including resolution 778 (1992) of 2 October 1992, shall no longer apply;

11. *Reaffirms* that Iraq must meet its disarmament obligations, *encourages* the United Kingdom of Great Britain and Northern Ireland and the United States of America to keep the Council informed of their activities in this regard, and *underlines* the intention of the Council to revisit the mandates of the United Nations Monitoring, Verification, and Inspection Commission and the International Atomic Energy Agency as set forth in resolutions 687 (1991) of 3 April 1991, 1284 (1999) of 17 December 1999, and 1441 (2002) of 8 November 2002;

12. *Notes* the establishment of a Development Fund for Iraq to be held by the Central Bank of Iraq and to be audited by independent public accountants approved by the International Advisory and Monitoring Board of the Development Fund for Iraq and looks forward to the early meeting of that International Advisory and Monitoring Board, whose members shall include duly qualified representatives of the Secretary-General, of the Managing Director of the International Monetary Fund, of the Director-General of the Arab Fund for Social and Economic Development, and of the President of the World Bank;

13. *Notes further* that the funds in the Development Fund for Iraq shall be disbursed at the direction of the Authority, in consultation with the Iraqi interim administration, for the purposes set out in paragraph 14 below;

14. *Underlines* that the Development Fund for Iraq shall be used in a transparent manner to meet the humanitarian needs

of the Iraqi people, for the economic reconstruction and repair of Iraq's infrastructure, for the continued disarmament of Iraq, and for the costs of Iraqi civilian administration, and for other purposes benefiting the people of Iraq;

15. *Calls upon* the international financial institutions to assist the people of Iraq in the reconstruction and development of their economy and to facilitate assistance by the broader donor community, and *welcomes* the readiness of creditors, including those of the Paris Club, to seek a solution to Iraq's sovereign debt problems;

16. *Requests* also that the Secretary-General, in coordination with the Authority, continue the exercise of his responsibilities under Security Council resolution 1472 (2003) of 28 March 2003 and 1476 (2003) of 24 April 2003, for a period of six months following the adoption of this resolution, and terminate within this time period, in the most cost effective manner, the ongoing operations of the "Oil-for-Food" Programme (the "Programme"), both at headquarters level and in the field, transferring responsibility for the administration of any remaining activity under the Programme to the Authority, including by taking the following necessary measures:

(a) to facilitate as soon as possible the shipment and authenticated delivery of priority civilian goods as identified by the Secretary-General and representatives designated by him, in coordination with the Authority and the Iraqi interim administration, under approved and funded contracts previously concluded by the previous Government of Iraq, for the humanitarian relief of the people of Iraq, including, as necessary, negotiating adjustments in the terms or conditions of these contracts and respective letters of credit as set forth in paragraph 4 (d) of resolution 1472 (2003);

(b) to review, in light of changed circumstances, in coordination with the Authority and the Iraqi interim administration, the relative utility of each approved and funded contract with a view to determining whether such contracts contain items required to meet the needs of the people of Iraq both now and during reconstruction, and to postpone action on those contracts determined to be of questionable utility and the respective letters of credit until an internationally recognized, representative government of Iraq is in a position to make its own determination as to whether such contracts shall be fulfilled;

(c) to provide the Security Council within 21 days following the adoption of this resolution, for the Security Council's review and consideration, an estimated operating budget based on funds already set aside in the account established pursuant to paragraph 8 (d) of resolution 986 (1995) of 14 April 1995, identifying:

> (i) all known and projected costs to the United Nations required to ensure the continued functioning of the activities associated with implementation of the present resolution, including operating and administrative expenses associated with the relevant United Nations agencies and programmes responsible for the implementation of the Programme both at Headquarters and in the field;
>
> (ii) all known and projected costs associated with termination of the Programme;
>
> (iii) all known and projected costs associated with restoring Government of Iraq funds that were provided by Member States to the Secretary-General as requested in paragraph 1 of resolution 778 (1992); and
>
> (iv) all known and projected costs associated with the Special Representative and the qualified representative

of the Secretary-General identified to serve on the International Advisory and Monitoring Board, for the six month time period defined above, following which these costs shall be borne by the United Nations;

(d) to consolidate into a single fund the accounts established pursuant to paragraphs 8 (a) and 8 (b) of resolution 986 (1995);

(e) to fulfil all remaining obligations related to the termination of the Programme, including negotiating, in the most cost effective manner, any necessary settlement payments, which shall be made from the escrow accounts established pursuant to paragraphs 8 (a) and 8 (b) of resolution 986 (1995), with those parties that previously have entered into contractual obligations with the Secretary-General under the Programme, and to determine, in coordination with the Authority and the Iraqi interim administration, the future status of contracts undertaken by the United Nations and related United Nations agencies under the accounts established pursuant to paragraphs 8 (b) and 8 (d) of resolution 986 (1995);

(f) to provide the Security Council, 30 days prior to the termination of the Programme, with a comprehensive strategy developed in close coordination with the Authority and the Iraqi interim administration that would lead to the delivery of all relevant documentation and the transfer of all operational responsibility of the Programme to the Authority;

17. *Requests further* that the Secretary-General transfer as soon as possible to the Development Fund for Iraq 1 billion United States dollars from unencumbered funds in the accounts established pursuant to paragraphs 8 (a) and 8 (b) of resolution 986 (1995), restore Government of Iraq funds that were provided by Member States to the Secretary-General as

requested in paragraph 1 of resolution 778 (1992), and *decides* that, after deducting all relevant United Nations expenses associated with the shipment of authorized contracts and costs to the Programme outlined in paragraph 16 (c) above, including residual obligations, all surplus funds in the escrow accounts established pursuant to paragraphs 8 (a), 8 (b), 8 (d), and 8 (f) of resolution 986 (1995) shall be transferred at the earliest possible time to the Development Fund for Iraq;

18. *Decides* to terminate effective on the adoption of this resolution the functions related to the observation and monitoring activities undertaken by the Secretary-General under the Programme, including the monitoring of the export of petroleum and petroleum products from Iraq;

19. *Decides* to terminate the Committee established pursuant to paragraph 6 of resolution 661 (1990) at the conclusion of the six month period called for in paragraph 16 above and *further decides* that the Committee shall identify individuals and entities referred to in paragraph 23 below;

20. *Decides* that all export sales of petroleum, petroleum products, and natural gas from Iraq following the date of the adoption of this resolution shall be made consistent with prevailing international market best practices, to be audited by independent public accountants reporting to the International Advisory and Monitoring Board referred to in paragraph 12 above in order to ensure transparency, and *decides further* that, except as provided in paragraph 21 below, all proceeds from such sales shall be deposited into the Development Fund for Iraq until such time as an internationally recognized, representative government of Iraq is properly constituted;

21. *Decides further* that 5 per cent of the proceeds referred to in paragraph 20 above shall be deposited into the Compensation Fund established in accordance with resolution 687 (1991) and subsequent relevant resolutions and that, unless an

internationally recognized, representative government of Iraq and the Governing Council of the United Nations Compensation Commission, in the exercise of its authority over methods of ensuring that payments are made into the Compensation Fund, decide otherwise, this requirement shall be binding on a properly constituted, internationally recognized, representative government of Iraq and any successor thereto;

22. *Noting* the relevance of the establishment of an internationally recognized, representative government of Iraq and the desirability of prompt completion of the restructuring of Iraq's debt as referred to in paragraph 15 above, further *decides* that, until December 31, 2007, unless the Council decides otherwise, petroleum, petroleum products, and natural gas originating in Iraq shall be immune, until title passes to the initial purchaser from legal proceedings against them and not be subject to any form of attachment, garnishment, or execution, and that all States shall take any steps that may be necessary under their respective domestic legal systems to assure this protection, and that proceeds and obligations arising from sales thereof, as well as the Development Fund for Iraq, shall enjoy privileges and immunities equivalent to those enjoyed by the United Nations except that the above-mentioned privileges and immunities will not apply with respect to any legal proceeding in which recourse to such proceeds or obligations is necessary to satisfy liability for damages assessed in connection with an ecological accident, including an oil spill, that occurs after the date of adoption of this resolution;

23. *Decides* that all Member States in which there are:

(a) funds or other financial assets or economic resources of the previous Government of Iraq or its state bodies, corporations, or agencies, located outside Iraq as of the date of this resolution, or

(b) funds or other financial assets or economic resources that have been removed from Iraq, or acquired, by Saddam Hussein or other senior officials of the former Iraqi regime and their immediate family members, including entities owned or controlled, directly or indirectly, by them or by persons acting on their behalf or at their direction, shall freeze without delay those funds or other financial assets or economic resources and, unless these funds or other financial assets or economic resources are themselves the subject of a prior judicial, administrative, or arbitral lien or judgement, immediately shall cause their transfer to the Development Fund for Iraq, it being understood that, unless otherwise addressed, claims made by private individuals or non-government entities on those transferred funds or other financial assets may be presented to the internationally recognized, representative government of Iraq; and *decides further* that all such funds or other financial assets or economic resources shall enjoy the same privileges, immunities, and protections as provided under paragraph 22;

24. *Requests* the Secretary-General to report to the Council at regular intervals on the work of the Special Representative with respect to the implementation of this resolution and on the work of the International Advisory and Monitoring Board and *encourages* the United Kingdom of Great Britain and Northern Ireland and the United States of America to inform the Council at regular intervals of their efforts under this resolution;

25. *Decides* to review the implementation of this resolution within twelve months of adoption and to consider further steps that might be necessary;

26. *Calls upon* Member States and international and regional organizations to contribute to the implementation of this resolution;

27. *Decides* to remain seized of this matter.

UNITED NATIONS S/RES/1511 (2003)
Security Council
Distr.: General
16 October 2003
Resolution 1511 (2003)

Adopted by the Security Council at its 4844th meeting, on 16 October 2003

The Security Council,

Reaffirming its previous resolutions on Iraq, including resolution 1483 (2003) of 22 May 2003 and 1500 (2003) of 14 August 2003, and on threats to peace and security caused by terrorist acts, including resolution 1373 (2001) of 28 September 2001, and other relevant resolutions,

Underscoring that the sovereignty of Iraq resides in the State of Iraq, *reaffirming* the right of the Iraqi people freely to determine their own political future and control their own natural resources, *reiterating* its resolve that the day when Iraqis govern themselves must come quickly, and *recognizing* the importance of international support, particularly that of countries in the region, Iraq's neighbours, and regional organizations, in taking forward this process expeditiously,

Recognizing that international support for restoration of conditions of stability and security is essential to the well-being of the people of Iraq as well as to the ability of all concerned to carry out their work on behalf of the people of Iraq, and *welcoming* Member State contributions in this regard under resolution 1483 (2003),

Welcoming the decision of the Governing Council of Iraq to form a preparatory constitutional committee to prepare for a constitutional conference that will draft a constitution to embody the aspirations of the Iraqi people, and *urging* it to complete this process quickly,

Affirming that the terrorist bombings of the Embassy of Jordan on 7 August 2003, of the United Nations headquarters in Baghdad on 19 August 2003, of the Imam Ali Mosque in Najaf on 29 August 2003, and of the Embassy of Turkey on 14 October 2003, and the murder of a Spanish diplomat on 9 October 2003 are attacks on the people of Iraq, the United Nations, and the international community, and *deploring* the assassination of Dr. Akila al-Hashimi, who died on 25 September 2003, as an attack directed against the future of Iraq,

In that context, *recalling* and *reaffirming* the statement of its President of 20 August 2003 (S/PRST/2003/13) and resolution 1502 (2003) of 26 August 2003,

Determining that the situation in Iraq, although improved, continues to constitute a threat to international peace and security,

Acting under Chapter VII of the Charter of the United Nations,

1. *Reaffirms* the sovereignty and territorial integrity of Iraq, and *underscores*, in that context, the temporary nature of the exercise by the Coalition Provisional Authority (Authority) of the specific responsibilities, authorities, and obligations under applicable international law recognized and set forth in resolution 1483 (2003), which will cease when an internationally recognized, representative government established by the people of Iraq is sworn in and assumes the responsibilities of the Authority, inter alia through steps envisaged in paragraphs 4 through 7 and 10 below;

2. *Welcomes* the positive response of the international community, in fora such as the Arab League, the Organization of the Islamic Conference, the United Nations General

Assembly, and the United Nations Educational, Scientific and Cultural Organization, to the establishment of the broadly representative Governing Council as an important step towards an internationally recognized, representative government;

3. *Supports* the Governing Council's efforts to mobilize the people of Iraq, including by the appointment of a cabinet of ministers and a preparatory constitutional committee to lead a process in which the Iraqi people will progressively take control of their own affairs;

4. *Determines* that the Governing Council and its ministers are the principal bodies of the Iraqi interim administration, which, without prejudice to its further evolution, embodies the sovereignty of the State of Iraq during the transitional period until an internationally recognized, representative government is established and assumes the responsibilities of the Authority;

5. *Affirms* that the administration of Iraq will be progressively undertaken by the evolving structures of the Iraqi interim administration;

6. *Calls upon* the Authority, in this context, to return governing responsibilities and authorities to the people of Iraq as soon as practicable and *requests* the Authority, in cooperation as appropriate with the Governing Council and the Secretary-General, to report to the Council on the progress being made;

7. *Invites* the Governing Council to provide to the Security Council, for its review, no later than 15 December 2003, in cooperation with the Authority and, as circumstances permit, the Special Representative of the Secretary-General, a timetable and a programme for the drafting of a new constitution for Iraq and for the holding of democratic elections under that constitution;

8. *Resolves* that the United Nations, acting through the Secretary-General, his Special Representative, and the United

Nations Assistance Mission in Iraq, should strengthen its vital role in Iraq, including by providing humanitarian relief, promoting the economic reconstruction of and conditions for sustainable development in Iraq, and advancing efforts to restore and establish national and local institutions for representative government;

9. *Requests* that, as circumstances permit, the Secretary-General pursue the course of action outlined in paragraphs 98 and 99 of the report of the Secretary-General of 17 July 2003 (S/2003/715);

10. *Takes note* of the intention of the Governing Council to hold a constitutional conference and, recognizing that the convening of the conference will be a milestone in the movement to the full exercise of sovereignty, *calls for* its preparation through national dialogue and consensus-building as soon as practicable and *requests* the Special Representative of the Secretary-General, at the time of the convening of the conference or, as circumstances permit, to lend the unique expertise of the United Nations to the Iraqi people in this process of political transition, including the establishment of electoral processes;

11. *Requests* the Secretary-General to ensure that the resources of the United Nations and associated organizations are available, if requested by the Iraqi Governing Council and, as circumstances permit, to assist in furtherance of the programme provided by the Governing Council in paragraph 7 above, and encourages other organizations with expertise in this area to support the Iraqi Governing Council, if requested;

12. *Requests* the Secretary-General to report to the Security Council on his responsibilities under this resolution and the development and implementation of a timetable and programme under paragraph 7 above;

13. *Determines* that the provision of security and stability is essential to the successful completion of the political process as outlined in paragraph 7 above and to the ability of the United Nations to contribute effectively to that process and the implementation of resolution 1483 (2003), and *authorizes* a multinational force under unified command to take all necessary measures to contribute to the maintenance of security and stability in Iraq, including for the purpose of ensuring necessary conditions for the implementation of the timetable and programme as well as to contribute to the security of the United Nations Assistance Mission for Iraq, the Governing Council of Iraq and other institutions of the Iraqi interim administration, and key humanitarian and economic infrastructure;

14. *Urges* Member States to contribute assistance under this United Nations mandate, including military forces, to the multinational force referred to in paragraph 13 above;

15. *Decides* that the Council shall review the requirements and mission of the multinational force referred to in paragraph 13 above not later than one year from the date of this resolution, and that in any case the mandate of the force shall expire upon the completion of the political process as described in paragraphs 4 through 7 and 10 above, and *expresses* readiness to consider on that occasion any future need for the continuation of the multinational force, taking into account the views of an internationally recognized, representative government of Iraq;

16. *Emphasizes* the importance of establishing effective Iraqi police and security forces in maintaining law, order, and security and combating terrorism consistent with paragraph 4 of resolution 1483 (2003), and *calls upon* Member States and international and regional organizations to contribute to the training and equipping of Iraqi police and security forces;

17. *Expresses* deep sympathy and condolences for the personal losses suffered by the Iraqi people and by the United Nations and the families of those United Nations personnel and other innocent victims who were killed or injured in these tragic attacks;

18. *Unequivocally condemns* the terrorist bombings of the Embassy of Jordan on 7 August 2003, of the United Nations headquarters in Baghdad on 19 August 2003, and of the Imam Ali Mosque in Najaf on 29 August 2003, and of the Embassy of Turkey on 14 October 2003, the murder of a Spanish diplomat on 9 October 2003, and the assassination of Dr. Akila al-Hashimi, who died on 25 September 2003, and *emphasizes* that those responsible must be brought to justice;

19. *Calls upon* Member States to prevent the transit of terrorists to Iraq, arms for terrorists, and financing that would support terrorists, and *emphasizes* the importance of strengthening the cooperation of the countries of the region, particularly neighbours of Iraq, in this regard;

20. *Appeals* to Member States and the international financial institutions to strengthen their efforts to assist the people of Iraq in the reconstruction and development of their economy, and *urges* those institutions to take immediate steps to provide their full range of loans and other financial assistance to Iraq, working with the Governing Council and appropriate Iraqi ministries;

21. *Urges* Member States and international and regional organizations to support the Iraq reconstruction effort initiated at the 24 June 2003 United Nations Technical Consultations, including through substantial pledges at the 23-24 October 2003 International Donors Conference in Madrid;

22. *Calls upon* Member States and concerned organizations to help meet the needs of the Iraqi people by providing

resources necessary for the rehabilitation and reconstruction of Iraq's economic infrastructure;

23. *Emphasizes* that the International Advisory and Monitoring Board (IAMB) referred to in paragraph 12 of resolution 1483 (2003) should be established as a priority, and *reiterates* that the Development Fund for Iraq shall be used in a transparent manner as set out in paragraph 14 of resolution 1483 (2003);

24. *Reminds* all Member States of their obligations under paragraphs 19 and 23 of resolution 1483 (2003) in particular the obligation to immediately cause the transfer of funds, other financial assets and economic resources to the Development Fund for Iraq for the benefit of the Iraqi people;

25. *Requests* that the United States, on behalf of the multinational force as outlined in paragraph 13 above, report to the Security Council on the efforts and progress of this force as appropriate and not less than every six months;

26. *Decides* to remain seized of the matter.

Dominique de VILLEPIN

Named Interior Minister of France in April, 2004, Dominique de Villepin previously served in the French Foreign Ministry starting in 1980. He was posted to the French embassy in Washington DC from 1984–1989, and subsequently served in India and Africa before becoming Foreign Minister of France in 2002. De Villepin is also France's representative at the Convention on the Future of the Union. Among his books are *Le Cri de la Gargouille* (*The Cry of the Gargoyle*), a collection of essays about politics and culture; *Les Cent-Jours ou l'esprit de sacrifice* (*The Hundred Days or the Spirit of Sacrifice*), a biography of Napoleon; and *Éloge des voleurs de feu* (*Tribute to the Fire Thieves*), a book of poetry.